THE M. & E. HANDBOOK SERIES

MANAGEMENT ACCOUNTIN[G]

MANAGEMENT ACCOUNTING

won the Annual Textbook Award, 1969 of the Society of Company and Commercial Accountants.

THE M. & E. HANDBOOK SERIES

MANAGEMENT ACCOUNTING

W. M. HARPER, A.C.W.A., A.M.B.I.M.

Senior Lecturer in Management and Cost Accountancy at the City of London Polytechnic

MACDONALD AND EVANS

MACDONALD & EVANS LTD.
8 John Street, London WC1N 2HY

First published June 1969
Reprinted June 1971
Reprinted May 1972
Reprinted June 1973
Reprinted March 1974
Reprinted March 1975
Reprinted March 1976

ISBN: 0 7121 1341 X

Printed in Great Britain by Richard Clay (The Chaucer Press), Ltd., Bungay, Suffolk

GENERAL INTRODUCTION

The HANDBOOK Series of Study Notes

HANDBOOKS are a new form of printed study notes designed to help students to prepare and revise for professional and other examinations. The books are carefully programmed so as to be self-contained courses of tuition in the subjects they cover. For this purpose they comprise detailed notes, self-testing questions and hints on examination technique.

HANDBOOKS can be used on their own or in conjunction with recommended textbooks. They are written by college lecturers, examiners, and others with wide experience of students' difficulties and requirements. At all stages the main objective of the authors has been to prepare students for the practical business of passing examinations.

P. W. D. Redmond
General Editor

NOTICE TO LECTURERS

Many lecturers are now using HANDBOOKS as working texts to save time otherwise wasted by students in protracted note-taking. The purpose of the series is to meet practical teaching requirements as far as possible, and lecturers are cordially invited to forward comments or criticisms to the Publishers for consideration.

AUTHOR'S PREFACE

MANAGEMENT accounting is a difficult subject to write about. There are differing opinions as to what topics are included in the subject and also controversy as to the correctness of matter within given topics. Moreover, the roots of the subject extend so far down into cost accountancy and the upper branches mingle so inextricably with operational research that no matter what decision is made as to where to start, and where to finish, it will inevitably provoke the objections of some (if not most) authorities. However, a student, faced with the relatively early prospect of sitting an examination entitled *Management Accounting* (or some similar title) needs *something* upon which he can base his studies. This book was written with such a student wholly in mind and in the hope that it will provide him with a text that makes a distinct contribution to his understanding of the subject.

"Cost Accountancy" and "Management Accounting." As was mentioned above, the roots of management accounting lie in the subject matter of cost accountancy, and to understand much in management accounting it is necessary to know certain cost accounting topics well. In writing this book I decided it would be best for most students if I assumed that the reader had no prior knowledge of cost accountancy. Therefore, although the reproduction of previously published material seemed slightly improper, I have occasionally incorporated passages from my previous HANDBOOK, *Cost Accountancy*. I hope that those students familiar with *Cost Accountancy* will find that reading matter they had previously met in that book will aid their comprehension of the new and more advanced subject of management accounting.

Progress Tests. Progress Tests are divided, where appropriate, into two parts—one headed "Principles" and the other "Practice." Questions in the "Principles" section are aimed at testing whether ideas, definitions, etc., given in the chapter have been grasped and remembered. Questions in the "Practice" section, on the other hand, are designed to test if the student can apply the principles learnt in the chapter, and answers to these questions will be found in Appendix III.

The student must be warned that many questions in the "Practice" sections are not easy, for, after all, management accounting is a Finals subject. The student should attempt all such questions, but if he finds them rather over-taxing then he should at least study the answers, for in order to keep the book down to a HANDBOOK size I have sometimes used the answers to illustrate points which otherwise would have needed illustrating in the chapter. The answers are, therefore, in effect often part of the text and should be studied as such.

Corporation Tax. Corporation Tax is a fact of life that must always be allowed for by the management accountant. He, naturally, must know the rates and regulations appertaining at any given time. However, in an examination paper on management accounting all that will be tested is the student's ability to integrate corporation-tax factors into his appraisals and computations. For this reason the Corporation Tax rates and allowances have been selected on the basis of simplifying the mathematics and are not, therefore, the rates and allowances currently ruling.

Decimalisation. In this book I have followed the recommendations of the various accountancy bodies and of the examining bodies responsible for National Further Education syllabuses and examinations on making the transition to decimal currency. Where appropriate, examples have now been given in the new decimal currency, in accordance with the rules laid down by the Decimal Currency Board, set out in *Decimal Currency: Expression of Amounts in Printing, Writing and in Speech*, H.M.S.O., 1968.

Reporting and Flow-charting. Examiners sometimes request students' answers to be in the form of reports or flow-charts. For this reason the essential principles of these two techniques are briefly outlined at the end of the appendix on examination technique (Appendix II) and the student is advised to study them carefully.

Bibliography. To aid further study the student is referred to the following books:

For further discussion of management accounting as a whole:

J. L. Brown and L. R. Howard: *Principles of Management Accounting*. Macdonald & Evans.

J. Batty: *Management Accountancy*. Macdonald & Evans.

For appreciation of the broader field of managerial economics in which management accounting lies:

Joel Dean: *Managerial Economics*. Prentice-Hall Inc.

For a more detailed coverage of cost accountancy:

H. J. Wheldon: *Cost Accounting and Costing Methods*. 11th Edition. Macdonald & Evans.

W. M. Harper: *Cost Accountancy*. Macdonald & Evans.

For a more detailed coverage of accounting in inflation:

I.C.W.A.: *The Accountancy of Changing Price Levels*.

For a more detailed coverage of the evaluation of capital projects:

A. J. Merrett & Allen Sykes: *The Finance and Analysis of Capital Projects*. Longmans.

For a more detailed coverage of financial management:

Robert W. Johnson: *Financial Management*. Allyn & Bacon.

F. W. Paish: *Business Finance*, Pitman.

Acknowledgments. I gratefully acknowledge permission to quote from the past examination papers of the following bodies:

Association of Certified and Corporate Accountants (*A.C.C.A.*)

Institute of Chartered Accountants in England and Wales (*C.A.*)

Institute of Cost and Works Accountants (*I.C.W.A.*)

I would also like to acknowledge my thanks to the Centre for Interfirm Comparisons Ltd. for allowing me to reproduce their interfirm comparison diagrams in Figs. 23 and 24. I also acknowledge that the concept of obsolescence insurance outlined in Chapter XVIII, paragraph **20**, was originally expounded in an article "Living with Obsolescence" by Thrasher and Leach and published in the November 1966 issue of *Management Today*.

May 1969 W. M. H.

CONTENTS

PART FOUR: CONTROL

Part Five: PERFORMANCE EVALUATION

Part Six: DATA-PROCESSING

LIST OF FIGURES

PART ONE

INTRODUCTION

In this Part the subject of management accountancy is introduced and emphasis given to the fact that management accountancy is primarily concerned with *management*, and only secondarily with accountancy as traditionally understood. It is hoped that as a result of a careful reading of the first chapter, the student will develop an attitude to the subject that will enable him to grasp more effectively the issues discussed in the rest of the book and also subsequently to apply management accounting techniques in their most managerially useful manner.

In the second chapter the technique of cost ascertainment is outlined. This technique is not normally regarded as falling within the field of management accountancy, but as a significant proportion of a management accountant's raw data includes figures which have been subjected to this technique, it is essential that the procedures and assumptions involved in its application are fully appreciated.

CHAPTER I

INTRODUCTION TO MANAGEMENT ACCOUNTANCY

MANAGEMENT accountancy is concerned with *management*. It is concerned with management first, last and at all times. The student who opens this book in the belief that management accountancy is the application of a set of accounting techniques which happen to be particularly useful to management should pause, take a deep breath and then expunge from his mind all his previous misconceptions on the subject. To realign his view correctly he should imagine himself as an equal member of a top management team which has been set the collective task of managing an enterprise. Members of the team will naturally undertake specialist activities—one may manage the factory, another handle research. The management accountant's particular task will be to provide information to his colleagues relating to the economic aspects of the operation of the enterprise. While he will take from the field of accountancy such techniques as will be useful, he will always look at the enterprise with eyes of a *manager*, conscious of management's problems, responsibilities, opportunities, limitations, hopes and fears. Every moment that he fails to take this viewpoint he is ceasing to be a management accountant.

Management accountancy, then, starts with management.

MANAGEMENT

1. The management function. What management is, and what managers should do, is the subject of endless books and controversies. In this section all that will be attempted is to indicate the breadth of the function so that students can appreciate that there is more to managing than simply cutting costs, selecting the project that on paper maximises enterprise profits, or giving orders.

From the first it should be appreciated that the fate of the enterprise is in the hands of the managers. Although a certain amount of luck enters any real-life situation, in the ultimate analysis they are responsible for the results. The onus for enterprise performance does *not* lie on unions, government, society or any other group—and though occasionally the actions of these bodies may be crippling to the enterprise, management cannot hold them responsible. It is management's job to manage and not be managed, and so on the shoulders of management, and also the management accountant as a member of the management team, lies the whole responsibility for the success or failure of the enterprise.

2. The primacy of the future. At all times management are concerned about the future. Always they must be looking ahead, for the instructions they issue in the present must be based on what they envisage the future will bring. This continual involvement with the future affects everything the management accountant does. Past and present figures only have value insomuch as they pre-shadow the future. The management accountant is constantly concerned with what *will be* and every aspect of his work is ultimately orientated to enabling him to see into the future. The past is of no interest whatsoever save in the power it gives him to predict.

3. The certainty of uncertainty. Management is concerned with the future. The only thing certain about the future is that it is uncertain. All management work involves constant assessment of probabilities. Although this is usually done by managers subjectively (and often unconsciously) this dimension of management pervades all aspects of its work. It must, therefore, pervade all aspects of the work of the management accountant.

4. Technological factors. Managers, in managing their enterprises, must consider simultaneously a variety of factors which are relatively distinct from each other. The first of these relates to technology. What a manager's plant can produce and what his product can achieve must be known to him and taken into account at all times. Economically it may appear more profitable to operate twenty-four hours a day, but if technically this risks serious plant breakdown then such a course must be avoided. Managers must also consider the possible emergence of new products and it is, therefore, important to keep a watch on research and development. It may prove necessary to manufacture a new product and so occupy factory space that could well be more profitably devoted to an established product, but if short-term maximisation of profits risks complete enterprise failure because the established product becomes obsolete at a time when the enterprise has no foot in the new market, then immediate profits must be sacrificed. Again, scrap costs may appear excessive and yet for sound technical reasons it may cost more to eliminate such scrap than the saved production would be worth.

5. Commercial factors. It is no use producing high-quality goods or providing a first-class service if there is no market. Managers must always be considering if there is a sufficient demand for the products they can manufacture or services they can provide, and if so, just how that demand can best be met, for it may be cheaper to produce only one model but more profitable to produce a dozen. Demand both at home and abroad must constantly be considered by management.

6. National and international events. In the modern world there is continuous and rapid change, both nationally and internationally. What is profitable today may be definitely unprofitable tomorrow and managers must watch and even foresee events in the world at large. They must appreciate that a civil war in a very distant and relatively insignificant country could seriously affect their raw material supply, or that an economic crisis in a European state could precipitate an economic freeze at home.

7. Industrial relations. It is no use economising in staff if the result is a six-month strike. Every act of management must be considered in terms of the effect on industrial relations and, unfortunately, many an otherwise profitable scheme has been reluctantly rejected because of its potential disruption of industrial relations. Students should not take this to mean, however, that sound projects may have to be scrapped because of "union blackmail": more often than not staff have a genuine case in opposing a scheme designed to benefit the shareholders only. Bad managers can usually make profits by exploiting labour; only good managers can satisfy everybody and still make good profits.

8. Organisation and staff. When considering any plan managers must view it in conjunction with the form of organisation within the enterprise and the quality of the staff. This means ideas must sometimes be turned down because of the inappropriateness of the organisation or the lack of suitable staff. Although both weaknesses can ultimately be overcome this is usually a long-term operation and viable short-term improvisations frequently cannot be made. Similarly, systems that the keen accountant may wish to install may easily be unworkable in this regard. Detailed shop-floor records kept by the operators are rarely possible; such operators are not likely to have clerical skills or interests, and also because of the dirty or heavy work they are engaged on, they find it virtually impossible to carry out meticulous clerical work.

9. Legal factors. At all times managers must bear in mind the legal aspects relating to their work. These can range through contract law, tort, industrial law and the legal requirements regarding record-keeping. Sometimes the reason for a rejection of an otherwise admirable idea is simply that it would be illegal.

10. Public relations. On some occasions the acceptance, rejection or amendment of a scheme is determined by its probable effect on public relations. Management must continuously keep this issue at the back of their minds and avoid quite innocuous acts which could, however, be misunderstood.

11. Social responsibility. The social responsibilities of management is a topic subject to much controversy. This, however, is not the place to discuss such an issue and it is sufficient simply to say that whatever management considers its social responsibilities to be, it must take into consideration such responsibilities when making decisions.

12. Economic factors. Last of all, but obviously not least, management must consider all the economic factors involved in any situation. This, of course, is the realm of management accounting and the subject of this book.

13. Decision-making: the ultimate act of management. When all the work of a manager is considered it will be appreciated that in the final analysis there emerges a management decision. Managers may plan, divine, discuss and cogitate, but ultimately all these activities lead to the making of a decision. Management accounting, then, is concerned with assisting managers to make decisions.

14. Conclusion. From all the above it can be seen that a manager has a considerable range of factors to consider in his work. If a management accountant is really to be of assistance to management he should have a keen appreciation of these factors. In addition he should be well acquainted with the various branches of management he will need to work alongside, such as production, marketing, personnel, stores, purchasing, research and development, sales, advertising, distribution, office, plant and maintenance, as well as having an understanding of the more important management techniques such as work study, quality control, market research, production planning and control, personnel selection and training, stores control, safety and welfare, materials handling, O and M, incentives and forecasting.

There is clearly much more to management accounting than the mere ability to handle monetary figures.

MANAGEMENT ACCOUNTANCY

15. The function of management accountancy. Consideration of the previous section should quickly lead to an appreciation of the complexity of managing. Clearly any management team will function most effectively if individual members specialise, and to the management accountant falls the task of specialising in enterprise economics. This means that management accountancy is concerned with:

(*a*) management's *need for information* regarding the economic operation of the enterprise; and
(*b*) the actual direct *management of cash*.

The provision of information is, of course, a service and the service should extend to every manager in the enterprise from the chief executive down to the most junior of foremen or office supervisors. The management of cash is more akin to actual operations and is by and large the more traditional form of accountancy. These two branches of management accountancy arise because of the dual role of money in modern economic society.

16. The dual role of money. It is vitally important that the student appreciates that money plays a dual role in the running of enterprises, being used both as an economic factor of production and also as a measure of economic performance.

(*a*) *Money as an economic factor of production.* Money in its physical form of currency is as necessary to an enterprise as any other economic factor such as materials or labour. In this form it is usually referred to as *cash* and consists, of course, of coins, bank notes, cheques. Without cash (or credit, which is essentially a form of cash to a business man) an enterprise would quickly grind to a halt.

(*b*) *Money as a measure of economic performance.* Basically the object of an enterprise is to combine a variety of economic factors (materials, labour, land, machines), so that from the combination some utility emerges that can be exchanged for cash. Since the combination can be varied (*e.g.* machines can be used in lieu of labour) it is necessary to be able to measure the economic value involved in any combination together with the value of the utility. Unfortunately, tons of material cannot be added to hours of labour nor compared with units of production. To make measurements in such circumstances, therefore, calls for the use of a common denominator, and *money* is the chosen measure. Money, therefore, is used as a measure of economic performance.

NOTE: In some ways the use of money as such a measure is unfortunate. People may confuse *money* used in this way with *cash*, and learning that on average it costs one shilling a mile to run a particular type of vehicle, wrongly assume that by running the vehicle 20 miles less they will have £1 more cash in their pockets. Moreover, money is an unstable unit, continuously affected by inflation so the same economic performance one year has a different monetary value from an identical performance another year. Despite these serious disadvantages it is the most practical measure we have.

17. Financial, cost and management accountancy. Now the dual role of money has been indicated it becomes possible to make some distinction between financial, cost and management accountancy. In practice hard-and-fast lines between the functions are pointless, since the modern concept of accountancy covers all aspects of enterprise economics; though it should be appreciated that the personal qualities required to carry out work at one end of the spectrum are different from those required for work at the other end (*e.g.* a good cashier should be strong on attention to minute detail but may be permitted to be weak in mathematics, while the converse holds true for an accountant engaged in operational research work).

(*a*) *Financial accountancy*. Clearly this function is concerned with money as an economic resource, *i.e.* cash. Consequently cheques, notes, bank balances and overdrafts, debtors and creditors feature largely in this type of accounting. The dominance of the balance sheet in financial accounting emphasises the *financial* aspect of this function which, it should be remembered, historically arose in order literally "to account for" cash entrusted to the enterprise.

(*b*) *Cost accountancy*. This function, on the other hand, is concerned with money as a measure of economic performance. Cost accounting aims at measuring the economic performance of departments, methods, equipment, and so forth, and of ascertaining the value of the economic resources consumed in producing goods and services.

(*c*) *Management accountancy*. Management accountancy evolved from, and is still inextricably linked to, cost accountancy. It may be said to differ from cost accountancy by its fundamental principle of looking at all situations from a *management* viewpoint (though all good cost accountants adopt this principle anyway) as against simple *economic* measurement. Also, by being concerned with the whole of enterprise economics it goes beyond cost accountancy with its involvement with *cash management*, demanding knowledge, therefore, of cash sources, cost of cash (*e.g.* interest), and the techniques of cash planning and cash control.

18. Return on capital. Since management accountancy is concerned very much with measuring economic performance it may be asked if there is any fundamental measure of such performance. Naturally, economic activity in modern society is so varied that there cannot be one definitive all-embracing measure, but for many practical purposes the rate of return on capital approximates to this. Such a rate of return is essentially the *ratio of profit earned to capital employed*.

(*a*) *Profit earned*. Profit, of course, in genuine competitive circumstances it itself a measure—a measure of the efficiency of an enterprise in converting a combination of economic resources (materials, labour, etc.) into utilities. Enterprise costs reflect the value the community places on resources consumed by the enterprise, while enterprise sales reflect the community's valuation of its products. Clearly, the larger the profit the more effective the enterprise has been in converting lower valued resources into more highly valued utilities.

(*b*) *Capital employed.* However, although profit measures the effectiveness of the conversion of resources into utilities it does not take into account in any way the economic resources *tied up in the production of such utilities* (*e.g.* land, buildings, machines, stocks). Now it is obviously more economically efficient to earn £1000 profit from a single machine than £1001 from three. Consequently it is not enough to look at the profit only—in addition the *value of capital* must be considered.

To find the *rate of return* the profit earned is simply expressed as a percentage of the capital tied up. By bringing together profit and capital employed (*i.e.* all the economic factors involved in economic activity), the rate of return can lay claim to being a fundamental measure of enterprise economic performance.

Having said this, however, one word of warning must be given. *How* profit is measured and *how* the capital employed is determined depends on various circumstances (*see* XX, **17, 18**) and also to some extent on personal judgment. The student, therefore, should not set too much store by this measure. Before a rate of return figure can be validly employed, the basis of its calculation must be fully detailed.

19. Uncertainty and management accountancy. In 3 above the continual uncertainty that surrounds all management work was referred to. Management accountants, then, should always be incorporating these uncertainties into their work, preferably in the form of *probability* assessments. Strangely enough this has hardly been done up to the present time, perhaps because accountants are used only to handling exactly known figures that arose in the past. However, this is changing now and as the emphasis in management accountancy swings away from "accountancy" towards "management," probability concepts will certainly become more and more a feature of management accountancy.

20. Profitability and productivity. There are two terms used in the measurement of economic performance which are frequently misunderstood, but which it is vital for a management accountant to understand thoroughly. These terms are profitability, and productivity. The important thing to note is that they are *relative* measures and so must not be confused with profit, and production, which are *absolute* measures. The distinction may perhaps be made clearer by discussing each separately:

(*a*) *Profitability.* When we use the concept of profitability we are concerned only with which of two or more alternatives is the *more* profitable. Note that we do *not* need to find the profit from each alternative to do this. For example, if an article can be sold to A for £40 or to B for £50 then, other things being equal, it is clearly more profitable to sell to B. This is true whatever the costs are (provided they are the same in either case), and so we know which alternative is the more profitable without knowing the profit to be earned from either. Indeed, even if the costs exceed £50 (so that we make a loss either way) it is still more "profitable" to sell to B since this results in a smaller loss than selling to A. Profitability, then, is a relative measure—it indicates the *most profitable alternative.* Profit, on the other hand, is an absolute measure—it indicates the overall amount of profit earned by a transaction.

(*b*) *Productivity.* Productivity is a ratio of economic output to economic input, *i.e.*

$$Productivity = \frac{Economic\ output}{Economic\ input}.$$

Thus if the same goods can be produced (*i.e.* output unchanged) for less labour hours (*i.e.* input reduced) then productivity has increased. Note that in this example the *production* has remained unchanged though the productivity has altered, and indeed it is obviously possible for production to fall while productivity increases (*e.g.* if output drops by 20% but labour hours drop by 30%).

Although discussions on productivity usually revolve round labour hours, the input can be any economic resource. For example, if one is considering those resources the consumption of which remains unaltered for small changes of output (*e.g.* land), then an increase in output clearly leads to increased productivity (since the input remains constant in this respect). Actually, of course, a number of input factors usually change from one situation to another so a common denominator is again required to enable the different forms of consumption to be added together. Hence more sophisticated productivity measurements tend to use the formula, *Productivity = Output/Cost* (*i.e.* output per £ cost), while situations where the forms of output differ and change require a *Sales/Cost* formula. Even with this formula the capital employed figure is excluded, so productivity measures are not as comprehensive measures of economic performance as the rate of return on capital (*see* **18**).

MANAGEMENT ACCOUNTING TECHNIQUES

Now that we have briefly examined all the factors that managers must take into account and considered the function of management accountancy in the context of management, it should be obvious that all management accounting techniques will be devised and operated with the management situation foremost in mind. This chapter ends, then, with a brief look at the broad categories of these techniques.

21. Decision-making. Management accounting uses a number of decision-making techniques and, in fact, the whole of Part Three in this book is devoted to this topic. These techniques include break-even charts, marginal and differential costing, cash and discounted cash flow and, used in a more sophisticated way than normal, total absorption costing. (Total absorption costing, because it throws fixed and variable costs indiscriminately together, is currently under a cloud. However, the technique does give information that is useful to management if the figures produced are interpreted in an appropriate manner.)

22. Planning. The management accountant's main contribution to planning lies in the preparation of budgets. Budgets, however, cover such a wide sector of management activity that it has proved impossible to deal with them at just one point in this book. Essentially there are the following four different kinds of budgets:

(*a*) *Operating budgets.* These budgets detail the economic resources to be consumed and the utilities to be produced during the budget period (normally one year). Such budgets culminate in a budgeted profit statement (*see* IV, **8–13**).

(*b*) *Capital budgets.* These budgets detail the capital assets to be acquired and disposed of during the budget period (usually of many years) together with the associated working capital changes and main forms of financing. Such budgets usually culminate in a series of budgeted balance sheets (*see* IV, **14–26**).

(*c*) *Cash budgets.* These budgets overlap the operating and capital budgets. They show the planned cash resources at any moment during both the operating budget period and the capital budget period, and where a shortage is indicated they will detail the amount and source of the cash required either to tide the enterprise over the shortage period or to finance permanently major capital acquirements (*see* IV, **11**).

(*d*) *Control budgets.* Whereas the three types of budgets referred to above are concerned with setting the definitive overall plans required to achieve major enterprise objectives, control budgets (usually better known perhaps as *flexible budgets*) are designed to enable management to pinpoint where, and for what reason, individual intermediate detailed plans were not achieved, so that action can be taken to ensure the ultimate attainment of the major planned objectives (*see* XIV, **1–4**).

Control budgets obviously should be discussed in Part Four, which is concerned with control, and cash budgets naturally form part of the subject of financial management. Strictly speaking, operating and capital budgets should be discussed under control, but it is felt that in this book the student will probably find them more conveniently situated just prior to and after cash budgets. This, then, is where these two kinds of budgets will be found.

23. Control. The management accounting techniques used for control work can be summed up in the phrase "standard cost and budgetary control." These techniques form the whole of Part Four, "Control."

24. Forecasting. Forecasting is a major function of management, but it is a function that management accountants have rather neglected in the past. Apart from using break-even charts (*see* VII) to predict costs relative to activity, they have passively left management to forecast on their own as best they could. Clearly, however, this is not satisfactory, for of all the members of the management team who should have both details of economic trends, external and internal, and the knowledge of statistical forecasting techniques at his fingertips, none are more obviously qualified than the management accountant.

25. Financial management. When the management accountant turns to financial management he is very much a line manager and many of his techniques are, in effect, management techniques. His cash and credit control are akin to production control; internal audit, a form of inspection; while his cashiers, wage and invoice clerks make up his work force. Financial management, therefore, deserves a book on its own—in this book, for reasons of space, we can only be concerned with financial management to the extent that the economic effectiveness of the enterprise is involved. This includes planning of finance, cash budgets and sources of finance.

26. Systems. Whatever techniques involving arrangement of data the management accountant may elect to use, or whatever financial objectives he may aim to attain, it will be necessary for him to devise systems to collect such data or reach such objectives. Devising systems is a technique and art in itself (as the presence of systems analysts shows), but to help the student tackle an examination question calling on him to devise a system, the following two simple definitions are offered:

> *System:* an integrated set of procedures.
> *Procedure:* a formal and organised way of carrying out a task.

When detailing a system it is frequently much quicker, and the system much more easily comprehended, if a *flow-chart* is used rather than a narrative form. (For the student to whom flow-charting is an unknown technique, a brief outline of the subject is given in Appendix II.)

It should always be remembered that in management accounting virtually every system is tailor-made for the specific enterprise and circumstances involved.

27. Reporting. Of all the techniques used by the management accountant none is more crucial than reporting. Whatever invaluable data the accountant may collect, whatever inspired ideas he may have, unless he can present the data and his conclusions in a lucid and meaningful manner he will have wasted his time. In management accountancy it is not enough to have completed all the "technical" work competently, it is also necessary to report to one's colleagues on the management team so that they too are as well-informed and fully alert regarding the economic significance of events as the management accountant. And it should be appreciated that the onus of effective reporting is wholly on the person reporting—not the person reported to. Reporting is especially important in control work and so an entire chapter of this book has been devoted to reporting in this context (*see* XVI).

Examination questions frequently call for a report and to assist the student to deal with this form of question, Appendix II includes an outline on how to write such a report.

28. Book-keeping and management accounting. Book-keeping is so much associated with accounting in the popular mind that it is a measure of how far the subject has recently developed for a book such as this one with "accounting" in its title to contain so few ledger accounts. Yet management accounting is much more concerned with the economics of business than with the recording of historical monetary data. Book-keeping is, of course, a necessary part of management accounting, but in this book it is assumed that the student can cope with virtually all aspects of book-keeping. Apart from a short section at the end of the next chapter outlining integral accounts (II, **17–22**), and a brief mention of the ledger accounts involved when adjusting asset values in an inflationary period (a topic rarely discussed in book-keeping texts) (XVIII, **26-28**), there are no references to book-keeping entries.

29. New techniques in management accountancy. Recently a whole new group of techniques has emerged in the world of management accountancy. Many of these emerged as a result of using a mathematical approach to the measurement of economic performance and efficiency, and were developed in the field of operational research. These techniques include linear programming, PERT/COST, model-building and a range of probability-based techniques that embrace topics such as decision theory and queuing. More and more, too, statistics is playing an important part in the work of the management accountant.

As yet examiners are only rarely asking questions involving these techniques in examination papers in management accounting, and so they are omitted from this short handbook. Nevertheless, the student should be aware that knowledge of these techniques is becoming increasingly necessary for the management accountant and should be prepared to study such techniques and learn ultimately how to incorporate them into his day-to-day work. For better or worse, accounting is becoming less and less a recording skill and more and more a skill appertaining to quantitative measurement.

PROGRESS TEST 1

Principles

1. Why are the following important in management accountancy:

   (*a*) the future? (2)
   (*b*) uncertainty? (3)

2. What factors must managers bear in mind when engaged in management? (4–12)
3. Briefly indicate the function of management accountancy. (15)
4. Distinguish between the two roles of money. (16)
5. Is there a fundamental measure of economic performance? (18)
6. What is:

   (*a*) profitability?
   (*b*) productivity? (20)

7. What four different kinds of budgets are used in management accountancy? (22)
8. What is:

   (*a*) a system?
   (*b*) a procedure? (26)

9. Why is reporting an important management accounting technique? (27)

CHAPTER II

COST ASCERTAINMENT

INTRODUCTION

COST accountancy to a large extent overlaps management accountancy; indeed, it may be argued that there is no longer any point in referring to them as two distinct techniques. Consequently many topics discussed in this book can also be found in books on cost accountancy. Cost ascertainment, however, appears to be a part of cost accountancy that is not regarded as being part of the core of management accountancy. This, no doubt, is because such ascertainment is an historical technique (*i.e.* concerned with *past* events) and so not sufficiently involved with the future for close study by students of management accountancy. Nevertheless, it is important for the management accountant to be aware of how costs are ascertained so that he can appreciate the underlying assumptions and limitations of the figures put in front of him by his cost office. In this chapter the main points involved in cost ascertainment are discussed, and the recording of actual costs by a system of integral accounts outlined. (For a fuller treatment of the subject see *Cost Accountancy*, W. M. Harper, Macdonald & Evans.)

BASIC COST CONCEPTS

1. The meaning of "cost" in cost ascertainment. When used in cost ascertainment the word "cost" refers to *the value of economic resources used* as a result of producing or doing whatever is being costed. Such a cost can be broken down into cost elements, a cost element being, in effect, the cost of an individual resource (*e.g.* material) consumed by whatever is being costed. Note that all cost elements have two components: a *quantity* of the resource used and the *price* of that resource. This means the costs of all cost elements can be shown by the formula:

$$Cost = Usage \times Price$$

It should, incidentally, be appreciated that in costing it is the economic resources used that is really important; multiplying by price to give cost is only the conversion to the common denominator of money. Improvement by management of economic performance hinges on the more economical use of resources or the substitution of cheaper resources for more expensive resources. A management accountant should never forget, then, that it is the *resources* underlying the £ figures that are really significant.

2. Cost units. We cannot have "costs" unless there are things being costed (such as pens, bridges, theatre performances, departments or factories) and when these are the things that the enterprise or department is set up to provide, then such "things" are termed "cost units." A *cost unit*, then, can be defined as a unit of quantity of produce, service or time in relation to which costs may be ascertained or expressed. These cost units may be:

(*a*) Units of production, *e.g.* jobs, contracts, tons of material, gallons of liquid, books, pairs of shoes.
(*b*) Units of service, *e.g.* kilowatt-hours, cinema seats, passenger-miles, consultancy hours.

NOTE: Students should learn and understand this definition as the term is frequently used in costing. In most cases cost units are simply the individual items of production, and provided the student appreciates the wider meaning (*e.g.* service units) he may regard them as such for study purposes.

3. Cost centres. Costs can relate to things other than cost units. They can refer to individual parts of the enterprise. Such parts can range from an entire factory (in the case of a company with a group of factories) down to a single machine or a single salesman. Any part of an enterprise to which costs can be charged is called a *cost centre*. A cost centre can be:

(*a*) *Geographical*, *i.e.* an area such as a department, store-yard or sales area.
(*b*) *An item of equipment*, *e.g.* lathe, fork-lift truck, delivery vehicle.
(*c*) *A person*, *e.g.* salesman.

Charging costs to a cost centre simply involves charging to that centre those costs which relate to it. Thus a lathe will be charged with its costs of depreciation, maintenance, power and cleaning and also with a share of the rent, rates, heat and light costs of the enterprise. A salesman "cost centre" similarly will be charged with his salary, commission, expenses, entertainment, telephone, postage, samples, car costs (and the car itself may, of course, be a cost centre charged with depreciation, petrol, oil, maintenance, tyres, licence, insurance), and so on.

4. General costing principles. The following general costing principles should be observed:

(a) *Costs should be related as closely as possible to their causes.* A foreman's salary, for instance, could not usually be pinned down to a single cost unit, but it should be so recorded that such a cost can only be shared among the cost units passing through that foreman's department and *not among any units remaining outside his department.* This relating of cost to cause, pinning the cost down so that it covers neither more nor less than the cost units or cost centres which caused it, is an important aspect of good costing. Grouping overheads into one single "general expenses" category is to be avoided if at all possible.

(b) *A cost is not charged until it is incurred.* This appears obvious, but is often forgotten. For instance, care should be taken that a cost unit is not charged with any selling costs while it is still in the factory, since units cannot incur selling costs until they are sold. Similarly, when the cost of lost units must be carried by good units such a charge cannot be imposed on units which have not passed the point of loss.

NOTE: A cost can be incurred at a different time to that when it is paid. A cost is incurred the moment something happens that makes ultimate payment inevitable.

(c) *Abnormal costs are excluded from costs.* Costing aims to provide information on economic performance to assist managers to manage. Abnormal costs, however, do not promote this object, since they do not relate to normal economic performance that management can influence but instead to infrequent accidents that cannot be controlled. Their presence in the costs, therefore, would tend to distort cost figures and mislead management as to their economic performance as managers under normal conditions. To charge gale damage costs (for instance) may result in a doubling of normal costs per unit, but such a figure gives production managers no real information as to their production efficiency. Abnormal costs are therefore excluded from costs.

(*d*) *Past costs are never charged to future periods.* There is often a temptation to charge past costs, or unrecovered costs, to a later period on the grounds that these costs have to be recovered somewhere, and since the past has gone they can only be recovered in future periods. This is quite wrong. Inclusion of past costs in future periods results in the distortion of the performance figures for those periods and gives rise to a risk of misleading management.

Care should be taken, however, in deciding whether a cost is "past" or not, a *past cost* being one from which no more benefit can be expected. If, however, the *benefit* of a particular cost comes in a later period, then such a cost is not a past cost and can, indeed must, be capitalised and charged in the period of benefit. (This is simply the old accountancy convention of charging expenditure to the period to which it relates.)

(*e*) *Profit appropriations are excluded from costs.* Profit appropriations are *not* regarded as costs. Thus dividends and taxes based on profits are excluded from costs. Note, however, that in *management* accountancy (particularly decision-making) such items do enter into the calculations.

5. Direct and indirect costs. All costs fall into one of the two categories of direct and indirect costs.

(*a*) A *direct cost* may be defined as a cost that arises *solely* from the existence of whatever is being costed. With a direct cost there can be no suggestion of sharing the cost between the things being costed. If the individual "thing" being costed had not existed the cost would not have arisen at all.

(*b*) An *indirect cost* is simply a cost that is not direct, *i.e.* its existence does not depend solely on what is being costed. It therefore implies some element of sharing a cost that is common or jointly incurred by two or more things being costed. When the things being costed are cost units indirect costs can also be referred to as *overheads*.

It should be noted in passing that the definitions refer to

"whatever is being costed." Thus, if departments, sales areas or even customer classifications are being costed, then the definitions should be applied with these in mind. For example, a departmental manager's salary is a direct cost if the department is being costed, though indirect if costing the cost units in the department. However, the terms direct and indirect costs are used far more often in relation to the costing of cost units, and so, unless the context clearly indicates differently, they should be regarded as relating to cost units.

COST DATA

All cost figures which appear on any cost statement must, of course, have some source. Sometimes the source may not be wholly reliable and in order to judge how much one may depend on any cost figure it is necessary to have some knowledge of how the basic cost data were collected. This section briefly outlines the sources of cost data.

6. Labour costs. The basic principle of labour costing is to record the number of hours an employee is engaged on whatever is being costed and then multiply this figure by his rate of pay. In labour costing the following points should be noted:

(*a*) The normal recording medium of the time a man spends on any activity is the *time-sheet*. This is a form on which a man *books his time*, *i.e.* records the time spent on each activity. It is important that a check is made to ensure that all time paid for by the enterprise (*i.e.* as normally recorded on the man's clock-card) has been booked on the time-sheet. Labour bookings are often subject to inaccuracies (*see* **9** below) and in order to improve the accuracy bookings are sometimes made by shop clerical workers or on special time-recording clocks.

(*b*) Where possible a man's time should be charged to *cost units* (*see* **4** (*a*)). If this is not possible then the time must be charged to a *cost centre*. In this latter case it is important also to record the nature of the work done in the cost centre (*e.g.* cleaning, maintenance, supervision, materials handling, idle time).

(*c*) Sometimes when computing a labour cost the man's actual wage rate is inflated to allow for holiday pay, national health insurance stamp, graduated pensions, and so on. Really, of course, this should always be done as it is in accord with the costing principle given in **4**(*a*).

7. Material costs. Material costing is, unfortunately, made much more complex by the fact that materials are frequently stored after purchase for some time before use. Essentially materials are put into store at their purchase price plus an addition for the cost of delivery. When the materials are issued for use on whatever is being costed the quantity used is multiplied by the price. In material costing the following points should be noted:

(*a*) Materials are normally issued by the storekeeper on the production of a *material requisition*. Such a requisition acts as:

(*i*) an authority to the storekeeper to release the materials;
(*ii*) a record of issue for stores control purposes; and
(*iii*) a record of material usage for the cost office.

In its latter capacity the requisition will indicate the cost unit or cost centre to be charged with the materials and there will be columns on the requisition in which the price and total value of the materials can be recorded.

(*b*) Since materials can be held in the store for some time it is possible to price issues in a variety of ways. The following are the main *methods of pricing stores issues:*

(*i*) *FIFO* (*First in, first out*). In this method it is assumed that issues of items are made in the same order as they were received in the store and are priced accordingly, *i.e.* issues are priced at the purchase price of items in the first batch received until that batch has been exhausted, after which items are priced at the purchase price of the second batch, and so on.

(*ii*) *LIFO* (*Last in, first out*). In this method it is assumed that issues of items are made from the batch *last received*, and priced accordingly. (If this batch is exhausted before another arrives then the purchase price relating to the batch received prior to that is used.) Note that using this method does not imply that the storekeeper will in fact be issuing materials on this basis. Materials should always be *physically* issued on a FIFO basis—LIFO is simply a book-keeping device.

(*iii*) *Average price*. Here the average price for all items of the material in question held in store is found at the time of each receipt and this price used to price all subsequent issues. The formula used in this method is:

$$\textit{New average price} = \frac{(\textit{Remaining balance of items} \times \textit{Old average price}) + \textit{Total cost of new receipt}}{\textit{Total of old balance and new items received}}$$

(*iv*) *Replacement price*. Under this method items are issued at the price that would currently have to be paid to replace them. There is no reference to what had been the actual purchase price.

(*v*) *Standard price*. Here items are issued at a predetermined price and the actual purchase price is disregarded.

8. Other costs. The sources of other cost data generally call for much less involved procedure than labour or material cost data. Items such as rent, rates, telephone and bank charges are clearly and unambiguously recorded on one or another of the commercial documents located in the enterprise files. Complications arise to some extent if costs are apportioned between beneficiaries (*see* **16**), but provided the management accountant has familiarised himself with the apportionment procedures employed by the enterprise, he should have no difficulty in assessing the significance of apportioned figures on any cost statement he may receive.

9. Reliability of cost data. Management accountants should never forget that cost data may not always be reliable. Much of them come from the shop-floor—time-sheets, material requisitions, material returned notes, transfer notes, piece-work tickets and scrap returns—and it should be appreciated that many shop-floor employees:

(*a*) Are not clerks, nor are they really paid for clerical accuracy.
(*b*) Rarely have good clerical facilities (either office desks or even proper pencils).
(*c*) Often regard paper-work as an unnecessary obstacle to "getting the job out." (It should be noted, however, that the accountant who thinks the paper-work should have priority makes an even graver error.)
(*d*) Often have to record information from memory, because no written reference exists or because it is not at hand.
(*e*) May deliberately falsify the data.

This last possibility may be common where time-sheets are involved, particularly if an incentive scheme is in operation. Two points should be noted here. Firstly, if management use a single record for both computing bonuses and preparing costs, they cannot really complain if the employees use them as instruments to maximise their bonuses in preference to recording accurate cost information. Secondly, attempts to enforce accurate time-recording usually prove abortive; loopholes are almost invariably found unless the scheme is so elaborate that it is uneconomic.

In view of such possible unreliability in their basic data, accountants must beware of jumping to conclusions from such data. For instance, when booking time to a mixture of small and large jobs employees may easily forget they worked on some small jobs. Moreover, they are conscious that their excessive time is much more noticeable on a small job than a large job involving a number of other employees. As a result, small jobs are almost always underbooked and large jobs overbooked and accountants should allow for this.

COST METHODS AND TECHNIQUES

There are a number of cost methods and techniques, but as all methods are really only variants of two fundamental kinds, job and unit, and as all the techniques other than the total absorption costing technique are discussed later in this book, only job, unit, and total absorption costing are dealt with in this section. First, however, since all methods and techniques ultimately employ cost statements, we shall start with a look at the relationship between cost data and cost statements.

10. Role of cost data. Costing is essentially the use of cost data to construct cost statements. Cost data in this context may be looked on as cost atoms, *i.e.* the smallest divisions of cost that exist. For instance, we may know that a tin of paint worth £2 was drawn from stock for general use in department A. There is no further breakdown of this £2 cost, and it is therefore similar to an atom. Clearly, in any cost office there will be a great many such "atoms." As the different combinations of chemical atoms in chemistry give different substances, so the different combinations of cost atoms give different kinds of cost statements.

Yet another way of looking at cost data is to consider them as building bricks. Such bricks can be used to construct "buildings" of quite different designs, *i.e.* used to construct quite different statements.

The important point to note here is that *the same cost data can be arranged and rearranged to give a number of quite different statements*, and that no one way is *the* only correct way.

11. The basic principle of cost data arrangement. It must be emphasised at this point that all costing and all cost statements must always be prepared with the following question in mind: *for what purpose is the information required?* This question lies at the heart of all costing, and every cost statement should be prepared with its particular purpose in the forefront of the accountant's mind. One is always faced in costing with the problem of choosing which pieces of data should be used, and if at every point one considers whether or not use of the data will help achieve the purpose, then it becomes much easier to pass through the labyrinth of alternative treatments of data that are a feature of costing. Remember, too, that there are no definitive rules or statute laws that make the choice for one; books may point the way, but always the final decision must be left to the judgment of the individual accountant.

12. Distinction between cost methods and techniques. The distinction between cost methods and cost techniques can best be made by examining each in turn.

(*a*) *Cost methods.* The cost method selected in any instance depends upon the *nature of the cost units.* Fundamentally there are only two different forms of cost units—one where every cost unit is different and one where the cost units are all identical. These forms dictate whether *job costing* or *unit costing* (or variants thereon) respectively shall be used (*see* **13** and **14**).

(*b*) *Cost techniques.* On the other hand, the cost technique selected depends upon the *purpose for which the information is required.* Information is required for a variety of purposes, such as decision-making, control, cost forecasting, performance evaluation and price-determination, and the exact purpose determines the technique to be used.

13. Job costing. The method of job costing is used where the *cost units are all different* and each unit is to be costed *individually.* In this method:

(*a*) Each cost unit is given an individual *job number.*
(*b*) As far as possible all costs incurred are charged to job numbers.
(*c*) For each cost unit there is a *job card* on which all cost data relating to that unit is collected (*see* Fig. 1).

14. Unit costing. The method of unit costing is used where *all cost units are identical* and are costed *collectively.* In this method:

(*a*) The cost of running each cost centre and the number of cost units passing through each centre is ascertained.

(*b*) For each cost centre the total cost of running the centre is divided by the number of cost units passing through, to obtain a cost centre cost-per-unit figure.

(*c*) As units pass through the various cost centres the cost-per-unit figures are cumulatively added so that the total cost-per-unit at any point in the production process is known.

JOB CARD

Description of Job.. Job No..............................

Customer .... Sales Order No.....................

Date of Despatch.. Order No. Date.....................

Direct Materials						Labour				Direct Wages		Factory O'h'ds	
Date	Req. No.	Description	Quan-tity	Price	Cost	Date	Dept.	Clock No.	Hrs.	Rate	Cost	O'h'd Rate	Cost
				Total £									

Direct Expenses:

Total £	

Total £	

Comments:

Summary	
Direct Materials	
Direct Expenses	
Direct Labour	
Factory Overheads	
Factory Cost £	
Selling Overheads	
Distrib. costs—Dist. job card...	
Freight	
Total Cost £	
Profit	
Selling Price £	
Returnable containers, allowances, etc.:	

FIG. 1.—*Job card*

This card is for a small job. Where jobs are large, usually only periodic totals are shown on the job card.

15. Total absorption costing. The technique of total absorption costing is based on the concept that *all* normal costs of running an enterprise should be charged in some way or other to all the cost units produced, *i.e.* the cost units absorb the total costs. Following this concept involves charging cost units with:

(*a*) their direct costs; and
(*b*) a fair share of the indirect costs or *overheads* as they are termed in this context.

Direct costs are, of course, mainly charged from time-sheets and material requisitions. The charging of a fair share of the overheads is, however, a rather involved procedure and is outlined separately in the next paragraph.

16. The allocation, apportionment and absorption of overheads. In order to charge overheads fairly to cost units the following procedure is adopted:

(*a*) All the overheads are collected together on an analysis sheet called an *overhead analysis*, the columns of which are headed with the names of the cost centres.

(*b*) Any overheads that are known to have been specifically incurred by a particular cost centre are *allocated* to that centre.

(*c*) Those overheads that were not specifically incurred by a particular centre must be shared out on a fair basis between all benefiting cost centres. This sharing is known as *apportionment*, and the basis on which the apportionment is made is known as the *basis of apportionment*. Selecting a suitable basis of apportionment is very much a matter of judgment, though the bases of the more common costs have been settled by custom (*e.g.* rent is apportioned on a basis of floor area and general administration costs on a basis of numbers of employees or employee hours in each cost centre).

(*d*) The cost centre costs are then added and the cost of the *service centres* are themselves then apportioned to the various cost centres, this apportionment continuing until ultimately all costs have been charged to production cost centres exclusively.

(*e*) The total cost of each production centre is then shared out fairly between the cost units passing through that centre. This is known as *overhead absorption*. There are different methods of overhead absorption though the *hourly rate method* is perhaps the commonest. In this method:

(*i*) The total cost centre cost is divided by the total production hours worked in the centre (labour or machine hours as the cost accountant judges is the better) to give an overhead rate per hour.

(*ii*) The production hours spent on each cost unit are recorded and this time is then multiplited by the overhead rate found in (*i*). This gives the overheads chargeable to that cost unit in respect of that cost centre.

Of course, to find the *total* overhead charge to be borne by a cost unit it is necessary to add together all the charges made to the unit in respect of all the different cost centres through which it passed.

INTEGRAL ACCOUNTS

In modern accounting the financial and cost ledgers are integrated into a single system, other methods of accounting now being regarded as obsolete. In this section the main points relating to such a system are outlined.

17. Definition. The term *integral accounts* relates to a single accounting system which contains both financial and cost accounts. In theory, all accounts are in a single ledger.

18. Chart of integral accounts. Fig. 2 shows a chart representing the essential accounting flow involved in a *system of integral accounts*. The following points should be noted:

(*a*) The accounts are usually drawn up on a monthly basis.

(*b*) The direct and indirect materials figures, and the direct and indirect wages figures, are abstracted from previously prepared analyses of materials and wages respectively.

(*c*) The Overhead Control Account in this chart summarises what would in practice be a large number of separate overhead and departmental accounts.

(*d*) Prepayments and accruals can be taken into consideration by the usual procedure of carrying them down, in this case in the Overhead Control Account.

(*e*) The debit in respect of overheads to the Work-in-Progress Account is the *absorbed* overheads and is found by multiplying the total cost unit factor of direct labour hours for the period by the overhead absorption rate. For instance, if 20,000 direct labour hours were booked to cost units and the overhead rate was £0·75 hour, then £15,000 would be debited to the Work-in-Progress Account for overheads.

(*f*) Selling and distribution overheads are *not* included in the charges to the Work-in-Progress Account. As these overheads are incurred at the time of sale and delivery, they are

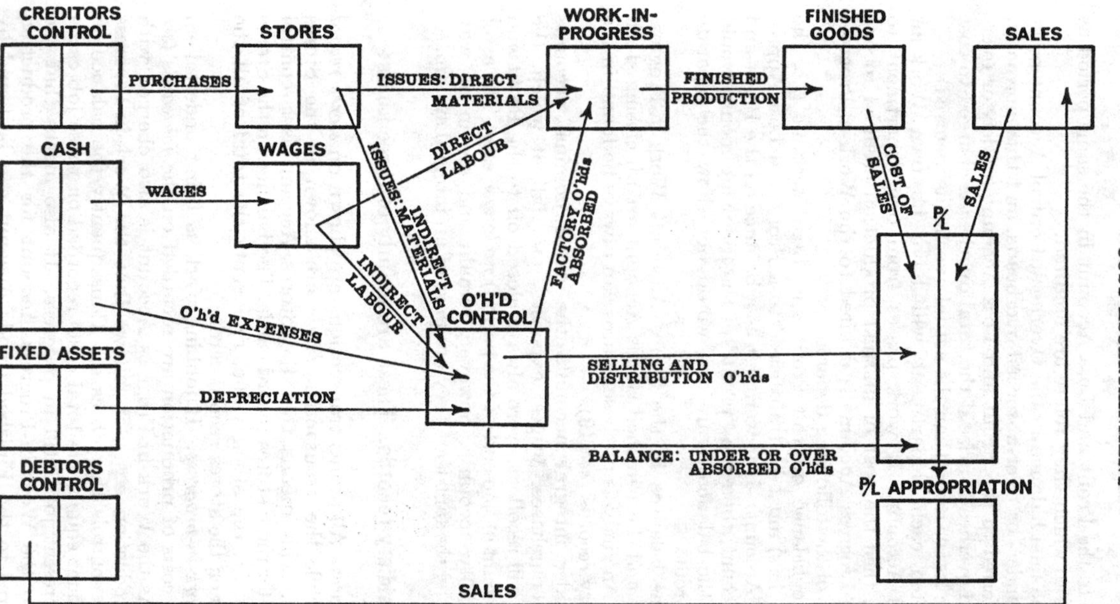

FIG. 2.—*Chart of accounting flow in an integral accounts system*

This is a single system containing both financial and cost accounts. The chart has been considerably simplified for purposes of clarity; *e.g.* in practice the Overhead Control Account would be split into many separate overhead and departmental accounts.

charged to the Profit and Loss Account in the same period as the sales to which they relate are credited.

(*g*) The final balance in the Overhead Control Account must be any under- or over-absorbed overheads, and this, normally, is transferred to the Profit and Loss Account (under- or over-absorbed overheads arise if the total overheads charged to cost units are less or more than the actual overheads incurred).

(*h*) Often each department will have its own Work-in-Progress Account. If work passes from one department to another, then the cost of finished production credited to one Work-in-Progress Account is debited to the Work-in-Progress Account of the following department.

(*i*) The balance on the Profit and Loss Account (*i.e.* the profit or loss) must be transferred to a Profit and Loss Appropriation Account. If it were left as a balance on the Profit and Loss Account, then the "profit" of the following month would include the balance figure and would not show the separate period profit.

(*j*) The balances in the Stores Account, Work-in-Progress Account and the Finished Goods Account are all closing stock values. An analysis of these figures can always be found in the subsidiary records (*see* **19**).

(*k*) Under integral accounts the usual nominal accounts showing purchases, wages, expenses, etc. (all of which, the student will recollect, were always closed off to the Profit and Loss Account at the end of the period) *no longer exist*. The asset and liability accounts, however, remain and are in no way affected by the fact that they are part of an integral system.

19. Subsidiary records. These are mainly of three kinds:

(*a*) *Stores.* All stores transactions are shown on *stores record cards*, while the transaction *totals* are shown in the Stores Account. This means that the Stores Account is a control account for these stores record cards. The balance on the Stores Account, *i.e.* the stock value, represents the total of all the balances on the stores record cards.

(*b*) *Work-in-progress.* If jobbing work is being undertaken, then all costs of production are recorded on the *job cards* (*see* **13**(*c*)). As the Work-in-Progress Account is also charged with these production costs, it follows that the Work-in-Progress Account controls the job cards. Consequently the balance on this account equals the total costs recorded on those job cards that represent jobs still in progress. It also means that the credit to the Work-in-Progress Account for the production transferred to the Finished Goods Account can be found by totalling all job cards representing jobs completed during the accounting period.

(c) *Finished goods.* In the same way that the Stores Account controls the stores record cards, so the Finished Goods Account controls the *finished goods stock records,* and therefore the balance on this account represents the balances on all the record cards. Also the cost-of-sales figure credited to the Finished Goods Account can be found by using the finished goods stock record cards to price all items removed from the finished goods store.

20. Cost Control Account. In practice, it is generally found to be physically inconvenient to keep all the accounts in a single ledger. The Ledger is therefore physically divided into two, a Financial Ledger under the responsibility of the financial accountant and a Cost Ledger under the responsibility of the cost accountant. This does *not* affect the double entry given in Fig. 2, but in order to assist balancing, a Cost Control Account is opened up *in the Financial Ledger.* This control account is similar to any other control account (*e.g.* Creditors Control, or Debtors Control) in that:

(a) It records in total all amounts that enter into the Cost Ledger.
(b) It enables the Financial Ledger to be balanced independently of the Cost Ledger.
(c) The balance on the Cost Control Account must equal the net balance in the Cost Ledger as a whole.

21. Rules for operating a Cost Control Account. Although the operation of a Cost Control Account is identical to the operation of any other control account, it does sometimes appear more complicated. The student may therefore find the following rules helpful when operating a Cost Control Account. (These rules are illustrated in Fig. 3.)

(a) Establish a clear distinction between the Financial Ledger accounts and the Cost Ledger accounts. Students often find it useful to imagine the ledgers being divided by a distinct line. Which accounts are to be in which ledger is purely a matter of choice, although a division similar to that shown in Fig. 3 is usual.

(b) The double-entry shown earlier in Fig. 2 is adhered to without change, but in addition whenever the double-entry spans the two ledgers (and therefore crosses the dividing line)

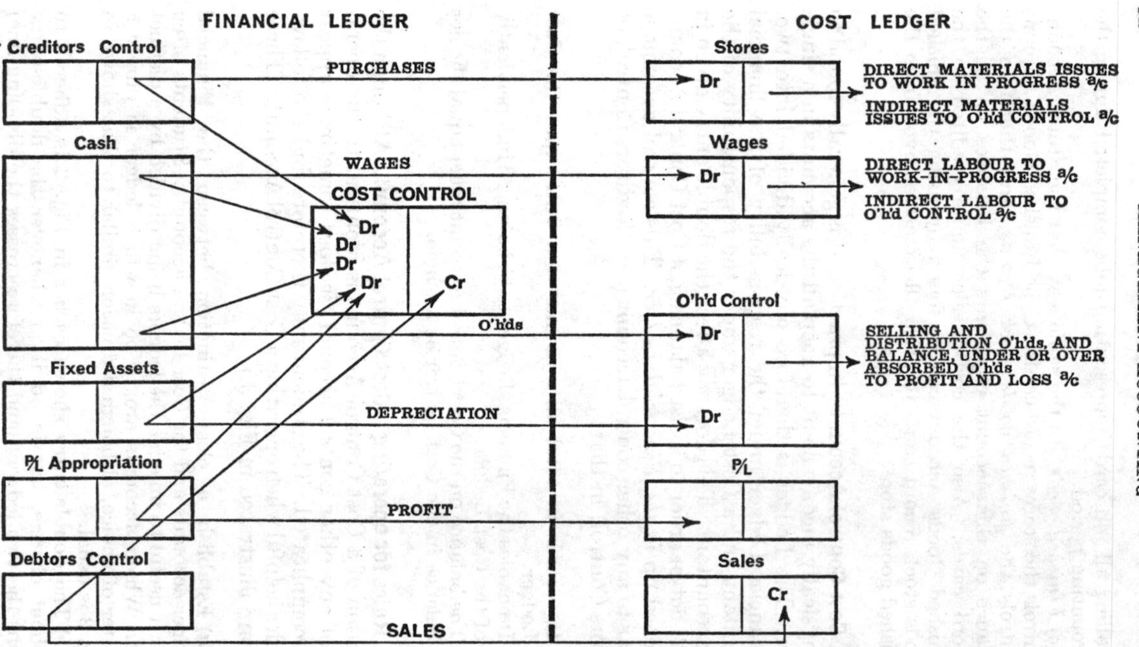

FIG. 3.—*Effect of including a Cost Control Account in an integral accounts system*

the entry made in the Cost Ledger account is duplicated in the Cost Control Account.

NOTE: This results in *all* entries within the Financial Ledger being balancing entries. Hence this ledger is self-balancing.

22. Financial and Cost Profit and Loss Accounts. In practice, there are often certain expenses which do not enter the cost accounts, *e.g.* cash discounts and interest. These expenses, therefore, must be recorded in the Financial Ledger. Before the profit on the *Cost* Profit and Loss Account can be transferred to the Appropriation Account such expenses have to be brought in. This is usually dealt with by transferring the cost profit to a *Financial* Profit and Loss Account in the Financial Ledger. These missing items are then incorporated into the cost profit and the resulting figure, *i.e.* the financial profit, transferred to the Appropriation Account. It is important to appreciate that *in integral accounts there is no contradiction between the cost profit and the financial profit;* reconciliation is unnecessary. The financial profit is simply the cost profit as transferred from the Cost Profit and Loss Account with a few small non-cost items incorporated.

PROGRESS TEST 2

Principles

1. What is the meaning of "cost" in cost ascertainment? **(1)**
2. What are:

(*a*) Cost units? **(2)**
(*b*) Cost centres? **(3)**

3. Distinguish between direct and indirect costs. **(5)**
4. On what main document is recorded data in respect of:

(*a*) Labour costs? **(6)**
(*b*) Material costs? **(7)**

5. State and distinguish between the five main methods of pricing stores issues. **(7)**
6. Why are cost data sometimes not reliable? **(9)**
7. State the basic principle of cost data arrangement. **(11)**
8. Distinguish between job costing and unit costing. **(13, 14)**
9. What concept underlies total absorption costing? **(15)**
10. Outline the procedural steps in the allocation, apportionment and absorption of overheads. **(16)**

11. What is meant by integral accounts? (17)

12. What are the rules for operating a Cost Control Account? (21)

13. Why is it unnecessary to reconcile cost and financial profits under a system of integral accounts? (22)

PART TWO

FINANCIAL MANAGEMENT

As we have seen (I, **25**) one aspect of the management accountant's work does involve actual management and that is the one relating to the management of cash and cash resources. There is much that can be written about this facet of management accountancy, but in this book discussion will be restricted to that part of the subject concerned with the use of cash in the most effective economic manner.

We start first by briefly examining the need for financial management (III), and observe that the essence of such management is to ensure that a correct balance of cash is maintained, *i.e.* not too much and not too little. Next, Chapter IV on budgets illustrates how the cash forecasts essential for effective cash management can be made, and this is followed by a chapter in which the planning of the finance shown to be necessary by the budgets is discussed (V). Finally, Chapter VI briefly examines the sources from which the planned finance may be obtained.

CHAPTER III

THE NEED FOR FINANCIAL MANAGEMENT

WHY do we need to manage finance? Obviously, until we have decided on the answer to this question the techniques required to carry out this management function cannot be intelligently discussed. In this chapter, then, the need for financial management will be outlined.

THE FINANCIAL CONTEXT

1. The need for cash. In our modern economic environment possession of cash is essential. In most trading and virtually all manufacturing situations it is necessary to possess cash to acquire economic resources before cash is received from customers for the goods produced from the acquired resources. This is particularly so in respect of capital equipment such as buildings or plant.

2. Cash: an economic factor of production. As we have seen, cash is an economic factor of production (I, **16** (*a*)). This means one must pay to acquire cash. The price one must pay to acquire cash varies, as it does with any economic factor, with supply and demand. Moreover, different "qualities" of cash (or "finance" as we should say in this context) can be acquired, *e.g.* finance can be short-term or long-term, and naturally the value differs with the "quality."

Since cash is an economic factor of production it follows that in any efficient enterprise only the minimum amount of cash should be acquired, excessive acquirement leading to excessive costs and a subsequent lowering of the efficiency of the enterprise.

3. The need for liquidity. If efficiency can be directly measured by how little cash is acquired, it would seem that financial management would simply involve ensuring that the absolute minimum necessary for operations is acquired, and that which is acquired is obtained in the cheapest form. Unfortunately, however, use of the cheapest "quality" of cash acquired almost invariably carries with it the obligation of early repayment. If this repayment is not made then the enterprise may well be taken over by the people who provided the finance.

There is no point in being financially efficient if such efficiency leads to the loss of the enterprise. Such a policy would be akin to under-fuelling an aircraft to economise in operating costs! Financial management, then, involves ensuring that there are always sufficient funds available to avoid defaulting on the payment of debt and so being taken over. The extent to which it is possible to do this is measured by what is termed *liquidity;* the more "liquid" one is, the more funds one has, or can obtain, relative to the size of the debt.

4. Efficiency v. liquidity. From the preceding paragraphs we can see that financial management revolves very much around the balancing of efficiency against liquidity. Too much cash will ensure a comfortable liquidity situation but at the expense of financial efficiency (and hence enterprise profit), while too little cash may feature high efficiency but ultimate self-destruction.

The right balance here is really a matter of human judgment, though there are a number of techniques that are of help to the Financial Manager in reaching a decision and which will be outlined in this Part of the book. The student, however, should be aware that temperament often enters the making of the decision in practice: businessmen tend to be optimistic and risk liquidity for the sake of profit, while cautious accountants are more likely to be prepared to forego profits for the sake of liquidity. The good management accountant, of course, must steer a more realistic middle course.

ACHIEVING FINANCIAL BALANCE

5. Financial ratios. One way the management accountant can approach the problem of balancing efficiency against liquidity is to study relevant financial ratios. For ease of reference all financial ratios are detailed in Chapter XX, and of those ratios the following four are particularly relevant to this situation:

(a) *Current ratio:* ratio of current assets to current liabilities (XX, 8).

(b) *Vulnerability:* extent to which current assets would need to be realised to pay all current liabilities (XX, **9**).
(c) *Liquid ratio:* ratio of liquid assets to current liabilities (XX, **10**).
(d) *Profit to capital employed:* usually percentage of net profit before tax to net worth (XX, **16**).

6. Applying the ratios. The ratios must naturally be applied with commonsense. A current ratio that contained a large debtor known to be in financial trouble would need to be discounted to this extent. Conversely, an imminent dispatch of finished goods (with certain early payment) would be allowed for in the liquid ratio.

Net profit to net worth is, of course, a valid measure of the efficiency of financing since the more cash that can be raised from sources other than shareholders, then the less the shareholders need to have invested to earn the enterprise profit. Nevertheless, this percentage is mainly influenced by the basic trading or manufacturing efficiency of the enterprise, to which financing efficiency is of little relevance. To obtain a better measure of financing efficiency, a comparison may be made between the percentage of net profit before interest to total capital employed, on the one hand, and percentage of net profit to net worth, on the other. The difference between the percentages would then indicate the financing efficiency of the enterprise, as the following illustrative figures show:

EXAMPLE

	Company A	*Company B*
Net worth	£200,000	£100,000
Debt at 8% interest	100,000	200,000
Total capital employed	£300,000	£300,000
Net profit before interest	£30,000	£30,000
Net profit after interest	£22,000	£14,000
Net profit before interest/Total capital employed	10%	10%
Net profit after interest/Net worth	11%	14%

Clearly, although A and B earned exactly the same profit from exactly the same total capital employed, B's financial structure gave its shareholders a significantly larger return on their investment. By comparing the percentages as suggested it can be seen that in the case of A there is a difference of +1% and in the case of B of +4%.

7. Unused overdraft = cash? When an enterprise has an overdraft limit the question sometimes arises as to whether any unused balance can be considered cash. For example, if there is an overdraft limit of £50,000 but at a given time only an actual overdraft of £10,000, could the enterprise consider itself to have a cash balance of £40,000 and a creditor for £50,000? Probably this approach can be regarded as acceptable, provided that the enterprise appreciates that the unused balance could be cancelled by the bank at any moment if conditions warranted it.

8. The need for planning. If the correct balance between efficiency and liquidity is to be maintained, it is vitally important for the management accountant to forecast accurately cash movements and plan his receipts and payments so that neither efficiency nor liquidity suffer unnecessarily. A good forecast allows the management accountant to submit suggestions regarding enterprise operations so that the peaks and valleys of cash resources are evened out. For example, it may be a sensible policy to hold a store's sale just prior to the due date for the payment of corporation tax, so that a heavy cash receipt immediately precedes a heavy cash payment. Again, it may be a very sound move to defer capital expenditure until the slack season of trading when low stocks and debtors result in a peak of cash resources. Evening out cash peaks and valleys naturally aids the enterprise, since during periods that it is holding unnecessarily large cash balances it is failing to operate at its maximum potential financial efficiency, while in periods that it is starved of cash it risks possible serious financial embarrassment.

Forecasting and planning, then, are essential requisites for good financial management.

9. Short- and long-term financing. Financing divides itself into two forms, short-term and long-term, though the dividing line between them tends to be indistinct and arbitrary.

(a) *Short-term financing.* This form of financing ensures that cash resources are available to tide the enterprise over temporary low cash points. This is particularly necessary if the business is seasonal; inevitably at one moment in the year the financial resources of the enterprise are under strain (if they are not then the enterprise is probably being inefficient in its use of cash). As this strain is only temporary the financing also need only be temporary.

(b) *Long-term financing.* This form of financing ensures that cash resources of a more permanent kind are available in situations where cash outflows will not be offset by an early subsequent inflow, *e.g.* when a major fixed asset item is acquired.

10. Planning horizons. A problem that always arises in planning involves deciding on how far ahead to plan. Although there is rarely any definite solution to this problem there is usually little to be gained by planning beyond the furthest point one can reasonably foresee with some certitude. Thus if a business is operating in an unstable environment (*e.g.* depending for much of its success on a world-wide but temporary material shortage) or in an uncertain situation (*e.g.* marketing a brand new product) then firm planning may be limited to a few months, while in a stable environment (*e.g.* the forestry industry) plans may run into decades. This furthest point that one can reasonably foresee is termed the *planning horizon* and when making most plans an early decision must clearly be made regarding the position of the planning horizon.

PROGRESS TEST 3

1. What is liquidity and why is it an important concept? **(3)**
2. What are the advantages and disadvantages of:
   (a) a cash excess?
   (b) a cash deficiency? **(4)**
3. What four ratios may aid the management accountant in finding the balance between efficiency and liquidity? **(5)**
4. Why is planning needed for good financial management? **(8)**
5. Distinguish between short- and long-term finance **(9)**
6. What is a planning horizon? **(10)**

CHAPTER IV

BUDGETS

INTRODUCTION

As we saw in the last chapter financial management involves plans, and the first plans that must be prepared relate to the receipts and payments of cash that will follow the planned running of the enterprise. When these have been prepared it is then possible to plan the form of financing to be employed.

This chapter looks at the preparation of these initial plans, the planning of the appropriate form of finance being left until Chapter V.

1. Definition. A *budget* is a cost plan relating to a period of time. Time is a fundamental factor in any budget. This definition is easily remembered, but it is important to appreciate the implications of the word "cost." As we saw in II, **1**, a cost is the value of economic resources used. Thus a ***cost plan*** is essentially a resources plan in terms of value (*see* **5**).

2. Forecasts and budgets. It is important to note carefully the distinction between a forecast and a budget:

(*a*) A *forecast* is a prediction of what will happen as a result of a given set of circumstances.

(*b*) A *budget* is a planned result that an enterprise aims to attain.

From this it follows that a *forecast* is a judgment that can be made by anybody (provided they are competent to make judgments), whereas a *budget* is an enterprise objective that may be issued only by the authorised management. (Moreover, the announcement of a plan is an implicit instruction to employees to work to achieve that objective.)

3. Main steps in preparing a budget. In preparing a budget there are five steps to take:

(*a*) Prepare forecast.

(*b*) Determine enterprise policy (*e.g.* product range; normal hours of work per week; channels of distribution; stocks; research and development appropriation; investments).

(*c*) Compute requirements in terms of quantities required to comply with forecasts and policies (*e.g.* men; machines; tons of material) and convert to money values. This results in the initial budget.

(*d*) Review the forecast, policies and initial budget. Amend the policies or budget or both, until an acceptable budget emerges.

(*e*) Formally accept the budget. It then becomes the "master budget," and as such an executive order.

4. Essentials of budget preparation. Budget preparation involves two essentials, clear thinking and commonsense. Unfortunately no book can help students with these, and so budgeting is the easiest technique to learn and the hardest to apply. In this chapter a few useful words are defined and a logical approach suggested. In the majority of budget problems, however, the student must use his own initiative.

5. The importance of quantities. In practice, it is important never to lose sight of the fact that it is the *quantities* which are budgeted, not money figures. The money figures are merely a way of expressing quantities in the form of a common measure (*see* I, **16** (*b*)).

6. Budget period. A *budget period* is the period of time for which a budget is prepared and employed. Budget periods naturally depend very much on the planning horizons. However, other factors also influence the period, for example if there is a natural cycle time (such as one year for trading) then it is logical to use the cycle time as the budget period. The budget periods for the main budgets are usually as follows:

(*a*) Trading budget—one year.
(*b*) Capital budget—many years.
(*c*) Research and development budget—some years.

7. Budgets and financing needs. When preparing budgets that will indicate financing needs it is clear that the need for short-term finance will be revealed by the operating budgets of the enterprise, while the need for long-term finance will be revealed by the capital budgets. Study of these two types of budgets, then, is the first task.

OPERATING BUDGETS

8. Definition. An *operating budget* is a budget that lays down the planned requirements for day-to-day operations of an enterprise over a normal cycle of operations, *e.g.* one year. It details the sales and expenditure plans, firstly by nature and secondly by moment in time. Capital receipts and expenditures relevant to the budget period are, of course, included, but these amounts are essentially direct abstractions from the capital budget.

9. Principal budget factor. There is always some factor that prevents an enterprise from immediately expanding to infinity. This factor is usually sales, the enterprise being unable to sell all it can produce. However, there are other possible factors which may limit enterprise activity, such as shortage of machinery, cash, labour, space, materials and managerial ability.

Such a factor is termed the *principal budget factor*, for, clearly, it must be determined and its value assessed before any other factors can be budgeted. Indeed, part of the art of management is to make plans so that use of the principal budget factor is maximised.

The principal budget factor does not remain constant. If the limitations imposed by one factor are removed, then another takes its place and becomes the principal budget factor. In practice, it is important that one is aware when this type of switch-over is imminent.

10. Functional budgets. When budgeting, each function within the enterprise prepares its own *functional budget* on a basis of the enterprise objectives. Obviously these budgets are interrelated, data from one being required in the preparation of another (*see* Fig. 4).

On the assumption that sales is the principal budget factor, the basic information required for each functional budget is given by the answers to the following questions:

(*a*) *Sales.* In view of this being the principal budget factor, what quantities can be sold and at what prices?

(*b*) *Finished goods stock.* What finished goods stock will be required to support the budgeted sales?

(*c*) *Production.* What production must be achieved to meet budgeted sales and secure the budgeted finished goods stock?

(*d*) *Materials.* What materials will be required to meet the budgeted production?

(*e*) *Raw material stores.* What raw material stocks will be required in view of the materials budget?

(*f*) *Purchases.* What purchases must be made to secure the budgeted materials and raw material stocks, and at what prices?

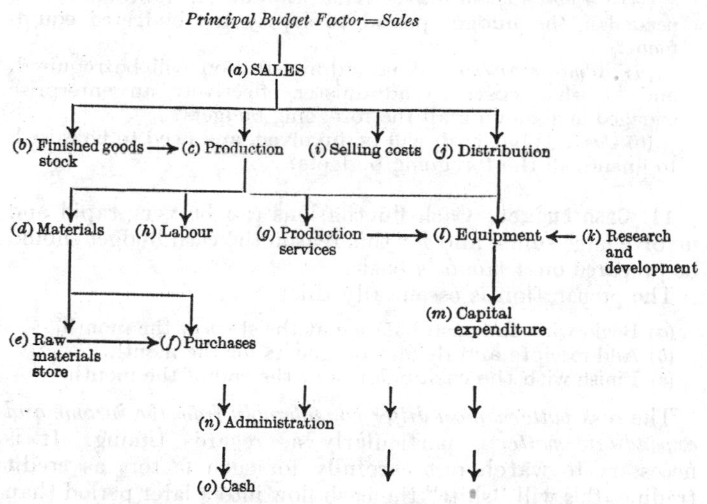

FIG. 4.—*Inter-relationship of functional budgets*

It is assumed here that the principal budget factor is sales. The letters in brackets refer to the sections of paragraph 10.

(*g*) *Production services.* What production services will be required to support the budgeted production, and at what cost?

(*h*) *Labour.* What labour must be employed to achieve the budgeted production and man the budgeted services, and at what rates?

(*i*) *Selling costs.* What selling services will be required to achieve the budgeted sales, and at what cost?

(*j*) *Distribution.* What distribution services will be required to distribute the budgeted sales, and at what cost?

NOTE: Students often make the error of basing these last two budgets on production instead of *sales*.

(*k*) *Research and development.* What research and development will be needed and at what cost?

NOTE: This budget in practice is often set independently of the others.

(*l*) *Equipment.* What equipment will be needed to enable budgeted production, research and development to be achieved, and budgeted services to be set up?

(*m*) *Capital expenditure.* What capital expenditure will be needed in the budget period to supply the budgeted equipment?

(*n*) *Administration.* What administration will be required, and at what cost, to administer effectively an enterprise engaged in achieving all the foregoing budgets?

(*o*) *Cash.* What cash will be involved, and need to be raised, to finance all the foregoing budgets?

11. Cash budget. Cash fluctuations can be very rapid and involve large sums, and for this reason the cash budget should be prepared on a *monthly* basis.

The preparation is essentially this:

(*a*) Begin with the cash balance at the start of the month.
(*b*) Add receipts and deduct payments for the month.
(*c*) Finish with the cash balance at the end of the month.

The *cash pattern may differ considerably from the income and expenditure pattern*, particularly as regards timing. It is necessary to watch out carefully for such factors as credit trading (this will "shift" the cash flow into a later period than the date of the sales or purchases), capital payments and receipts, tax and dividend payments, non-trading income and expenditure.

12. Summary budget. A *summary budget* is a budget that is prepared from, and summarises, all the functional budgets. The end products of the summary budget are:

(*a*) *The budgeted Profit and Loss Account.* By abstracting the budgeted income found in the sales budget, and the budgeted costs found in the other budgets, a budgeted Profit and Loss Account can be built up.

(*b*) *The budgeted balance sheet.* This is built up by:

(*i*) Taking the final cash balance in the cash budget.
(*ii*) Bringing in the budgeted values of the other assets and liabilities at the end of the budget period.

(*iii*) Adding the budgeted profit retained to the opening net worth.

13. Master budget. The budgeted Profit and Loss Account and Balance Sheet will indicate the enterprise results to be expected by the end of the period. If the results are judged to be unsatisfactory the functions are rebudgeted. This process continues until an overall satisfactory budget is drafted. The budget is then accepted by top management (or, often, the Board of Directors), and upon acceptance the budget is termed the *master budget*. From that moment on it ceases to be merely a plan; it is also an executive order.

CAPITAL BUDGETS

14. Definition. A *capital budget* is a budget that lays down the planned requirements for the long-term running of an enterprise. It indicates the fixed assets, working capital and forms of finance that will be needed over the future years.

15. Factors to consider in the preparation of capital budgets. When preparing capital budgets the following factors should be carefully considered:

(*a*) *Economic change.* The economic situation is never static. It is important to try and foresee future economic developments, *e.g.* new national groupings such as the Common Market, the steady rise in the standard of living of various countries. One development that must be quickly detected is the emergence of new industrialised nations, for these provide both new competitors and new markets.

(*b*) *Technological change.* Nowadays change in the technological field is very rapid. Faster communication, increasing automation, new forms of materials and the endless product of more and more research and development make it essential that any plan spanning the years predicts the broad development of technology.

(*c*) *Growth of industry.* Closely related to the two previous factors is the growth of one's own industry. If the industry is in a field of fast technical growth (*e.g.* computers) and is located in a booming economic environment, then the industry growth will be very rapid. Conversely, a technically declining industry (*e.g.* coal) situated in a depressed economy must inevitably shrink.

(*d*) *Growth of enterprise.* A competitive enterprise can

normally expect to obtain its share of the growth of its particular industry. However, a concerted effort by one's competitors may deprive the enterprise of its full share of the industry growth, while conversely a major effort by the enterprise can result in it capturing more than its previous share.

(*e*) *Future additional equipment.* Having forecast enterprise growth, it is simply an exercise in production planning to determine what future additional equipment will be needed to meet the future demand. (Note that in this context equipment includes land and buildings.)

(*f*) *Replacement of equipment.* Students very frequently forget that equipment, particularly existing equipment, needs to be replaced—possibly more than once over a long budget period. Capital budgeting, then, requires a careful assessment of when equipment must be replaced.

(*g*) *Future administration costs.* There is a danger that in capital budgeting costs that remain relatively steady in the short term will be forgotten, administrative costs being perhaps the most important. However, over a long period of time there may be considerable change. A head office set-up that has lasted some 20 years may quickly fail to be adequate if there is any further growth. Consideration, then, must be given to such an eventuality.

(*h*) *Future policy costs.* Consideration must also be given to future policy costs (*i.e.* costs that are incurred as a result of the *policy* of the enterprise such as research and development or advertising). Budgets for such costs are sometimes based on what remains after everything else has been decided. It should be obvious that this is a completely back-to-front method of planning.

(*i*) *Credit and stock policies.* Clearly the policy of an enterprise in respect of credit period and stock levels will affect the working capital requirements and can often be a very sizeable part of a capital budget.

(*j*) *Financing.* In all capital budgeting one ultimately arrives at the question, how will needs be financed? This depends very much, of course, on the financing policy of the enterprise and is the subject of the next chapter (V).

16. Preparation of capital budgets: cash flow method. One method of preparing a capital budget for ascertaining cash needs is by using a *cash flow* technique. Using this technique one simply lists the *cash* receipts and payments for each subperiod of the budget so that the cash resources available at any moment can be ascertained.

It should be appreciated that although the technique simply

requires the listing of cash receipts and payments, very often the preparation of some form of small operating budget is necessary in order to ascertain what the receipts and payments will, in fact, be.

17. Cash flow method illustrated. The following problem can be used to illustrate the cash flow method of capital budgeting.

EXAMPLE

A trading enterprise commences business by issuing 75,000 £4 ordinary shares £2 paid and £100,000 10% debentures. Subsequent finance will be in the first instance by an overdraft (limit £60,000) and then by calls on capital of £1 each. Fixed assets (which, incidentally, will not depreciate) worth £200,000 will be acquired in the first year, and an additional £40,000 worth acquired in each of the following three years. Sales are expected to be £120,000, £160,000 and £200,000 in the first, second and third years respectively and £240,000 in the fourth and subsequent years. Purchases will be for sales (purchase price = 50% selling price) plus such purchases as will be necessary to hold the stock up to 50% of annual sales value. Overheads (including debenture interest) will run at all times at £60,000 per annum. Credit will be given such that debtors will be 25% of annual sales while creditors will be paid on receipt of goods. No dividends will be paid for at least five years. Corporation tax is expected to be 40%, payable one year after the end of the trading period.

A capital cash budget for the first five years is to be prepared (overdraft interest to be ignored).

Solution: To prepare this budget it is first necessary to know the stock increase year by year and also the tax payable. This means a small operating budget must first be prepared and then the cash flow statement can be drawn up.

Operating Budget (£000s):

1. *Year*	2. *Sales*	3. *Cost of Sales* (½ × Col. 2)	4. *Overheads*	5. *Profit* (Col. 2 − (3 + 4))	6. *Tax* (40% × Col. 5)	7. *End of Year Stock* (½ × Col. 2)	8. *Stock Increase*
1.	120	60	60	Nil	Nil	60	60
2.	160	80	60	20	8	80	20
3.	200	100	60	40	16	100	20
4.	240	120	60	60	24	120	20
5.	240	120	60	60	24	120	Nil

Capital Cash Budget—Cash flow (£000s):

Year	CASH PAYMENTS					
	Fixed Assets	*Purchases*		*Overheads*	*Tax*	*Total*
		For Sales	*For Stock*			
1.	200	60	60	60	Nil	380
2.	40	80	20	60	Nil	200
3.	40	100	20	60	8	228
4.	40	120	20	60	16	256
5.	Nil	120	Nil	60	24	204

CASH RECEIPTS				NET CASH FLOW	CASH BALANCE *Overdraft*‡
Sales		*Capital Receipts*	*Total*		
Last year's Debtors	*This year's Debtors*				
Nil	90	250*	340	−40	*40*
30	120	75†	225	+25	*15*
40	150	Nil	190	−38	*53*
50	180	75†	305	+49	*4*
60	180	Nil	240	+36	32

* 75,000 £4 shares £2 paid + £100,000 10% debentures.

† Call of £1 a share made on 75,000 shares to keep overdraft below limit of £60,000.

‡ Overdraft figures shown in italics.

18. Preparation of capital budgets: projected balance sheet method. An alternative method of preparing a capital budget is by means of the *projected balance sheet* method. To apply this method all the asset and liability figures at the end of each sub-period of the budget period are forecast, with the exception of cash. The cash figure is then computed by finding the difference between the assets and the liabilities. If this balancing figure shows an undesirable cash situation, a planned change is made to one or more of the balance sheet figures so that an acceptable balance sheet is ultimately attained.

19. Projected balance sheet method illustrated. The projected balance sheet method can be illustrated by means of the same problem as was used for the cash flow method. Application of this method still necessitates the preparation of a small operating budget and to save duplication the figures required here will be directly taken from the operating budget given in **17**.

Capital Cash Budget—Projected balance sheet (£000s):

Year:	*1.*	*2.*	*3.*	*4.*	*5.*
ASSETS					
Fixed assets	200	240	280	320	320
Stock	60	80	100	120	120
Debtors	30	40	50	60	60
Total	290	360	430	500	500
CAPITAL AND LIABILITIES:					
Capital	150	150	225	225	300
P/L appropriation*	—	12	36	72	108
Debentures	100	100	100	100	100
Provision for tax	—	8	16	24	24
Total	250	270	377	421	532
CASH BALANCE					
Initial balance†	*40*	*90*	*53*	*79*	32
Capital called up	Nil	75	Nil	75	Nil
Final balance†	*40*	*15*	*53*	*4*	32

* After corporation tax (*i.e.* this item is the cumulative after-tax profits).

† Overdraft indicated by italics.

When using this method the easiest approach is usually to draw up a tabular framework similar to the above and then fill this in *horizontally* as far as possible rather than vertically, for it is easier to consider an asset or liability for a period of years than consider all the different assets and liabilities at the end of a given year.

WORKING CAPITAL BUDGETS

20. Definition. A *working capital budget* is a budget that lays down the planned requirements for working capital, *i.e.* it details the planned current assets and current liabilities with special reference to the cash needed to finance the working capital. Working capital budgets are rarely prepared as such for the whole enterprise—they usually relate to a specific enterprise project. There may, therefore, be many working capital budgets within a single enterprise.

21. Profit: retained or remitted? Before a working capital budget can be prepared for a project it is important to decide whether or not the project may retain the profits it earns to finance itself. This is important, for most projects build up slowly and although more and more additional finance is required throughout the initial phases of the operation, some profit may well be earned during this period and so, if retained, be available to reduce the ultimate peak financial demand made by the project on the parent organisation. If, however, the profit must be remitted to the parent organisation then the peak working capital financial requirement will be that much higher.

Although either method may be adopted most examination questions appear to assume that profit is remitted.

22. Remitted profit: remitted at moment of sale or payment? If profit is to be remitted the next question relates to when such remission is deemed to take place—at the moment a sale is made or at the moment payment is received from the debtor. If the former (*i.e.* the moment of sale) then, since the project will not receive the profit in cash until the debtor pays, the working capital financing demand made by the project will include a sum that relates to the profit remitted to the parent organisation but not received from the customer (*i.e.* the profit element in the debtors' figure). Although it would appear more logical to delay profit remission until the project had received payment from the debtor, most examination questions appear to assume the opposite arrangement, *i.e.* that profit is remitted at the moment of sale.

In the working capital budget the decision on this point primarily affects the debtors' figure, namely:

(*a*) If profit is remitted at the moment of sale, then debtors will be valued at *sales* value.

(*b*) If profit is remitted at the moment payment is received from the debtor, then debtors will be valued at *cost of sales* value.

23. The "worst moment" concept. Since a major objective of a working capital budget is to indicate to management the amount that will be required to finance the working capital, it is very important to appreciate that this amount must be computed *in relation to the worst possible moment of operations.*

To take this factor into account sometimes requires careful thought. For example, assume that purchases are made on the basis of paying suppliers at the end of the month in which deliveries are made. This seems to imply that there is on average half a month's credit. However, in the context of a working capital budget there is no credit at all. This is because at the end of the month suppliers must be paid *right up to date* and enough cash provided by the budget to enable this to be done. At this "worst moment," then, there is no credit at all. It is, of course, irrelevant that during the month no cash will be required for suppliers—what is relevant is that at month-end cash to pay *all* suppliers' invoices will be needed.

The student must remember, then, that there will always be peaks and valleys in respect of working capital cash requirements, and the relevant cash figure for financing purposes is the one that relates to the moment when the demand for cash is at its heaviest, *i.e.* at the worst moment.

24. Working capital budgets: method of preparation. A working capital budget can be prepared in the following manner:

(*a*) Decide the profit arrangements which are to apply (*see* 21 and 22).

(*b*) List all working capital assets (*e.g.* raw material stocks, debtors), excluding cash.

(*c*) Taking each class of asset in turn decide how many weeks must elapse from the moment of *payment* for an item within the asset class until payment is to be received from the customer in respect of that item; (*e.g.* an item of raw material may be bought in week 1, *paid for* in week 3, stored until week 4, incorporated in a product which is then despatched in week 5 and paid for by the customer in week 8, the elapsed time being, therefore, 8 − 3 = 5 weeks). Note that the "worst moment" concept must be applied at this point.

(*d*) Take the weekly *cost* relating to the item and multiply this by the time found in (*c*) to obtain the finance required for that item; (*e.g.* if £2000 per week is incurred on the raw material item referred to above, then the finance requirement is £2000 × 5 = £10,000).

(*e*) Add together all the amounts obtained in (*d*) plus any cash float that it is deemed desirable to hold. This gives the amount required to finance the working capital.

(*f*) To obtain a complete working capital budget this amount should then be analysed so as to show how much finance is required for each current asset and liability.

25. Working capital budget preparation illustrated. The following problem can be used to illustrate the preparation of a working capital budget.

EXAMPLE

A new project is being planned which will have weekly sales of 4000 units at £3 a unit, six weeks' credit being given to customers. Unit costs will be £1·25 for direct materials and £0·50 for direct labour, while overheads will run at £4000 per week. Planned stocks will include £25,000 raw materials and 20,000 units in the finished goods store. Creditors will be paid for materials at the end of the month that follows the month of delivery and for overheads four weeks after incurring the expense. Wages are paid at the end of each week for the whole of that week. Units are two weeks in production and profit is "remitted" to the parent company at the moment of sale. A cash float of £10,000 is considered desirable.

Prepare a working capital budget (1 month = 4 weeks):

Solution: First the weekly costs will be found as follows:

Materials: 4000 units at £1·25	£5,000
Labour: 4000 units at £0·50	2,000
Overheads	4,000
Cost of production	11,000
Profit	1,000
Sales: 4000 units at £3	£12,000

From this it follows that the time goods are in stock is:

Raw materials: $\frac{£25,000}{£5,000} = 5$ weeks.

Finished goods: $\frac{20,000 \text{ units}}{4,000 \text{ units}} = 5$ weeks.

Working capital requirements:

	Materials	Labour	Over-heads	Profit
Weeks:				
Raw materials stock	5	—	—	—
Work-in-progress	2	2*	1†	—
Finished goods stock	5	5	5	—
Debtors	6	6	6	6
	18	13	12	6
Less Creditors	4*	—	4	—
Elapsed time	14	13	8	6
Weekly cost	£5,000	£2,000	£4,000	£1,000
∴ Finance required =	£70,000	£26,000	£32,000	£6,000

Total finance required = (70,000 + 26,000 + 32,000 + 6,000) + Cash float = £134,000 + £10,000 = £144,000

* Applying the "worst moment" concept.
† Average overheads incurred over two weeks in progress.

Working Capital Analysis:

	Weeks	Weekly Cost	Total	
Raw materials stock:				
Materials	5	£5,000	£25,000	£25,000
Work-in-progress				
Materials	2	5,000	10,000	
Labour	2	2,000	4,000	
Overheads	1	4,000	4,000	18,000
Finished goods stock:				
Materials	5	5,000	25,000	
Labour	5	2,000	10,000	
Overheads	5	4,000	20,000	55,000
Debtors:				
Materials	6	5,000	30,000	
Labour	6	2,000	12,000	
Overheads	6	4,000	24,000	
Profit	6	1,000	6,000	72,000
Cash				10,000
				180,000
Creditors:				
Materials	4	5,000	20,000	
Overheads	4	4,000	16,000	36,000
Total				£144,000

26. Working capital budget preparation: an alternative approach. The thoughtful student on studying the above illustration may well decide that he could have prepared the budget very much more quickly by simply using the projected balance sheet technique in relation to the current assets and current liabilities. This is a perfectly valid approach *provided he remembers that he must apply the "worst moment" concept* (*e.g.* in the above illustration he must not assume that there is an average credit of six weeks for materials). If care is used, working capital budget problems can certainly be more quickly solved using the projected balance sheet method, but for the student who would prefer a longer but more certain method the technique illustrated above is advised.

BUDGET ADMINISTRATION

27. Budgeting, a management technique. Budgeting is almost wholly a management technique, for a budget lays down management's plans regarding the economic resources to be used and the utilities to be produced. Management, then, is responsible for the compilation of budgets. Since these usually involve managers throughout the whole enterprise, a *budget committee* with representatives from all sections of the business should be appointed to plan and co-ordinate the budgets.

28. Budget officer. In addition to the committee, a budget officer should also be appointed. His work is essentially that of secretary to the committee, and entails:

(*a*) Ensuring that the committee secretarial work is carried out (*e.g.* agendas, minutes, notice of meetings).
(*b*) Ensuring that committee instructions are passed to the appropriate people.
(*c*) Collecting data and opinions for consideration by the committee.
(*d*) Keeping managers to the budget time-table (*see* **29** below).
(*e*) Co-ordinating and briefing the members of the committee.

Clearly, the management accountant is well suited for, and often appointed to, this post.

29. Budget time-table. When preparing major budgets it is first necessary to prepare many of the smaller, but key, budgets. If these smaller budgets are not completed quickly, then the preparation of the major budgets will be held up, which in turn will hold up the summary budget and ultimately the master budget. Delay in issuing the master budget is clearly serious, for a budget issued after the start of a period has very much reduced value, and many even result in the delay of vital projects. In order, then, that the master budget can be issued before the period begins, it is necessary to prepare a carefully thought-out time-table for all budget activities. Such a time-table must be rigidly adhered to, since delays in this type of work tend to snowball and quickly assume serious proportions.

30. Budget manual. To assist everyone engaged in budgeting and budget administration, a budget manual should be issued. A *budget manual* is a manual that sets out such matters as the responsibilities of the people engaged in, the routine of, and the forms and records required for, budgeting and then, subsequently budgetary cost control (*see* XVI).

More generally, this manual will set out all information needed by all persons involved in budgeting and budgetary control to enable them to maximise both:

(*a*) their contribution to the budget compilation; and
(*b*) their benefit from the control data ultimately reported back to them.

PROGRESS TEST 4

Principles

1. Define a budget. (1)
2. Distinguish between a forecast and a budget. (2)
3. What is a budget period? (6)
4. Define:

(*a*) Operating budget; (8)
(*b*) Capital budget; (14)
(*c*) Working capital budget. (20)

5. What is a principal budget factor and why is it important in budgeting? (9)
6. Will a short-term cash budget be similar to the corresponding income and expenditure budget? (11)
7. What is a master budget and why is it important? (13)
8. What factors should be considered when preparing a capital budget? (15)
9. What is meant by the "worst moment" concept? (23)
10. What is the purpose of each of the following:

(*a*) Budget committee; (27)
(*b*) Budget officer; (28)
(*c*) Budget time-table; (29)
(*d*) Budget manual. (30)

Practice

11. Daniel Bencher, who founded D. Bencher Ltd some four years ago, has seen an ideal opportunity to expand his business.

He has the chance to double his sales next year, and then increase the turnover of each succeeding year by £20,000 over that of the year immediately preceding it. Since his profit before tax but after depreciation is 20% of sales, he feels this chance is too good to miss.

Unfortunately, to take advantage of the opportunity, he would need to buy an additional £70,000 worth of fixed assets similar to those he owns at the moment. As he is short of money he is thinking of issuing debentures for this amount to finance the purchase. He needs, however, to state a redemption date, and asks you to advise him as to the earliest date possible. He realises that he could be under-capitalised in future years and so feels it would be prudent not to redeem until he has sufficient cash not only to repay the debentures, but also to be in a position to pay one-half of all current liabilities (*i.e.* tax and creditors) and be able to maintain this position for all time.

He submits to you his balance sheet (*see below*) and advises you of his following policy decisions:

(*a*) Dividends to be 20% gross until repayment of debentures.
(*b*) Stocks, debtors and creditors to be 40%, 20% and 10% of sales respectively.

You also know the following facts:

(*a*) Current sales are £100,000 per annum.
(*b*) Debenture interest will be absorbed by economies of scale.
(*c*) Corporation tax is 50%, payable in one year.
(*d*) Fixed assets have a total life of eight years. Depreciation is $12\frac{1}{2}$% straight line.
(*e*) Inflation is to be ignored.

Current Balance Sheet

Fixed Assets	£50,000
Stocks	40,000
Debtors	20,000
Cash	5,000
	£115,000
Capital	£50,000
Reserves	20,000
Provision for depreciation	25,000
Tax (1 year)	10,000
Creditors	10,000
	£115,000

12. The Lee Kee Tent Company proposes to open a new branch shop on 1st January. Given the following data, compute the amount of cash that will be required to finance working capital.

Tent sales ($\frac{3}{4}$ Popular; $\frac{1}{4}$ De-luxe):

January (three weeks only)	£40,000	April	£160,000
February	£80,000	May	£120,000
March	£120,000	June	£120,000

From July onwards sales will stabilise at £100,000 per month for the rest of the year.

Gross Profit on sales:	Popular	10%	De-luxe	20%
Credit: Creditors (tents) (months)	Popular	1	De-luxe	$\frac{3}{4}$
Debtors (months)	Popular	1	De-luxe	2

The opening stock each month should be equal to that month's estimated sales quantity. Tents can only be delivered to the shop at the end of the first quarter of the month.

Salaries (paid month end) will be £4000 per month and shop overheads (one month's average credit) will be £2000 per month.

The local bank will provide overdraft facilities up to £50,000 (ignore interest).

As regards profit, head office is prepared to allow the shop to use any profits it makes up until the half-year. However, on the 30th June all profits must be remitted to Head Office, profit being regarded as taken at the moment of debtor payment.

CHAPTER V

PLANNING FINANCE

ONCE budgets have been prepared the moments when, and the periods for which, finance is needed can be seen. The next step is to decide what *kind* of finance should be used. This chapter discusses this point, the problem of *where* to obtain the finance being left until the next chapter.

BASIC CONSIDERATIONS

1. Types of finance. Broadly, planning finance involves selecting a mix of the following types of finance:

(*a*) *Debt:*

(*i*) Short-term, *e.g.* bank overdraft.
(*ii*) Long-term, *e.g.* debentures.

(*b*) *Equity:*

(*i*) Retained profits.
(*ii*) Capital issues.

2. Factors for consideration. The following factors should be considered when planning finance:

(*a*) *Cost.* The cost of finance is an obvious consideration; minimising cost is, of course, a major financial objective. Because of its importance, costs of the different kinds of finance are discussed in a section of their own (*see* VI, **19–23**).

(*b*) *Repayment date.* If the life of the management accountant is not to be one long, continual battle to borrow new short-term finance to repay old short-term debts (an exercise with considerable hidden costs and carrying the perpetual threat of insolvency), then due regard must be given to the period of time for which finance is required. To enter into a scheme with a repayment date that falls before the end of the full period for which the finance is needed means that at best extra trouble is involved raising a short-term loan to cover the balance of the time, while if conditions became particularly adverse, it may prove impossible to obtain such a loan.

(*c*) *Liquidity.* Low cost finance is usually associated with early repayment. If, then, an enterprise is to pass through a period of high liquidity (*e.g.* holding easily realisable assets), then it can risk employing a larger proportion of short-term finance continuously renewed than it could if a period of low liquidity was imminent (*e.g.* holding special-purpose equipment suitable only for the owning enterprise).

(*d*) *Reward payment dates.* A major consideration when deciding between debt and equity (1) is the fact that interest on debt must be paid on due dates, while dividends on equity need only be paid when circumstance render payment possible. Heavy interest charges can prove embarrassing, particularly, for example, to an enterprise that is fairly new and only gradually building up to its optimum level of operations.

(*e*) *Claim on assets.* Some forms of financing may result in a charge on certain assets, which in turn usually involves restrictions being placed on the use of the assets. This means that enterprise manœuvrability may be seriously impaired at a critical moment. On the other hand suitable debt finance may not be obtainable unless such a form of security is given. In this situation the final decision depends very much on personal judgment in weighing the balance.

(*f*) *Control.* When deciding whether or not to issue new capital, it is important to appreciate that such an issue may result in the new shareholders obtaining partial or even total control of the enterprise. This is a particularly important consideration where the majority of the existing shareholders are a small, well-knit group of people or family. The issue of non-voting shares is, incidentally, one way of overcoming this problem.

(*g*) *Risk.* The riskier a project is, the better it is to finance it out of equity. There are two reasons for this. Firstly, the more risk there is associated with a project the more nervous a lender of finance will be, and consequently the higher the interest rate and the more the restrictions will be. Secondly, the obligation to pay regular interest can, if the project fails, saddle an enterprise with heavy interest payments that continue long after the project ceased to exist. In other words, in the event of a gamble failing it is better to write off a part of one's equity than bequeath to the enterprise a legacy of crippling debt. The corollary to this, of course, is that it is better not to launch a risky project if equity to finance it is not available.

(*h*) *Availability of finance.* Planning one's finance depends very much in practice on what finance is available—a factor that can change from year to year. Sources of finance is a complete topic in its own right and will in fact be discussed in the next chapter (VI).

3. Capital gearing. An important concept in financial planning is that of *capital gearing*, which can be defined as *the ratio of debt to equity capital*, *i.e.* high capital gearing means a large amount of debt capital relative to equity. (The term is derived from the idea of a small equity gear wheel which, since equity controls the whole of the enterprise capital, drives a large total capital gear wheel; *see* Fig. 5 (*a*).)

The advantage and disadvantage of high capital gearing are as follows:

(*a*) *Advantage*. High capital gearing means that in a time of good profits shareholders obtain an exceptionally high reward, since debt capital is rewarded by fixed interest which, once paid, leaves all the remaining profit in the hands of a relatively small shareholding body (*see* Fig. 5 (*b*), (*i*)).

(*b*) *Disadvantage*. The disadvantage of high capital gearing is really the converse of the advantage, namely when profits are low the payment of fixed interest on high debt capital may easily absorb all the profit, leaving nothing for the shareholders (*see* Fig. 5 (*b*), (*ii*)).

NOTE. High capital gearing means that often only a handful of shareholders with a relatively small investment have *control* over a relatively very large amount of capital. This situation naturally appeals to ambitious owners and so high capital gearing may be employed more for reason of personal power than financial advantage. Needless to say, the providers of debt form a counterbalance to this attitude, as they will be understandably reluctant to lend large sums to a company in which the owners have only a small investment. In consequence the planned capital gearing may be very much a compromise between objective financial criteria and subjective personal desires.

ASPECTS OF FINANCIAL PLANNING

4. Debentures and mortgages: a feature of sound finance. When considering the appropriate proportions of debt and equity that an enterprise should plan, students should appreciate that unless an enterprise has borrowed large sums in some other form, *not* to have debentures or mortgages indicates a *lack* of financial skill rather than the converse. Clearly, a part of virtually all enterprise capital is used to finance very safe if not liquid assets (*e.g.* land). Now the function of a manufacturing or trading enterprise is to make profits from manu-

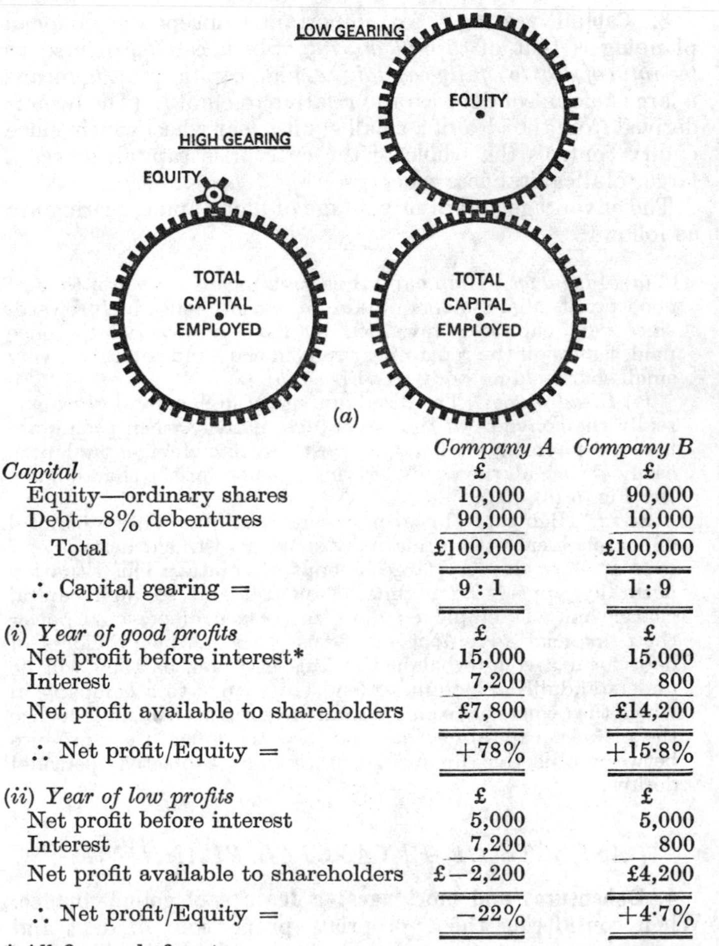

(*a*)

	Company A	*Company B*
Capital	£	£
Equity—ordinary shares	10,000	90,000
Debt—8% debentures	90,000	10,000
Total	£100,000	£100,000
∴ Capital gearing =	9 : 1	1 : 9
(*i*) *Year of good profits*	£	£
Net profit before interest*	15,000	15,000
Interest	7,200	800
Net profit available to shareholders	£7,800	£14,200
∴ Net profit/Equity =	+78%	+15·8%
(*ii*) *Year of low profits*	£	£
Net profit before interest	5,000	5,000
Interest	7,200	800
Net profit available to shareholders	£−2,200	£4,200
∴ Net profit/Equity =	−22%	+4·7%

* All figures before tax.

(*b*)

FIG. 5.—*Capital gearing*

(*a*) Diagrammatic representation; (*b*) Illustrative figures; it can be seen that the return to shareholders in the high geared company (A) is exceptionally high in a year of good profits, while the return to the low geared company (B) is much lower. When, however, profits slump to one-third in a year of low profits, the high geared company loses 22% of its capital while the low geared company still shows nearly a 5% return to shareholders.

facturing or trading operations, and so the capital supplied by the shareholders should be primarily used for this purpose and not to acquire simple ownership of capital assets. It follows, then, that the bulk of assets having continuing high value should be financed from sources more concerned with security and regular interest payments than with risk and the rewards for risk-taking. This means an enterprise not only can but should raise part of its capital by debentures or mortgages to finance such assets. Not to do so is to employ risk capital in non-risk situations with a consequent lower than optimun return to the shareholders.

5. Funding. Frequently when a large capital expenditure is planned (*e.g.* construction of a new factory) the amount of finance required is not known accurately in advance. To avoid making a share or debenture issue which may subsequently prove to have been either too small or unnecessarily large, arrangements are made to obtain short-term debt as expenditure proceeds, and then at the end when the total figure is known exactly, to make an issue of an appropriate size and use the proceeds to liquidate the short-term debt. This conversion of short-term debt into long-term debt is called *funding*.

6. Broad pattern of financing. Any enterprise must decide for itself in the light of its own circumstances the pattern of financing most suitable for it. However, to give the student some idea of the pattern of such financing a broad framework is outlined in the following paragraphs:

(*a*) *Short-term debts* should normally be self-liquidating, *e.g.* a loan to finance temporary stock build-up of a seasonal product, or a short-term loan for a funding operation. This, of course, implies that most short-term debt should be employed to finance fluctuations in current assets, *e.g.* stock build-up before sales; debtors' build-up during sales.

(*b*) The financing of the *basic current assets* should be done by *long-term debt* since the basic current assets will not be liquidated as long as the trading pattern remains essentially unchanged, normally for several years. In addition, long-term debt should also be arranged to finance an appropriate proportion of the *fixed assets* (*see* 4).

(*c*) Finally we come to the role of *equity*. Essentially equity should be used to finance all *risk elements* and also to give the providers of debt capital reassurance as to the security of their money. This reassurance will need to be in the form of a generous cushion of equity which would be able to absorb the worst reduction in the value of the enterprise's assets that could be reasonably contemplated (remember, the providers of debt have no control over the way the enterprise is run—they can only look to the assets for security regarding the eventual repayment of their money).

7. Enterprise cost of capital. A question that frequently arises in management accountancy is, what is the cost of capital to an enterprise? As we shall see in the next chapter (VI), different kinds of capital have different costs, but basically the two forms of capital that are most important in this context are long-term debt and equity. Now although debt capital can be attracted by a lower reward than that offered for equity capital (*i.e.* by an interest rate lower than the prospective dividend rate after adjustment to exclude growth, of course), as we saw in the paragraph on capital gearing (**3**), equity must to some extent match debt, otherwise providers of debt capital will be reluctant to lend. Just what the ratio of the two is to be depends, of course, on the planned capital gearing. However, as they are linked together by this ratio it is logical to compute the enterprise cost of capital by means of a weighted average. For example, assume that a debt/equity ratio of 2 : 3 is planned, that debt can only be raised at 8% and that equity requires a pre-tax return of 15%, then the cost of capital for such an enterprise can be computed as follows:

		Cost
Debt:	£200 at 8%	£16
Equity:	£300 at 15%	£45
	£500	£61

This means that to raise £500 in the planned ratio will cost £61. The enterprise cost of capital will, therefore, be $(61 \div 500) \times 100 = 12.2\%$. This, then, is the figure that will be used in any problems requiring a cost of capital figure, *e.g.* a discounted cash flow analysis (*see* XI, **6**).

8. Advantages of financial planning. The following advantages may be claimed for financial planning:

(*a*) The future needs for finance are revealed, both in respect of the amounts and also the moments in time.

(*b*) The enterprise is given time to arrange such finance

reasonably in advance of needs, without expensive panic (which usually ends in obtaining the wrong kind of finance anyway), and at the best negotiable rates.

(*c*) Knowing future financial requirements well ahead of needs enables the enterprise to select the most appropriate moment for arranging such finance.

(*d*) The existence of a well thought-out financial plan gives the providers of capital—be they potential shareholders or bank managers—some assurance that:

(*i*) the enterprise is being properly managed with managers acting to direct future events and not merely reacting to past events; and

(*ii*) the promises of management are properly based assessments within a realistic framework and not just optimistic and pious hopes.

(*e*) Having a financial plan means that a definite form of financial control can be devised. Comparing actual figures with planned will immediately indicate when factors affecting financial needs begin to move in an unplanned direction, *e.g.* stocks build up excessively or debtor payments drag.

PROGRESS TEST 5

Principles

1. Broadly, what types of finance are involved in financial planning? (1)
2. What factors should be considered when planning finance? (2)
3. What form of finance should be used for risky projects? (2) (*g*))
4. (*a*) What is meant by capital gearing? (3)

   (*b*) What is the advantage and disadvantage of capital gearing? (3)
5. Does the existence of debentures or mortgages in the capital structure of an enterprise indicate sound finance or otherwise? (4)
6. What is meant by funding? (5)
7. (*a*) What broad pattern of financing should an enterprise adopt?

   (*b*) What is the role of equity in the pattern of finance? (6)
8. What are the advantages of financial planning? (8)

Practice

9. An enterprise with a planned debt/equity ratio of 5:3 can raise debt capital at 10% but must offer 20% to attract equity capital. What will the enterprise cost of capital be?

CHAPTER VI

SOURCES OF FINANCE

ONCE the future financial needs of the enterprise are known and its financial policy decided, it then remains to select the sources of future finance. This chapter briefly examines the main sources that can be considered and their associated costs.

INTERNAL SOURCES

Before looking outside an enterprise the possibility of providing finance from internal sources should first be examined. In actual practice this source is much more used for enterprise expansion than many students would imagine and certainly should never be overlooked when planning finance.

1. Main internal sources of finance. The following are the main internal sources of finance:

(*a*) Retained profits.
(*b*) Depreciation provision.
(*c*) Tax provision.
(*d*) Reduction in current assets.

2. Retained profits. An enterprise can frequently provide itself with a steady source of finance by the simple act of retaining, or ploughing-back, profits. If an enterprise were to make, say, an annual profit after tax of $12\frac{1}{2}\%$ on total capital, then by retaining all profits such an enterprise will double its capital every six years, while an enterprise fortunate enough to make 20% profit after tax could *quadruple* its capital in less than eight years. Obviously, an enterprise in a highly profitable field could probably finance all the growth it could managerially handle simply from retained profits.

It should also be appreciated that current tax legislation is designed to encourage the retention of profits insomuch that undistributed profits remain free of income tax, whereas paid as dividends they suffer such tax. Consequently, most shareholders will find that for every £1 profit they allow to be retained and so invested in the company they will only forego about £0.60 dividend.

The disadvantage of using retained profits is, of course, the absence of dividends. A company with a large number of shareholders who look for a substantial and regular dividend would have difficulty adopting such a policy, but where there are only a few shareholders more concerned in growth than short-term dividends, retained profits often provide a rich source of funds.

3. Depreciation provision. Another internal source of finance is the provision for depreciation. Making such a provision, of course, simply results in reducing the stated profit without cash actually being paid out. Consequently, the annual depreciation provision represents cash retained by the enterprise over and above the normal undistributed profit. This can amount to a relatively large sum: in an enterprise having £300,000 total capital and using two-thirds of this to finance fixed assets which are depreciated at 10% on cost, an annual depreciation provision of £20,000 will be made, *i.e.* cash equal to one-fifteenth of the total enterprise capital will be made available for financing future expenditure.

Of course, in a stable enterprise such cash will normally be required to replace fully depreciated assets (*e.g.* in the enterprise above where there are £200,000 of fixed assets all with a life of ten years, on average one-tenth of such assets will need to be replaced, *i.e.* £20,000 worth). However, in a new enterprise for the first years such cash will be free for financing new investment. Indeed, a little thought shows that on average only half the cost of the fixed assets is really required to finance them, for if an enterprise had acquired fixed assets costing, say, £200,000 over a period of time such that the annual replacement was constant and the average age of all assets therefore one-half normal life, then the depreciation provision would always stand at £100,000, *i.e.* the enterprise would have a permanent "loan" from itself equal to one-half the original cost of its fixed assets.

The phenomenon of the depreciation provision actually resulting in cash funds is often referred to by the expression, *depreciation generates cash.* Of course, such cash may well have been spent by the time the provision is formally made, but if the enterprise is restricting its cash payments to essentially

Profit and Loss Account items then the whole of the provision will be additional cash available to the enterprise at the end of the year.

4. Tax provision. It should be noted that corporation tax is not payable until about one year after the profits have been earned. In a stable situation, therefore, there is an unchanging and virtually permanent tax provision in the accounts—in other words the enterprise has the continual use of the tax on one year's profits. This is, in effect, a permanent financing arrangement, though it must be appreciated that it does depend on profits remaining stable. If profits decrease, for instance, the provision, and therefore the amount of finance, also decreases in proportion.

5. Reduction in current assets. If current assets can be reduced then inevitably cash funds will be released. Only too often stocks creep to unnecessarily high levels and debtors' payments are allowed to fall behind. By reducing the level of current assets large sums may be made available. In this type of financing it is also important to appreciate that any obsolete stock or equipment should be sold for whatever it will fetch; however low the amount it does represent that much extra cash which can be applied to a more productive use.

6. Advantages of internal financing. The advantages of internal financing can be summarised as follows:

(*a*) No repayment is necessary.
(*b*) No interest payments have to be met.
(*c*) Managers are spared the cost and time of locating sources of suitable finance and negotiating terms.
(*d*) The costs involved in arranging a financing operation (*e.g.* share issue costs) are avoided.
(*e*) Internal financing often results in a more financially fit enterprise.

EXTERNAL SOURCES

7. Main external sources of finance. The following are the main external sources of finance available to an enterprise:

(*a*) Trade creditors (**8**)
(*b*) Bank overdrafts (**9**)

(*c*) Bank loans (**10**)
(*d*) Factoring (**11**)
(*e*) Debentures and mortgages (**12**)
(*f*) Hire purchase (**13**)
(*g*) Leasing (**14**)
(*h*) Sale-leaseback (**15**)
(*i*) Shares:

(*i*) New issue.
(*ii*) Rights issue (**16**)

(*j*) Special organisations (*e.g.* ICFC and FCI: *see* **17**(*a*) and (*b*)).

In the rest of this section these sources will be discussed individually.

8. Trade creditors. In the extreme short term and for relatively small amounts finance is sometimes raised by ceasing to pay creditors. Cash, of course, continues to flow in from debtors and can be used to finance whatever project is on hand. Later, when the situation eases, the creditors are paid.

In the absence of trade discounts this is is a very cheap method of financing. Goodwill, however, may suffer, though suppliers are usually so keen to do business that they accept the occasional delay in payment with as good a grace as they can muster.

9. Bank overdraft. Probably the bank overdraft is the commonest and most flexible method of obtaining short-term funds. It is also relatively cheap. However, banks do not look kindly on customers who use their overdrafts as permanent finance. In their minds the object of an overdraft is to help an enterprise to even out the peaks and valleys of its cash resources. Overdrafts, therefore, should always in theory be self-liquidating, although the extent to which an overdraft is in practice subject to a self-liquidating test depends very much on the policy of the bank and its managers.

Bank overdrafts are technically repayable on demand, though again in practice such a dramatic demand is rarely made, and the worst an enterprise is likely to suffer is a request for the progressive reduction of the overdraft over a reasonable period of time.

10. Bank loans. In addition to overdrafts banks may also grant loans. Unlike overdrafts these are not repayable on demand but at a specified future date, or by instalments at a series of future dates.

Bank loans are not normally made either for large sums or for long periods. They are, however a useful form of finance where the amount required hardly justifies a full-scale financing operation.

11. Factoring. Factoring is a method of raising finance under which a "factor" buys from the enterprise requiring finance the enterprise's invoiced debts, *i.e.* in effect he buys the debtors. This means an enterprise can obtain cash from credit sales virtually at the moment of sale. There is, of course, a charge for this service, but since most manufacturing and trading concerns can earn bigger profits from manufacturing and trading than can normally be earned from straightforward financing, the charge is economically worth accepting. A great advantage of this method of financing is that as sales increase there is no increase in enterprise debtors, in other words, no need to worry about financing debtors in a period of expansion.

12. Debentures and mortgages. Debentures and mortgages are really the standard form of financing long-term requirements. From these sources large sums can be obtained for relatively long periods of time.

(*a*) *Mortgages* are probably easier to obtain in terms of effort and initial cost, but are usually more expensive regarding interest, and have, of course, what may prove to be a serious disadvantage in the restriction of the uses to which the enterprise may put the mortgaged asset.

(*b*) *Debentures,* on the other hand, have one feature that makes them a particularly flexible method of financing: namely that the enterprise can buy back some or all of its own debentures on the open market if subsequent events provide the enterprise with an unanticipated surplus of funds. If, incidentally, interest rates have risen significantly since the issue was made, the enterprise can not only clear the debt, or part of the debt, in advance, but also may find it can buy back the debentures at a price below that which would be repayable on the specified redemption date.

13. Hire purchase. Hire purchase is a useful form of finance when large items of equipment are to be bought. As we saw above, depreciation generates cash and so the bulk of the hire purchase instalments can, in fact, often be made from the depreciation provision for the asset. This relieves the enterprise of either finding the large initial sum that would be required for an outright purchase or needing to locate a regular external source of finance to finance instalment payments.

14. Leasing. As we have already seen, fixed assets are to be used rather than owned (V, **4**). An enterprise, then, may be able to avoid the need for raising finance for such assets by leasing them, payment of leasing charges naturally being financed from sales. As there are also other advantages from leasing (*e.g.* avoidance of risk of obsolescence), this method of financing is sometimes rather expensive.

The student should, incidentally, appreciate that tax allowances and grants (XII, **5–9**)—particularly investment grants—will be given to the owner and not the lessee, though rental will, of course, be allowed when computing taxable profits.

15 Sale-leaseback. If an enterprise owns a large asset one method of raising finance is to sell the asset and simultaneously lease it back. This is called *sale-leaseback* and can result in a large sum of money being made available in exchange for contracted future payments. Again, sale-leaseback conforms to the view that fixed assets are to be used rather than owned.

16. Share issues. After a certain point it is no longer practicable to raise debt capital and consideration must be given to making an issue of shares.

(*a*) If a *new issue* is made (*i.e.* shares issued to the general public), however, many complications arise—so many, in fact, that the work is normally handled by an *issuing house*, a financial organisation specialising in such work. Moreover, the costs of such an issue may be very heavy.

(*b*) Alternatively, a very popular way of raising share capital that avoids the complications and costs of a new issue is a *rights issue*, under which existing shareholders are given the right to purchase additional shares. The shareholders are allowed to purchase shares at a very favourable price, though each shareholder is only allowed to buy new shares up to a stated proportion of his existing holding (*e.g.* 1 new share for every 2 currently held). If a shareholder does not wish to buy his allowance of shares he can *sell his rights* to any member of the public, who can then purchase the shares for himself. This method is not only a convenient way of raising share capital but also seems psychologically more effective in inducing investors to subscribe.

17. Special organisations: ICFC and FCI. There are in the capital market a few rather special organisations financed primarily by banks and formed to provide funds for enterprises which, while having a good economic case for being supplied with finance, find it difficult to raise such finance within the existing capital environment. The two most important of these are the following:

(*a*) *Industrial & Commercial Finance Corporation Limited* (ICFC), which provides longer-term finance for the expansion or development of small and medium size companies. The financing ranges in kind over share capital, long-term loans and plant purchase and leasing facilities; in size from £5000 to £500,000; and in time up to twenty years for loans and indefinitely, of course, for share capital. If it holds shares in a company it does not aim to interfere in the running of the company, its shareholding simply being directed at obtaining a reasonable dividend to reward it for its investment. ICFC has a number of associated companies formed to deal with specific financing situations, for example, Technical Development Capital Limited (TDC) aims to provide pioneer finance for technical innovation so that companies can finance technically new ideas up to the point when their commercial potential is demonstrated.

(*b*) *Finance Corporation for Industry Limited* (FCI) is, in effect ICFCs big brother. This organisation only concerns itself with financing amounts over £200,000, and only then if no other source of such large capital sums is available to the company.

18. Export Credit Guarantee Department. A mention should be made in this section of the Export Credit Guarantee Department (ECGD), a government department under the President of the Board of Trade which, while not providing finance, does assist finance to be raised. This department insures enterprises against losses connected with overseas trading, the guarantee it issues enabling a bank loan to be negotiated. Basically the procedure is as follows:

(*a*) An enterprise enters into a contract with an overseas buyer.

(*b*) The enterprise then insures with ECGD so that on acceptance of an economic premium ECGD guarantees payment on completion of the contract.

(*c*) The enterprise can then negotiate a bank loan of up to 90% (or even 100% depending on the type of guarantee) of the contract value, the loan being liquidated by payment on completion of the contract from either the overseas buyer or, in the event of his default, from ECGD.

COSTS OF FINANCE

The cost of finance naturally differs from type to type. Generally speaking, the longer the finance period the higher the cost. In this section the costs of the main types of finance will be briefly examined.

19. Trade creditors. This type of finance is often virtually costless, other than in terms of goodwill if payment is exceptionally delayed. If, however, a cash discount is offered, then to lose the discount is almost invariably an expensive loss. For example, assume an invoice for £100 carries a 3% discount if paid within one month. If then payment is made within one month only £97 is remitted, while if payment is delayed for an additional month £100 must be remitted. This means, in effect, that £3 has been paid for the use of £97 for one month, *i.e.* an interest payment equivalent to over 38% per annum. This is clearly a very expensive method of financing. Withholding payment beyond even the second month certainly reduces this rate of interest, but usually the insistence of the creditor, or his solicitors, results in payment long before the time necessary to make this form of financing economical is reached.

20. Bank overdraft. The cost of a bank overdraft is simply the rate of interest charged. (The need to keep constant the ratio of equity to debt, and therefore raise the true cost of debt, is not so relevant here since overdraft finance is provided more on the self-liquidating nature of the arrangements than the security provided by assets.) It should be appreciated that the great advantage of an overdraft is that interest is charged on the daily balance only and not on any fixed sum. Thus if one required a £10,000 loan that is to be liquidated by equal daily payments, then it is as cheap to use an overdraft at 10% as a fixed loan at 5%.

21. Leasing. Leasing essentially costs only the rent, though the restrictions placed on the use of the assets may form a hidden cost.

22. Loans, debentures and mortgages. The cost of this type of finance is in the first instance the rate of interest charged. However, as was shown earlier (V, **3**), there is a close link between debt and equity and any debt raised carries with it the later need to raise an appropriate balance of equity. The full cost, therefore, of such loans is the enterprise cost of capital (V, **7**). In addition, of course, there are costs incurred in arranging the finance.

23. Equity. Because there is no legal obligation to pay a dividend to equity holders this type of finance is often regarded as being costless. However, this is not so, for equity capital can only be raised if the prospect of reasonable dividends is held out to investors. Such a dividend will, of course, need to be significantly higher than the ruling interest rates. Basically, then, the cost of equity capital is the dividend rate required to induce investors to acquire such equity. However, the following points should also be noted in this respect:

(*a*) An increase in equity opens the way to an increase in debt capital (*see* **22** above). The cost of equity, therefore, is virtually the enterprise cost of capital.

(*b*) Raising finance in the form of a new issue (and to some extent a rights issue as well) means incurring issue costs that increase the cost of the finance. Raising finance in the form of retained profits, of course, avoids this cost.

(*c*) Under the existing tax laws investors are encouraged to finance companies by means of retained profits rather than to receive dividends for re-investment elsewhere, since income tax is payable on such dividends.

PROGRESS TEST 6

1. What internal sources of finance are available to an enterprise? (**1**)
2. Are retained profits likely to be a particularly significant source of finance? (**2**)
3. (*a*) What is meant by the expression "depreciation generates cash"?
   (*b*) To what extent can a depreciation provision provide finance for an enterprise? (**3**)
4. What are the advantages of internal financing? (**6**)
5. What are the main external sources of finance? (**7**)
6. What are the main features of the following forms of finance:
   (*a*) Trade creditors? (**8**)
   (*b*) Bank overdraft? (**9**)
   (*c*) Bank loans? (**10**)
   (*d*) Factoring? (**11**)
   (*e*) Debentures and mortgages? (**12**)
   (*f*) Hire purchase? (**13**)
   (*g*) Leasing? (**14**)
   (*h*) Sale-leaseback? (**15**)
   (*i*) Share issues? (**16**)
7. Can a company buy its own debentures? (**12**)
8. How can the bulk of hire-purchase instalments often be financed? (**13**)
9. When leasing, who can claim the tax allowances and grants? (**14**)
10. What is an issuing house? (**16**)
11. Is it better when raising capital by shares to have a new issue or a rights issue? (**16**)
12. What is:
    (*a*) ICFC? (**17**)
    (*b*) FCI? (**17**)
    (*c*) ECGD? (**18**)
13. What costs are involved in the following forms of financing:
    (*a*) Trade creditors? (**19**)
    (*b*) Bank overdraft? (**20**)
    (*c*) Leasing? (**21**)
    (*d*) Loans, debentures and mortgages? (**22**)
    (*e*) Equity? (**23**)
14. Why is it uneconomical to lose a trade creditor's cash discount? (**19**)
15. What special cost advantage does a bank overdraft have? (**20**)

PART THREE

DECISION-MAKING

In this Part the techniques used by the management accountant to assist management to make decisions are examined. In this type of work it is essential to appreciate that decision-making is basically *choosing between alternatives*. This means that the management accountant can help by showing management the *relative economic advantages* of one alternative as against another, and this in turn means that decision-making work should concentrate on analysing the economic *differences* between alternatives. Figures such as the total cost-per-unit, total sales or total enterprise profits are of little value here; what is required is the difference in profit that will arise as a result of selecting one alternative in preference to another.

Using always this basic approach of analysing differences, we will consider what happens if there are differences in activity (VII, Break-even Charts); if there are minor differences in products (VIII, Marginal Costing); if there are major differences in products or fixed costs (IX, Differential Costing and X, Cash Flow); and if there are differences in the timing of receipts and payments (XI, Capital Projects—Discounted cash flow). Finally, Chapter XII surveys the whole topic of decision-making as the management accountant sees it.

CHAPTER VII

BREAK-EVEN CHARTS

IN this chapter we look at break-even charts and in the next at marginal costs. A word of warning is necessary here. These two techniques are used essentially for making short-term decisions in a practical context. Students must beware, therefore, of applying them to long-term or extreme situations, for then much of the theory no longer applies. This warning relates particularly to references to changes in the level of activity. Such references relate to *normal* changes, between, say, 50% and 100% of capacity. Decisions involving activities outside these limits must be based on other decision-making techniques such as differential costing.

FIXED AND VARIABLE COSTS

1. Dual basis of costs. Making correct decisions depends very much on understanding how costs behave, and for short-term decisions this in turn depends upon appreciating that all costs are essentially either:

(*a*) *time*-based (*i.e.* change in proportion to time); *or*
(*b*) *activity*-based (*i.e.* change in proportion to activity).

2. Time-based (fixed) costs. Time-based costs are costs that change in direct proportion to the length of time that elapses. Typical of these is rent. Clearly, the amount of rent that one pays depends upon *how long* one uses the premises—the rent payable for two years' use is twice that for one year. Note that such costs are unaffected by activity; no matter whether the enterprise is busy or slack, the rent payable is the same.

Other examples of time-based costs include rates, debenture interest, audit fees, and to a large extent, management salaries.

Since time-based costs do not vary with activity then *for any given period of time they will remain unchanged regardless of the level of activity.* Rent, rates, loan interest and most management salaries, for example, will be the same whatever the level of activity. These costs are therefore termed *fixed costs.*

NOTE: Fixed costs are not costs that never alter. Obviously rent, rates and so on can alter—the point being made is that they do not alter as a result of *change of activity*.

3. Activity-based (variable) costs. Activity-based costs are costs that change in proportion to the level of activity undertaken. The most obvious of these costs is the direct material cost. If, for example, production is increased by 10%, then the direct material cost will clearly increase by 10%. Other such costs are direct wages, sales commission and power. Such costs are termed *variable costs* and can be defined as *costs that vary in direct proportion to activity.*

4. Mixed-base (semi-variable) costs. There are clearly a number of costs that are neither wholly fixed nor wholly variable. Such costs change with activity, but not in direct proportion to it. For example, activity may increase by 10% but a particular cost of this type may only increase 4% or 5%. Such costs are termed *semi-variable costs*, and include such costs as maintenance, supervision and storekeeping.

These costs are really mixed time and activity-based costs. For instance, maintenance can be analysed into time-based maintenance (*e.g.* weekly, monthly or annual preventive maintenance, the cost of which is independent of activity) and activity-based maintenance (*e.g.* 5000 mile services, breakdowns, the costs of which are wholly dependent on activity).

5. Segregation of semi-variable costs. All semi-variable costs can be segregated into their time-based and activity-based (fixed and variable) components. However, in practice it is virtually impossible to segregate the fixed and variable costs by simple inspection (as was suggested with maintenance above). Such segregation must be done statistically. The following is a simple method of segregation (*see* Fig. 6):

(*a*) Prepare a graph with axes for activity (horizontal) and costs (vertical).

(*b*) Take the figures from a number of past periods and for each period plot the activity and costs as a single point.

(*c*) Draw the "line of best fit" through the points and extend it to the cost axis. This is the *total cost line*.

(*d*) The point where the total cost line cuts the cost axis gives the *fixed cost*.

(*e*) The *variable cost* at any level of activity is given by the difference between the fixed cost and the total cost line.

NOTE: Students who have studied statistics may have realised that we have been constructing a scattergraph and that, indeed, the whole object has been to find the regression line of costs on activity (see Chapters XVI and XVII, *Statistics*, W. M. Harper, Macdonald & Evans).

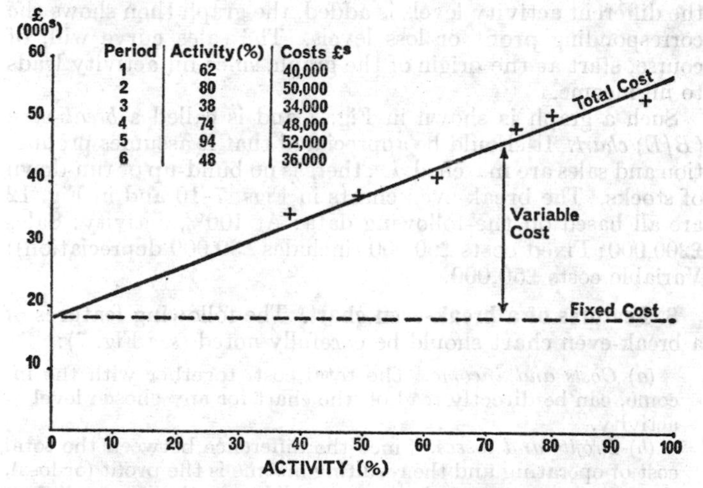

FIG. 6.—*Segregation of fixed and variable costs by scattergraph*

Activity and costs for each period are plotted as single points. The "line of best fit" is the total cost curve. The point where it cuts the cost axis gives the fixed cost.

This graph shows the fixed cost is approximately £18,000 and the variable cost is £380 per 1% of activity.

6. Total cost = fixed + variable costs. Since all semi-variable costs can be segregated into fixed and variable components, then *all* the costs in an enterprise can be analysed into fixed and variable categories. This means that the total cost for any period can be regarded as the sum of costs that are wholly fixed and costs that are wholly variable, *i.e.* total cost = fixed + variable costs.

7. Graphing costs and income. It is a simple matter to plot the foregoing equation on a graph having activity and money axes. On such a graph the fixed cost curve will show as a horizontal line at a height equal to the fixed cost and the total cost curve as a straight upward-sloping line starting from the fixed cost curve at nil activity (since at nil activity the variable costs must by definition be nil and the total cost, therefore, equal to the fixed cost).

If a third curve representing the income received (sales) at the different activity levels is added, the graph then shows the corresponding profit or loss levels. The sales curve will, of course, start at the origin of the graph, since nil activity leads to nil income.

Such a graph is shown in Fig. 7 and is called a *break-even* (*B/E*) *chart*. It should be appreciated that it assumes production and sales are matched, *i.e.* there is no build-up or run-down of stocks. The break-even charts in Figs. 7–10 and in Fig. 12 are all based on the following data: At 100% activity: Sales £200,000; Fixed costs £90,000 (includes £30,000 depreciation); Variable costs £50,000.

8. Features of a break-even chart. The following features of a break-even chart should be carefully noted (*see* Fig. 7):

(*a*) *Costs and income.* The total cost, together with the income, can be directly read off the chart for any chosen level of activity.

(*b*) *Profits and losses.* Since the difference between the total cost of operating and the resulting income is the profit (or loss), then the gap between the total cost line and the income line at any level of activity measures the profit (loss) at that level.

(*c*) *Break-even point.* When the income line crosses the total cost line income and total costs are equal, and neither a profit nor a loss is made, *i.e.* the enterprise *breaks even.* This point is called the break-even point, and is usually measured in terms of activity (*e.g.* break-even point of Fig. 7 = 60% activity).

(*d*) *Margin of safety.* This is simply the difference between the break-even point and any activity selected for consideration.

9. The importance of the break-even point. If a company is continually making losses, no matter how small, then its life is definitely limited. On the other hand, if it is making profits, no matter how small, then theoretically it can continue indefinitely. The break-even point is important to management, therefore, since it marks the very lowest level to which activity can drop without putting the continued life of the company in jeopardy. Occasionally working below break-even point is, of course, not necessarily fatal, but on the whole the company must operate above this level.

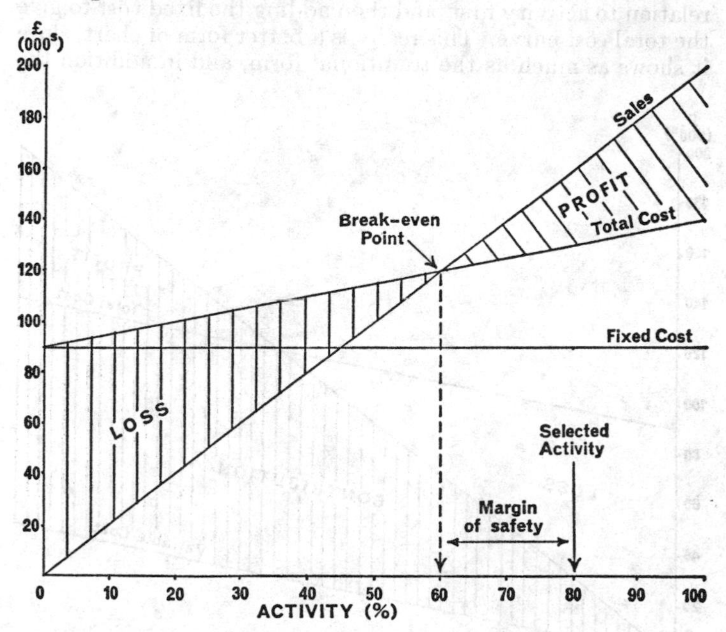

FIG. 7—*Traditional break-even chart*

Break-even point is measured in terms of activity. This chart shows that if the selected activity is 80%, then:

Expected sales	£160,000
Expected total cost	£130,000
Expected profit	£30,000
Margin of safety	20%

The following data are used in Figs. 7–10 and in Fig. 12:

At 100% activity:	Sales	£200,000
	Fixed costs	£90,000 (includes £30,000 depreciation)
	Variable costs	£50,000

BREAK-EVEN CHART VARIANTS

So far we have only examined the break-even chart in its traditional form. In this section we look briefly at a few break-even chart variants.

10. Break-even chart: variable costs at base (Fig. 8). Break-even charts can be drawn showing the variable cost and its relation to activity first, and then adding the fixed cost to give the total cost curve. This really is a better form of chart, since it shows as much as the traditional form, and in addition the

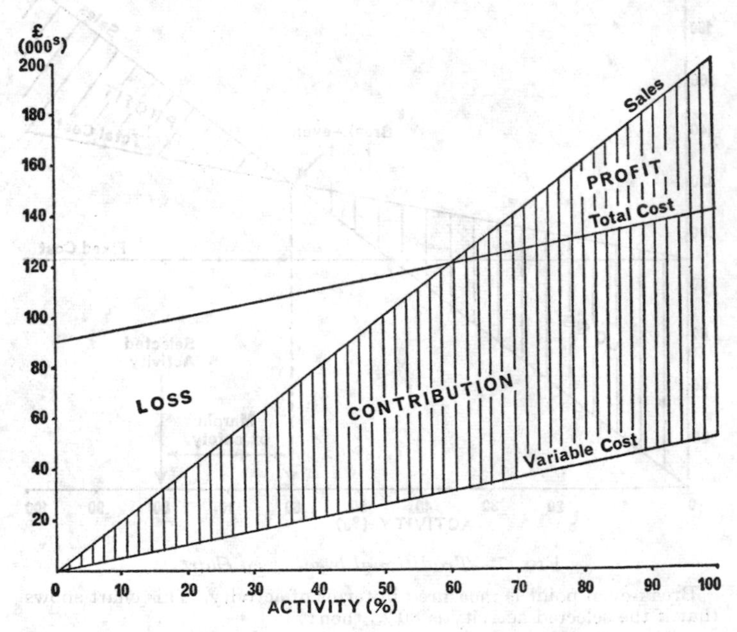

FIG. 8.—*Break-even chart with variable costs at base*

Here the variable cost curve is drawn first. This is an important improvement on the traditional break-even chart shown in Fig. 7, since it provides a direct measure of contribution (*see* VIII, 3).

gap between the variable cost and income curves is a direct measure of contribution (*see* VIII, 3).

11. Cash break-even chart (Fig. 9). Here only *cash* costs and income are graphed; book charges are ignored. The major effect of this is to eliminate depreciation, which results in a reduction of the fixed (and therefore, total) costs. On such a chart the cash break-even point measures the level of activity required to ensure that the cash received from income is sufficient to cover all costs requiring cash payments.

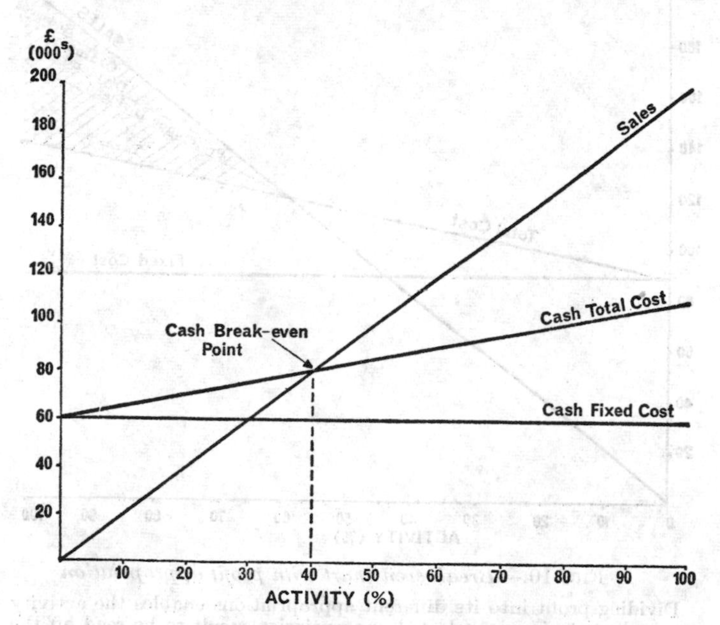

FIG. 9.—*Cash break-even chart*

In this type of break-even chart book charges are ignored, eliminating depreciation and lowering fixed costs. This chart shows that if activity reaches 40%, then enough cash will be received from sales to cover all *cash* costs; this excludes credit considerations, however.

12. Break-even chart with profit appropriation (Fig. 10). This is a normal break-even chart in which the profit wedge is split into the different profit appropriations. This enables the activity required to attain any selected appropriation result to be read off the chart directly (*e.g.* increase in reserves of £4500 after payment of 20% ordinary dividend requires activity of 90%).

13. Multi-product break-even chart (Fig. 11). (*This chart requires a knowledge of the matter discussed in the next chapter.*)

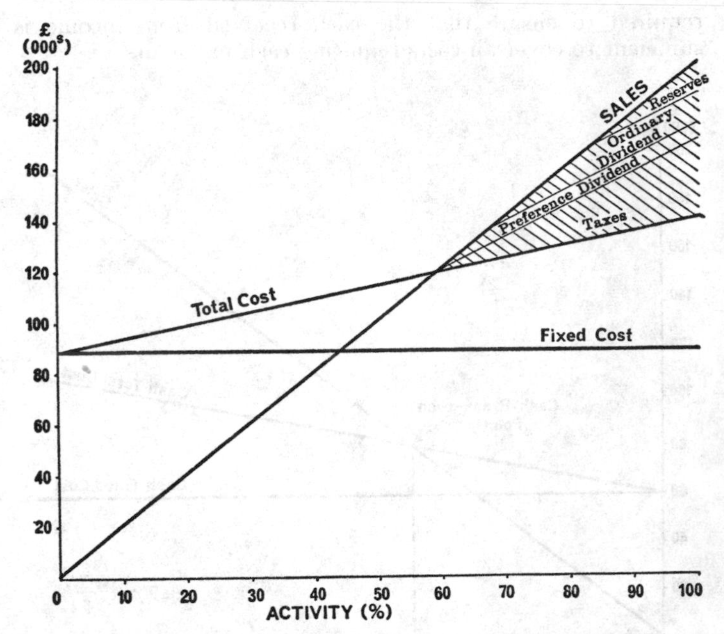

FIG. 10.—*Break-even chart with profit appropriation*

Dividing profit into its different appropriations enables the activity required to attain any selected appropriation result to be read off the chart directly. For purposes of illustration, it is assumed that corporation tax is 50%; Preference Shares are £75,000 at 8%; Ordinary Dividend is 20% maximum on £60,000.

It is not so easy to use break-even charts where there are multiple products. One way is to:

(*a*) Plot the total fixed cost line.

(*b*) Plot the *contribution* of the product with the highest profit-volume (P/V) ratio up to its normal level of sales, then add (cumulatively) the contribution of the product with the next highest P/V ratio, and soon.

(*c*) Join the origin to the end of the last line plotted. This gives the average contribution slope. The break-even point is where this line cuts the fixed cost line, assuming product sales proportions remain constant.

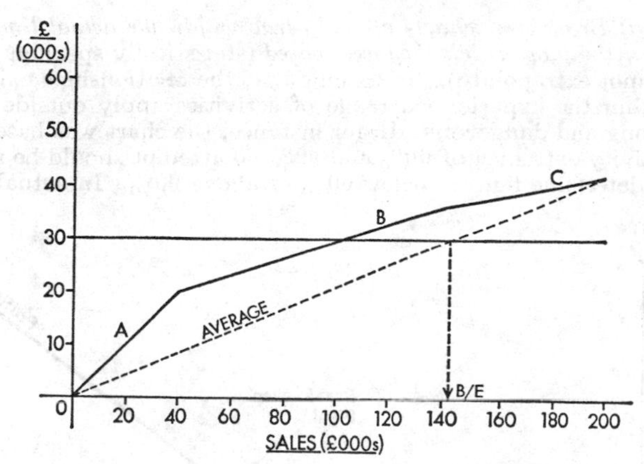

FIG. 11.—*Multi-product break-even chart*

Data	*Product*	*Sales*	*P/V ratio*	*Contribution*
	A	£40,000	50%	£20,000
	B	£100,000	16%	£16,000
	C	£60,000	10%	£6,000

Fixed cost £30,000

Break-even point is where the average contribution line cuts the fixed cost line (assuming product sales proportions remain constant).

14. Profit graph (Fig. 12). Profit cannot be read *directly* off a break-even chart—it is necessary to deduct the total cost reading from the income reading. A profit graph overcomes this by plotting the profit directly against activity. This means that at nil activity a loss equal to the fixed cost will be suffered (£90,000), and at break-even (*i.e.* nil profit) the profit curve will cut the activity axis (60%).

VALIDITY AND USE OF BREAK-EVEN CHARTS

15. Validity of break-even charts. As can be seen, the break-even chart is a useful tool for relating costs and profits to activity, but it does have certain limitations that must always be borne in mind. In practice, before jumping to any conclusions, the validity of any individual chart should be considered in the light of the following considerations:

(*a*) *Break-even charts are only true within the actual limits of the activity on which they were based* (statistically speaking, you cannot extrapolate). To assume that the relationships existing within the experienced range of activities apply outside it is wrong and dangerous. If, for instance, the chart was based on activity extremes of 60% and 90% no attempt should be made to determine figures below 60% or above 90%. In actual fact

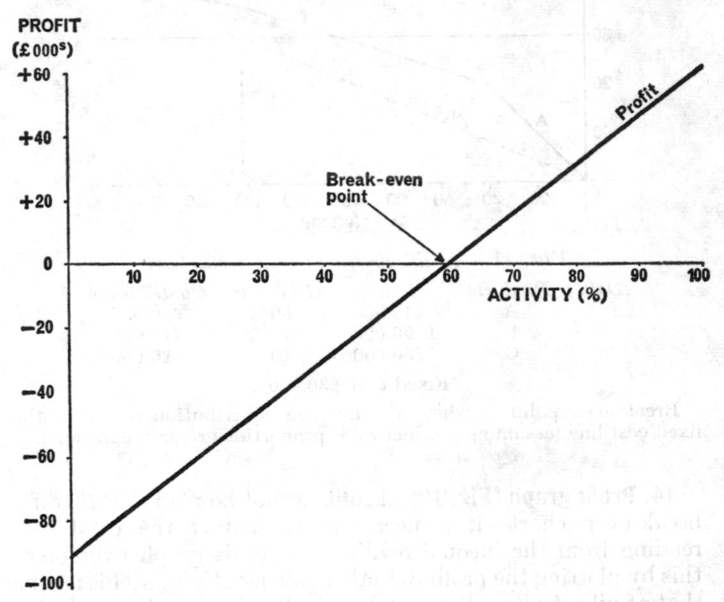

FIG. 12.—*Profit graph*

Profit is plotted directly against activity. At nil activity, therefore, loss equals the fixed cost.

the true cost curve is probably something like that in Fig. 13(*a*). Such a curve is relatively flat through the normal levels of activity and it is this that gives validity to the break-even chart. Clearly, to use break-even theory at other parts of the curve is quite wrong.

(*b*) *Fixed costs may change at different levels of activity.* For up to 80% activity, for instance, one storekeeper in a small company may suffice, but above that level he may need a full-time assistant. The wages of the assistant will therefore increase the fixed cost total.

It should be noted that such fixed costs tend to increase in steps, *i.e.* the increase takes place with a sudden jump at a critical activity level (*see* Fig. 13(*b*)).

(*c*) *Variable costs may not give a straight-line chart.* Attempts to sell more units may well entail transporting the extra units over longer distances to reach more distant markets. Thus distribution costs may increase at a *faster* rate than activity. Overtime and bulk discounts, too, have the effect of putting kinks in the cost line so that the angle of the slope changes. (These factors should not be over-estimated, however. In practice, within the normal range of activities, they are frequently of only slight significance.)

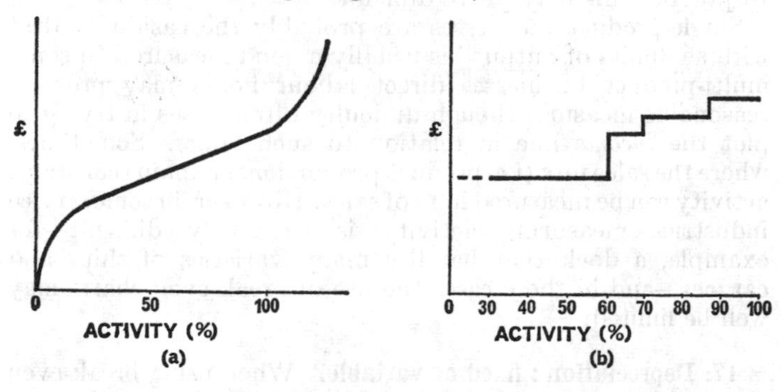

FIG. 13.—*Actual cost curves*

In (*a*) the true *total cost curve* is relatively flat only through normal levels of activity. It would be wrong to apply break-even theory outside the normal levels of activity.
In (*b*) a single *fixed cost curve* is seen to increase in steps, as the fixed cost changes at particular activity levels.

(*d*) *The income curve may bend a little.* It may be necessary to give extra discounts in order to sell extra units, and this will reduce the slope of the income curve at higher sales levels.

(*e*) *The relevant time span affects the chart.* If the chart is based on short-term considerations, then many costs will be fixed that, in a longer time context, would vary to some extent. For instance, if only the next day is being considered, even direct labour becomes a fixed cost, since men cannot be put off (or on) at such short notice. Conversely, a twenty-year time span means even debenture interest may become a variable cost (*i.e.* increased activity: increased loan required). This all means, of course, that different break-even charts are needed when different time spans are under consideration (*see* also **18**).

(*f*) *Managerial decisions can alter the fixed and variable balance.* Management can, at any time, interchange fixed and variable costs. For instance, they can replace a small labour team, a variable cost, by an automatic machine having mainly fixed costs. This means a break-even chart can be completely out-dated by a management decision, and so usually it is necessary to prepare a new chart every time break-even figures are required.

16. Measuring activity. Clearly, the value of a break-even chart depends very much on being able to measure activity. In practice this may prove difficult.

Single-product businesses are probably the easiest to deal with as "units of output" is usually a good measure. In some multi-product businesses direct labour hours may prove a reasonable measure, though difficulty often arises in trying to plot the *income* line in relation to such hours. Sometimes, where the sales mix (*i.e.* product proportions) remains constant, activity can be measured in £s of sales. However, in some service industries measuring activity is extremely difficult—for example, a dock that handles many varieties of ships and cargoes—and in these cases the use of break-even charts may well be limited.

17. Depreciation: fixed or variable? When using break-even theory it is necessary to determine whether depreciation is a fixed or variable cost. The test essentially is to ascertain whether depreciation increases with activity or not. Frequently it will be found to do so—if not entirely then to a significant extent. For example, lorries depreciate mainly with use, and the cost is therefore activity-based. On the other hand if obsolesence arises before the asset is worn out then the depreciation is time-based and so a fixed cost.

18. Relationship between time-based costs and activity. In **15** (*e*) it was pointed out that the time-span involved affects a break-even chart. Although in the short term fixed costs are not affected by activity, this becomes less true as the time-span increases. Over a period of a month rent will not be affected by activity, but over a period of ten years then the long-term trend in activity may well result in premises of a different size being obtained. This means that rent *will* be affected by activity. In the case of management salaries an even shorter period will see changes; an alteration in activity may well be partially reflected in such salaries within six months.

This means that there *is* a relationship between time-based costs and activity and the longer the time span the closer the relationship. This is what is meant by the saying, "In the long run all costs are variable." When making a decision, therefore, the time involved should be considered If only the short term is affected then fixed costs can be taken as wholly fixed, but if otherwise the effect of the relationship must be assessed and allowed for.

19. Use of break-even chart in decision-making. Study of the break-even chart and its variants should indicate clearly to students the many ways in which it can be used in decision-making. It is particularly useful when making decisions relating to planned levels of activity, fixing selling prices, or changing the fixed/variable cost structure.

At all times, however, the qualifications made in **15** above should be heeded. Provided this is done, the chart will be found to be of considerable help, showing as it does the inter-relationship between the main factors involved in enterprise economics.

PROGRESS TEST 7

Principles

1. On which two basic factors do costs depend for their values? **(1)**
2. What is a semi-variable cost and how does it arise? **(4)**
3. How can fixed and variable costs be segregated? **(5)**
4. Why is it important to know the break-even point? **(9)**
5. What are:

   (*a*) Cash break-even charts? **(11)**
   (*b*) Profit graphs? **(14)**

6. A well-known writer commenting on the break-even chart said:

   "It (the break-even chart) must be applied with an intelligent discrimination, with an adequate grasp of the assumptions underlying the technique and of the limitations surrounding its practical application."

   Expand on this statement, giving illustrations of the points which the writer had in mind (*A.C.C.A*) **(15)**

7. What is meant by the saying, "In the long run all costs are variable"? (18)

Practice

8. A company has abstracted the following data for the past two successive periods:

	Period 1	*Period* 2
Material costs	£30,000	£36,000
Labour costs	£21,200	£24,700
Overhead costs	£41,800	£45,300
Production	10,000 units	12,000 units

Sales throughout were made at £10 per unit.

(*a*) Use a break-even chart to find:

(*i*) the company fixed costs;

(*ii*) the current break-even point.

(*b*) A plan is proposed whereby:

Variable costs will be reduced by £1 per unit.

Fixed costs will rise by £11,600.

Find: (*i*) the new break-even point;

(*ii*) the minimum sales level that will justify changing from the current position to the proposed plan.

9. During 1968 the Even Brake Company obtained sales of £336,000. Their total variable costs for the year amounted to £340,000 and their fixed costs were £140,000. They had no finished goods at the beginning of 1968, but they did have a finished goods stock at the end of the year which they valued at marginal cost.

If their volume of sales had been 25% higher (*i.e.* if they had sold 25% more units with no change in their selling prices) they would have broken even.

(*a*) Construct a break-even chart for the Even Brake Company.

(*b*) Find the value of their finished goods stock at the end of 1968.

(You may assume there are no raw material or work-in-progress stocks involved.)

CHAPTER VIII

MARGINAL COSTING

WE can now develop the break-even chart technique into the even more useful technique of marginal costing.

MARGINAL COST THEORY

1. Marginal costs. *Marginal costs are the variable costs incurred as the result of undertaking a specified activity.*

Economists define marginal cost essentially as the extra cost of producing *one* additional unit, *i.e.* as the variable cost per unit. However, it should be noted that in business—particularly in decision-making—it is usually the *total* variable cost involved in a project that is relevant rather than the variable cost per unit. Consequently the term "marginal cost" can relate to either a single unit or an entire project, and the student must decide for himself from the overall context in which sense the term is used.

2. Importance of marginal costing. The importance of marginal costing in decision-making lies in the fact that in the short term the only extra costs involved in a project are the marginal costs. If, for example, we have on a given day a choice of manufacturing either a bedroom suite or a dining-room suite then clearly, since rent, rates, administration salaries, and so on, will be the same whichever we make, we need consider only the marginal costs of each when assessing the relative costs of the two alternatives.

3. Contribution. Costs, however, are not the only criteria for deciding which alternative to accept; the income from each is also relevant. For instance, our bedroom suite may have a marginal cost of £30 against a £20 marginal cost for the dining-room suite, but if we can sell the bedroom suite for £80 and the dining-room suite for only £60, then the bedroom suite is the more profitable, since it gives an excess of income over marginal cost of £50 against only £40 for the other suite. *This difference between income and marginal cost* is termed *contribution.*

"Contribution" is probably the most important word in

decision-making terminology, and it must be fully understood by students. Its importance warrants re-stating its significance in the following summary form:

When making a short-term decision between a number of alternatives the only relevant figures are the marginal costs and incomes of each alternative, as the fixed costs are the same whichever alternative is selected. The difference between the marginal cost and income—i.e. the contribution of an alternative—measures, therefore, the net gain to the business that will result from selecting that alternative. Consequently the profits of the business are maximised by selecting the alternative that gives the greatest contribution.

This principle, which is the basis for very many decisions, must however be qualified in the following two respects:

(*a*) Fixed costs must not alter. In short-term decisions this qualification usually holds.
(*b*) No key factors are involved. This qualification is discussed in **12** and **13** below.

4. Contribution and profitability. Students are often worried about the total disregard of fixed costs that the above principle demands. This worry is unfounded. Since essentially the fixed costs represent an unalterable flow of money out of the business, the only scope for action that we have is to find a project that brings into a business the maximum reverse flow in the form of contribution. Usually, of course, there will be a number of projects all in operation at once and their combined contributions will form a reverse flow well in excess of the actual outflow of fixed costs—the excess clearly being the profit to the business. The essential point to note, however, is that when one must *choose* between alternatives, that which gives the largest contribution must increase the profit the most (*see* Fig. 14). Thus contribution is a measure of profitability.

NOTE: Remember the difference between "profit" and "profitability." The contribution does not measure the actual *profit* earned by a project, but only which alternative will maximise the whole profit of the business—or minimise the loss—*i.e.* it measures *profitability; see* I, **20**.

5. Marginal cost statements. Since contribution is the vital figure in short-term decision-making, marginal cost statements

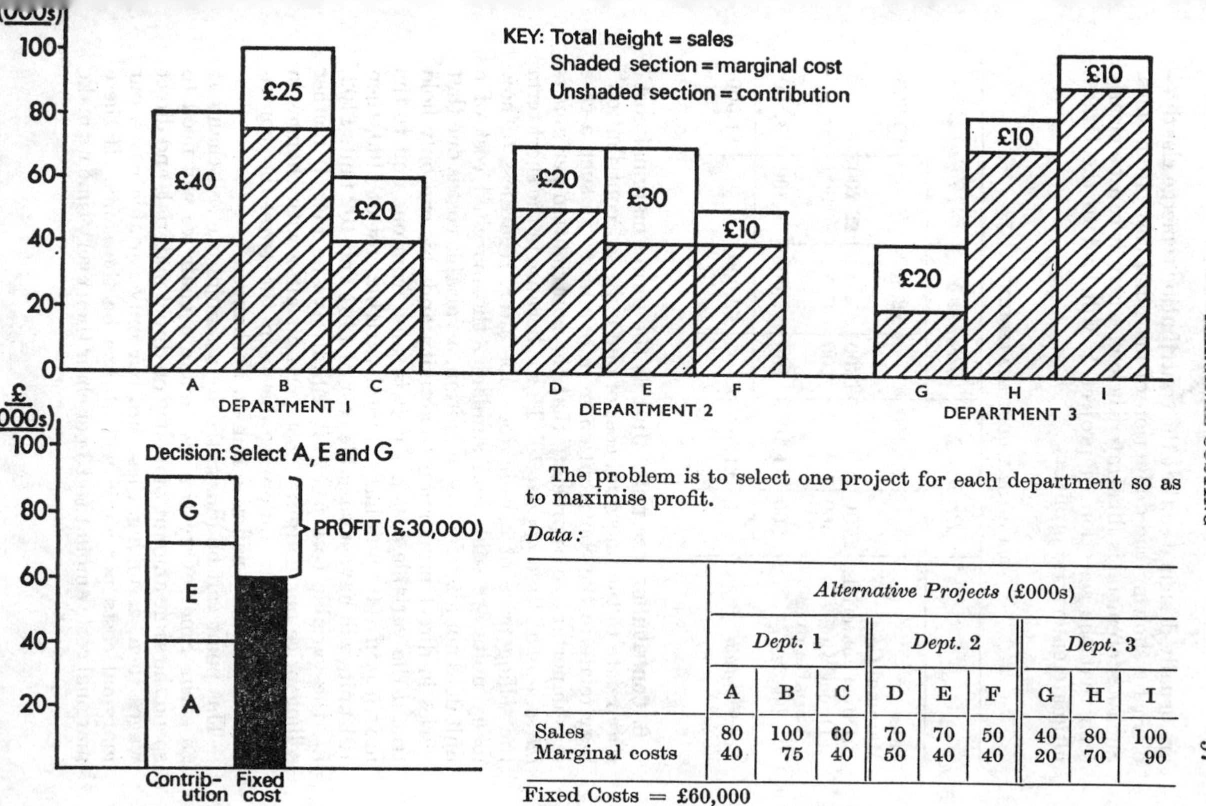

The problem is to select one project for each department so as to maximise profit.

Data:

	Alternative Projects (£000s)								
	Dept. 1			*Dept.* 2			*Dept.* 3		
	A	B	C	D	E	F	G	H	I
Sales	80	100	60	70	70	50	40	80	100
Marginal costs	40	75	40	50	40	40	20	70	90

Fixed Costs = £60,000

FIG. 14.—*Diagrammatic representation of contribution as a measure of profitability*

are usually designed so that the contributions emerge clearly—often by showing the deduction of marginal costs from sales. Such a statement is illustrated below, where it can be clearly seen that the selection of project Y will lead to the largest ultimate enterprise profit.

MARGINAL COST STATEMENT

	Project X		*Project Y*		*Project Z*	
Sales		£2,400		£2,600		£5,000
Marginal Costs						
Direct materials	£700		£300		£2,200	
Direct wages	500		200		900	
Variable overheads	200	1,400	100	600	400	3,500
Contribution		£1,000		£2,000		£1,500

6. Contribution per unit. Just as the term "marginal cost" may relate to the marginal cost of one unit, so "contribution" may relate to the contribution from one unit. In such a case it is important to appreciate that the contribution *per unit is the same at all levels of activity.* This is because in the short term the selling price of a unit does not alter, regardless of how many units are sold, and similarly, the marginal cost of a unit does not alter for, by definition, a variable cost is one that varies in direct proportion to activity and this can only hold true if the variable cost per unit is same from one unit to the next (*e.g.* if 100 units have a total variable cost of £100, then 101 units will have a variable cost of £101 and 102 units £102, *i.e.* the variable cost *per unit* will always be £1). If neither selling price nor marginal cost per unit alter with changes in activity then the difference between the two—the contribution per unit—will also remain unchanged.

This point can be illustrated by assuming we sell chairs at £5 each. Since every time we make a chair we will need to spend the same amount of money on direct materials and direct wages then, assuming these are our only variable costs, our marginal costs per chair will always be the same. If these marginal costs amount to £3 per chair then every time we make and sell a chair we will take £5 and pay £3, which leaves us with £2 contribution for each and every chair.

7. P/V (Profit/volume ratio). It follows that sales and contribution are in direct proportion to each other, *i.e.* if sales increase by 20% then the contribution increases by 20%. For example, if 10 chairs are sold sales are £50 and the contribution is £20. Increase sales by 20% (*i.e.* 2 chairs) and the contribution rises to £24, *i.e.* by 20%.

Since sales and contribution are always in direct proportion, then dividing one by the other will always give the same figure—*e.g.* contribution divided by sales in the above examples gives:

$\frac{2}{5}$; $\frac{20}{50}$; $\frac{24}{60}$; and the latter two both cancel down to $\frac{2}{5}$.

This fraction is called the *P/V ratio* and can always be calculated so:

$$P/V\ ratio = \frac{Contribution}{Sales}$$

This ratio is useful inasmuch as it enables the contribution to be quickly calculated from any given level of sales (or vice versa), since the formula can be turned round to *Contribution = Sales × P/V ratio* (*e.g.* given a sales figure of £180, the contribution will be £180 $\times \frac{2}{5} =$ £72).

8. Marginal cost mathematics. Using the break-even theory of the last chapter we are now in a position to build up a series of formulae linking total costs, marginal (variable) costs, fixed costs, break-even points (B/E) and profits with levels of activity, *i.e.*:

Total cost = Fixed cost + Variable cost
Contribution = Sales — Marginal cost
Profit = Contribution — Fixed cost

In a single-product enterprise or department the following additional formulae can be used:

Contribution = *Number of units* × *Contribution per unit.*

(∴ Profit = Number of units × Contribution per unit − Fixed cost.)

$$B/E\ point\ \text{(in units)} = \frac{Fixed\ cost}{Contribution\ per\ unit}$$

(*i.e.* the number of units required to build up a total contribution equal to the fixed cost, at which point, of course, the profit is nil).

To find the B/E point in £ sales, multiply both sides of the last formula by the selling price:

∴ Number of units at B/E × Selling price (= sales)

$$= \frac{\text{Fixed cost} \times \text{Selling price}}{\text{Contribution per unit}}$$

$$\therefore \text{Sales (at B/E)} = \text{Fixed cost} \times \frac{\text{Selling price}}{\text{Contribution per unit}}$$

$$= \text{Fixed cost} \times \frac{1}{\text{P/V ratio}}$$

9. Profit planning. Very often an enterprise plans its sales, costs and activity and then computes what profit will emerge. In profit planning this is reversed; the enterprise decides what profit it wants (which is usually based on a reasonable return on capital employed *see* I, **18**) and then works *backwards* to see what sales, costs and activity are needed to produce that profit.

In practice, certain factors are usually fixed before planning begins (*e.g.* capacity may be limited, or selling prices determined by competitors' activities) and then profit planning indicates the value that the remaining factors must take to achieve the profit target.

EXAMPLE

Data: A company manufactures a single product having a marginal cost of £3 a unit. Fixed costs are £48,000. The market is such that up to 40,000 units can be sold at £6 a unit, but any additional sales must be made at £4 a unit. There is a planned profit of £80,000. How many units must be made and sold?

Method:

Planned profit (£80,000) + Fixed costs (£48,000) = Planned contribution.

∴ Planned contribution = £128,000.

Now the first 40,000 units give a contribution of 40,000 × (£6 − £3) = £120,000.

This is £8000 contribution short of plan.

Since the contribution per unit on sales over 40,000 units is £4 − £3 = £1, then the number of additional units needed to give a contribution of £8000 = 8000.

∴ Total number of units to be made and sold = 40,000 + 8000 = 48,000 units.

APPLICATION OF MARGINAL COSTING

In this section we will examine how marginal costing can be applied to a variety of situations.

10. Selecting the most profitable project. This is the basic situation in which marginal costing is applied and has already been illustrated in **5** above.

11. Acceptance of a special contract. One type of decision often to be made is the acceptance or otherwise of a special contract under which units are sold below normal selling prices. In such circumstances the contribution is the relevant figure, since the whole of any contribution must be extra profit if the enterprise is over the break-even point, or a reduction of the loss if below this point. Either way the enterprise is better off by the amount of the contribution. From this we see that *it is always better to take a special contract if there is some contribution, no matter how small, than to reject the contract and have no contribution.*

Note, however, two qualifications to this:

(*a*) It is assumed that the fulfilment of the contract *will not affect normal sales.* Nothing is gained by selling units at £4 which otherwise would have been sold at £5.

(*b*) It is also assumed that *nothing better is likely to come along.* A business that fills its workshops with many low-contribution contracts and then has to turn away high-contribution work is not making the best decisions. Judging whether or not anything better is likely to come along is, of course, the responsibility of management.

12. Key factors. There is always something that limits an enterprise from achieving an unlimited profit as we saw when discussing the principal budget factor (IV, **9**). Usually this is sales, *i.e.* the enterprise cannot sell as much as it would like. Sometimes, however, an enterprise can sell all that it can produce, but output is limited by the scarcity of some economic *factor of production*, *e.g.* materials, labour, machine capacity or cash. Such a factor is called a *key factor*.

13. Contribution per unit of key factor. If a key factor is operating, then it is important that the enterprise makes as much profit as it can each time it uses up one of its scarce units of key factor. Since fixed costs do not alter, this means *maximising the contribution per unit of key factor*.

EXAMPLE

Data: Materials are limited to 1000 tons. A choice must be made between two jobs requiring such materials, A and B. Job details are as follows:

	Job A	*Job B*
Selling price	£300	£200
Marginal cost	£100	£120
Contribution	£200	£80
Tons required	4	1

Method: On the face of it A is in all respects the more profitable; it has a higher selling price, lower marginal cost and contribution over twice that of B. But in using 4 tons of materials it earns a contribution of only £50 a ton, *i.e.* if all jobs were of this type our 1000 tons would allow us to earn only £50,000 contribution. B, on the other hand, earns a contribution of £80 a ton, so jobs of this type would allow us to earn £80,000 contribution. Type B jobs are therefore more profitable in these circumstances, and so should be selected in preference to type A jobs.

Where a key factor is involved, therefore, the work that gives *the highest contribution per unit of key factor used should be chosen*.

14. Make-or-buy decisions. Another type of decision, called a *make-or-buy decision*, arises when the product being manufactured has a component part that can either be made within the factory or bought from an outside supplier. On the face of it, since the only extra cost to make the part is the marginal cost, then the amount by which this falls below the supplier's price is the saving that arises on making. However, this is a deception, as it is also important to consider what work would have been carried out using the relevant facilities if the part had not been made. This is necessary, since if making the part involves putting aside other work, then the business will *lose the contribution this work would otherwise have earned*. Such a loss of contribution must be added to the marginal cost of the part.

NOTE: In economics such a cost is called an *opportunity cost*. An opportunity cost is one that is represented not by money paid out but by the loss of income that would otherwise be obtained.

To summarise, in a make-or-buy decision compare:

(*a*) the supplier's price; with
(*b*) the marginal cost of making, plus the loss of contribution of displaced work.

This loss of contribution is usually best found by use of the contribution per unit of key factor (*see* 13).

EXAMPLE

Data: An X takes 20 hours to process on machine 99. It has a selling price of £100 and a marginal cost of £60. A Y (a component part used in production) could be made on machine 99 in 3 hours for a marginal cost of £5. The supplier's price is £10. Should one make or buy Ys?

Method: Now contribution per X = 100 − 60 = £40.

$\therefore$ Contribution earned per hour on machine 99 is $\frac{40}{20} = £2.$

If then a Y is made in 3 hours, £6 contribution is lost.

$\therefore$ Full cost to make Y = £5 + £6 = £11.

This is more than the supplier's price of £10, and so it is better to buy than make.

This decision assumes that machine 99 is working to full capacity and machine time then, is the key factor.

PROGRESS TEST 8

Principles

1. What are marginal costs? (1)
2. Why is contribution an important concept? (3)

3. How is a P/V ratio computed and how is it most commonly employed? (7)

4. What is involved in profit planning? (9)

5. (a) What is a key factor? (12)
   (b) Why is it important in decision-making to take the key factor into account? (13)

6. What figures are employed in a make-or-buy decision? (14)

Practice

7. (a) A company makes £5000 profit from £60,000 sales. Its fixed costs are £15,000. What is its break-even point?
   (b) A company has sales of £100,000, fixed costs of £20,000 and a break-even point of £80,000. What profit has it made?
   (c) A company has a profit of £5000, fixed costs of £10,000 and a break-even point of £20,000. What were its sales?

8. A company, currently operating at 80% capacity, has the following Profit and Loss Account:

Sales		£320,000
Costs:		
Direct materials	£100,000	
Direct labour	40,000	
Variable overheads	20,000	
Fixed overheads	130,000	290,000
Profit		£30,000

It has just received an offer of an overseas order that would require the use of half the factory's capacity. The order, which must be taken in full or rejected completely, must be supplied at prices 10% below current home prices.

Management are in a dilemma. They can either:

(a) Reject order and carry on with home sales only as currently;
(b) Accept order, split capacity equally between overseas and home sales, and turn away excess home demand; *or*
(c) Increase factory capacity so they can accept the export order and maintain the present home sales level by:
   (i) buying machine that will increase factory capacity by 10% and fixed costs by £20,000; *and*
   (ii) work overtime at time and a half to meet balance of required capacity.

Which is the most profitable alternative?

9. A company produces a standard product, each unit of which has a direct material cost of £4, requires 2 hours' labour and sells for £10. The company has no variable costs, only fixed costs of £18,000 a month. Labour, which is paid at £0·50 per hour, is currently very scarce, while demand for the company's product is heavy.

A contract worth £900 has just been offered to the company, and the Estimating Department has ascertained the following facts in respect of the work:

(*a*) The labour time for the contract would be 200 hours.
(*b*) The material cost would be £190 plus the cost of a special component.
(*c*) The special component could be purchased from an outside supplier for £50 or alternatively could be made by the company for a material cost of £20 and an additional labour time of 12 hours.

Advise management regarding the action they should take.

CHAPTER IX

DIFFERENTIAL COSTING

Now that we have examined decision-making in respect of short-term situations, we can expand our discussion to include decisions involving longer-term alternatives. This leads us to the technique of differential costing.

THE BASIC CONCEPT

1. Definition. *Differential costing* is a decision-making technique in which *only cost and income differences between alternatives are examined.* When laid out correctly these differences indicate the profitability differences between alternatives so the most profitable alternative can be identified.

2. Relationship between differential and marginal costing. If the basic decision-making approach given in the introduction to this Part of the book is referred to (p. 79), then it will be seen that differential costing is essentially the application of this approach—in other words differential costing embraces the other decision-making techniques. This means that marginal costing is a special application of differential costing. This point becomes clear when it is realised that marginal costing assumes that the only differences between alternatives lie in the marginal costs and incomes—fixed costs remaining unchanged. If the fixed costs do in fact differ between alternatives, then marginal costing cannot be employed and the more basic concept of differential costing must be used.

3. Alternatives with differing fixed costs. The application of differential costing to a situation where the fixed costs are different for different alternatives is straightforward enough —simply charge these fixed costs to the appropriate alternatives. The following example should be sufficient demonstration of the technique:

EXAMPLE

Department A produces units that have a marginal cost of £10, a selling price of £12 and an expected sales level of 1000 units per annum. If the department closes down there will be a saving of fixed costs associated with staffing and equipment depreciation of £3000 per annum. Should the department be closed?

Solution

Annual sales, 1000 units at £12	£12,000
Less marginal costs, 1000 units at £10	10,000
Annual contribution	2,000
Annual fixed costs identifiable with Dept. A	3,000
Net gain due to keeping Dept. A open	£−1,000

In this case the difference between closing Dept A and keeping it open is £1000 and it is therefore more profitable to close A, despite the fact that it is making an annual contribution of £2000.

4. Identifiable fixed costs. It is important to appreciate that when bringing fixed costs into a differential cost analysis only those fixed costs *that will alter* must be included. Such costs are called *identifiable fixed costs* since they can be positively identified with the alternatives under consideration. To test whether a fixed cost is identifiable with a given alternative, consider whether or not the cost would be incurred if the alternative was not selected. If it would *not* be incurred, then the cost is identifiable.

Clearly, no apportioned fixed costs can be identifiable since, whether or not the given alternative is selected, the cost apportioned will be incurred regardless. In a differential cost analysis, therefore, there must be no apportioned fixed costs charged to alternatives. Only costs specifically incurred (or incomes specifically earned) must be included.

FEATURES OF DIFFERENTIAL COSTING

5. Exclusion of key factor costs. It is interesting to note that if there is a key factor, the costs associated with this factor can be ignored in decision-making involving the determination of the most profitable product. This situation arises because, clearly, whatever the decision, the key factor will be utilised to the full and so its cost will always be the same. For example, if the key factor were labour hours, of which there were only

1000 paid at £0.50 per hour, then since we shall always use the full number available the total labour cost will always be £500 no matter what we produce. Since such costs do not alter they will be excluded from the differential cost analysis.

EXAMPLE

	Product A	*Product B*
Selling price	£30	£70
Material	£4	£20
Labour (at £0·50 hr)	20 hr	40 hr

Labour is the key factor, and only 1000 hours are available. Should A or B be produced?

Solution

	A	B
Maximum production in 1000 hours	*50 units*	*25 units*
Relevant figures: Sales	£1,500	£1,750
Materials	£200	£500
Net differential income	£1,300	£1,250

A should be selected as £50 more profit will be earned than would be if B were selected.

NOTE:

(*i*) Labour costs, being the same for both alternatives, are excluded.

(*ii*) The figures show only the *differences* between the alternatives and do not measure actual profit, only profitability.

6. Absolute and relative costs. When a comparison is required between two alternatives only, then the presentation of differential costs can be made using either absolute costs or relative costs.

(*a*) *Absolute costs.* Using this approach the full costs and incomes that differ are listed for each alternative so that the two net differential figures can be compared and the more profitable alternative identified, as in **5**.

(*b*) *Relative costs.* Using this approach one alternative is take as "base" and the gain or loss in respect of each item of income and cost that would result if the *other* alternative was selected instead is detailed. This results in a final figure that indicates the net total gain or loss that would follow if the second alternative was substituted for the "base" alternative, and so indicates whether or not such a substitution is profitable. If this method had been adopted for the problem in **5** the presentation would have been as follows:

Taking the production of A as base, the substitution of B would have the following consequences (+ = gain; − = loss):

Extra sales from product B: £1750 − £1500	£+250
Extra costs producing B: £200 − 500	−300
Net difference	£−50

Producing B will lose £50 as against A. Therefore A should be produced.

PROGRESS TEST 9

Principles

1. What is *differential costing*? (**1**)
2. What is an *identifiable fixed cost*? (**4**)
3. Distinguish between absolute and relative costs (**6**)

Practice

4. A company incurred a tooling cost of £50,000 for a product whose manufacture and sales were planned to be 5000 units a year for five years. The total cost build-up per unit is as follows:

Direct materials	£1
Direct labour (4 hr at £0·50 hr)	2
Share of tooling cost	2
Fixed overheads (at £1 hr)	4
	9
Profit	1
Selling Price	£10

After only six months' production the company learns there is a good market (lasting at least 4½ years) for another type of product which has a direct material cost of £1·50, a selling price of £4 and requires 1 hour's labour to make. Unfortunately labour is in short supply and to make this product would mean permanently abandoning the first product, scrapping the tools, and switching all labour over to the second product. This second product would, in addition, require an extra expenditure of £3000 p.a. on fixed costs.

Which product should the company manufacture?

5. A foundry sells for £200 a unit a product which is essentially two halves assembled together, a right-hand half and a left-hand half. The casting requirements to make either half are:

Material, 1 ton at £40 ton
Labour, £10.

The assembly cost for joining the two halves together is £20 per finished unit (*i.e.* per pair of halves).

Unfortunately material is in scarce supply and the foundry has only 200 tons available for the forthcoming period. It has, however, been offered a supply of completed right-hand halves. What is the maximum price the foundry would be prepared to pay to buy these halves if all units made could be sold and if a total cost of £400 would be incurred in transporting the load of purchased halves to the foundry?

CHAPTER X

CASH FLOW

IN this chapter we see how the differential approach in decision-making can be applied to cash alone in many situations—which needless to say simplifies much of the work involved in assessing the alternatives.

THE BASIC CONCEPT

1. Definition of cash flow. *Cash flow* is a phrase meaning the actual movement of cash in and out of an enterprise. Cash flow in (or *positive cash flow*) is cash received, and cash flow out (*negative cash flow*) is cash paid out. The difference between these two flows is termed the *net cash flow.*

2. The cash flow technique. The cash flow technique is yet another decision-making technique that uses differences—in this case the differences between the cash flows of alternatives. For each alternative a statement is made detailing the cash flows in and out that *will* arise (*i.e.* starting from the moment of the decision and ignoring any past cash receipts and payments) and hence showing the net cash flow of the alternative. The alternative having the most favourable net cash flow is then selected as the most profitable.

EXAMPLE

A finished goods stock item that cost £100 to make is in danger of becoming completely obsolete. There are two alternative ways of disposing of it: sell it to X for £100 or to Y for £108. Y is situated twice as far away as X (although owing to road conditions the delivery time will be the same) and the cost accountant has supplied the following cost estimates for delivery:

X—Petrol and oil £5; wages £6; share of licence, insurance and depreciation (based on mileage) £7.

Y—Petrol and oil £10; wages £6; share of licence, insurance and depreciation £14.

Should the item be sold to X or Y?

Solution

	X	Y
Cash flow in: Sales	£+100	£+108
Cash flow out: Petrol, oil and wages	−11	−16
Net cash flow	£+89	£+92

Since Y has the most favourable net cash flow the correct decision is to sell to Y.

NOTE:

(*i*) The £7 and £14 shares of licence, insurance and depreciation are not included as there is no actual future outflow of *cash* in respect of these costs.
(*ii*) The net cash flow does not measure the profit (there is a loss whichever alternative is selected) but only indicates which alternative is the more profitable.

3. Principle underlying cash flow technique. The principle underlying the cash flow technique can be stated quite simply as follows:

The most profitable alternative is that one which will, over the life of the problem for which a solution is required, most favourably affect the bank balance of the enterprise—other things being equal.

In other words, the most profitable alternative is that which makes one richest, and this conclusion is difficult to fault.

4. Qualification to the cash flow principle. Despite this logical conclusion, students are often concerned at the total disregard of those costs which are not represented by actual cash flows. In one respect they are right, for the principle above (3) does contain a vital qualification—*other things being equal.* In other words it is necessary that, whichever alternative is selected, at the very end the enterprise will be in exactly the same position except as regards its bank balance. Sometimes this is not so: under one alternative the enterprise may be left with goods in stock, or a plot of land, or an old machine. In such cases the net cash flow figures emerging as a result of employing the pure cash flow technique must be adjusted to allow for these left-over items.

5. Past flows irrelevant. In a second respect—that involving past flows—the concern of students is unfounded. If an enterprise had earlier paid out a sum of money for some item, then this amount does *not* enter the calculations, for no matter what alternative is selected the payment cannot be eliminated and therefore must be common to all alternatives. Being common it cannot affect the differences between alternatives and is, therefore irrelevant.

To summarise, *all past cash expenditure and incomes are irrelevant in decision-making.* It also follows from this that since book values of assets are based on past expenditures these, too, are totally irrelevant in decision-making.

FEATURES OF THE CASH FLOW TECHNIQUE

6. Depreciation and cash flow. It was noted in an example earlier (*see* 2) that since depreciation does not involve a flow of cash it does not appear in a cash flow analysis. This does not mean it is overlooked completely. What happens is that if one enters the purchase price of an asset into the analysis as a negative cash flow, and the ultimate residual value as a positive flow at the moment of sale, the complete loss in value due to use is taken into consideration.

In the case of a replacement decision the depreciation of the existing asset is automatically made, but in a somewhat roundabout way. Careful study of a cash flow analysis will show depreciation to be allowed for by the combined effects of:

(*a*) recording the positive flow that would ultimately arise from its residual value if kept; and

(*b*) reducing the cash flow out relating to the purchase price of the replacing asset by the amount of cash received on the sale of the replaced asset (*see* answer to Progress Test 10, Question 4).

7. Absolute and relative cash flows. Cash flows can be presented as absolute flows or relative flows in exactly the same way as costs (*see* IX, 6).

In 2 above a statement using absolute flows was given. The same problem can be reworked using relative flows as follows:

EXAMPLE

Taking the sale to X as base, the substitution of the sale to Y gives the following relative cash flows:

Sales—extra cash flow (in)	£+8
Costs—extra cash flow (out)	−5
Net relative flow	£+3

Selling to Y will improve the overall cash flow by £3. Therefore the sale should be to Y.

8. Advantages of using the cash flow technique. The advantages of using the cash flow technique are as follows:

(*a*) It is a relatively simple technique—only actual cash flows in and out have to be considered. There are no complications involving the matching of costs and revenue, no temptations to apportion fixed costs to alternatives, and no problems of depreciation.

(*b*) It automatically prevents past costs being unnecessarily included in the calculations and so avoids the possibility of erroneous treatment of such past costs (students all too often make errors in this respect).

(*c*) It avoids misguided attempts to saddle particular alternatives with unrecovered past costs. For example, some managements believe they cannot drop a specific product until it has "recovered" its tooling costs. They fail to appreciate that continued production of an inferior product often makes less profit than the introduction of a better product, despite heavy unrecovered costs.

(*d*) It is needed if a discounted cash flow analysis is required (*see* XI).

PROGRESS TEST 10

Principles

1. State the underlying principle of the cash flow technique and explain the qualification therein (**3, 4**)

2. Distinguish between absolute and relative cash flows. (**7**)

3. What are the advantages of using the cash flow technique? (**8**)

Practice

4. A company is considering replacing a sound but somewhat old-fashioned machine by a more up-to-date special purpose one.

Unfortunately, in five years' time the work done on these types of machine will end. The facts are as below and you are to determine whether or not to replace the existing machine.

	Existing Machine	*New Machine*
Book value	£24,000	—
Resale value now	10,000	—
Purchase price	40,000	£30,000
Residual value in 5 years	4,000	2,000
Annual cash running costs	9,000	6,000
Annual receipts from production	10,000	12,000

CHAPTER XI

CAPITAL PROJECTS

In this chapter we examine decision-making methods that relate to long-term projects, *i.e.* projects running into many years, and particularly capital projects. When evaluating long-term projects the fixed/variable analysis becomes less important, as the emphasis is on the *project* cost rather than the cost unit cost. On the other hand the *timing* of cash receipts and payments often becomes critical and this chapter deals in the main with the technique that allows for this factor in decision-making.

PRESENT VALUES

1. The importance of timing. The essence of the technique we shall consider is the fact that £1 in a year's time has not the same value as £1 now. There is more than one reason for this (*e.g.* inflation), but the *only* reason this technique recognises is that £1 *now can be immediately invested so that by the end of the year its value has grown by the amount of interest.* To pay £1 now, therefore, for a promise of £1 in a year is an unprofitable act—and to pay £1 for a promise of £1 in two, three or more years is increasingly more unprofitable. Consequently, when investing money now in long-term projects it is not only the amount of money that will be earned later that is relevant but also just when it is received, *i.e.* the timing of the subsequent cash flows is important.

2. Converting cash flows. To say that when evaluating projects £1 in a year has not the same value as £1 now is akin to saying they are in different currencies such as £s and $s. When amounts are in different currencies it is necessary to convert them all into a common currency using *conversion rates.* Which currency is selected as the common currency is not really important, though one may be rather more advantageous than another.

In exactly the same way it is necessary to convert all project cash flows into £s having the same value, *i.e.* a common currency. This involves selecting a moment in time and expressing the value of all flows in respect of that moment, and though again it is not important which moment is selected there are definite advantages to selecting the very beginning of the project. In other words, if the project is to begin *now*, then we shall convert all future cash flows into the amounts we would pay now for the promises of those future flows. Such amounts are termed *present values* since they are the value of those flows at this present moment. Note, incidentally, we are considering *cash* flows, not cost values, since only cash can be invested to earn interest.

3. The present value of the future £. Just what is the promise of £1 in one year's time worth today? Clearly, the amount would equal the sum of money we would need to invest *now* to end the year with a total of principal and interest of £1. This would obviously depend on the interest rate.

(*a*) *Illustration.* Assume that the rate is 100% per annum. If £1 is invested now, then in one year this will have increased to £2. This means that we would be prepared to exchange £1 now for the promise of £2 in one year's time, so if the promise was only £1 in one year we would only pay £0·5 now. *Therefore, the present value of £1 in one year at 100% is £0·5.* Continuing the illustration, if £1 is invested now then in two years it will amount to £4. (Note that compound interest is always used in this technique.) To buy a promise of £1 in two years' time, then, we would only pay £0·25 now, and so the present value of £1 in two years at 100% is £0·25.

(*b*) *Formula.* If the illustration were to be continued further a pattern would soon be noticed, namely that the present value of the future £ is the reciprocal of the amount to which £1 would accumulate by the end of the specified period. This holds true for all rates of interest, and so the following formula emerges:

$$\textit{Present Value of the Future £} = \frac{1}{\textit{Future Value of the Present £}}$$

Although this formula can always be used, in practice tables are employed to give present values. In Appendix I there is an abridged version of such a set of tables.

Although mathematically, present values should be viewed as in (*b*), conceptually the present value of the future £ should be thought of as the amount one would pay now for the promise of £1 to be received at a future specified date.

4. Applying present values to future cash flows. If we know what the present value of £1 at a specified date is, then we can find the present value of any number of pounds at that date by multiplying by our present value figure (*e.g.* present value of £1000 in two years at 100% = 1000 × £0.25 = £250). This means that we can convert any future cash flow into its present value by multiplying it by the appropriate present value of the future £.

If we now do this for all the cash flows relating to a project, then we have in effect converted these flows into a common currency, *i.e.* present values. This means we can add these figures knowing we are no longer in danger of adding together pounds having different values. The total of all the present values of all the cash flows involved in a project is the *present value of the project*, and measures what the project is worth to us in terms of pounds now.

NET PRESENT VALUE AND DISCOUNTED YIELD METHODS

There are two main methods of applying the discounted cash flow concept: the *net present value* and the *discounted yield*. In this section both are outlined, though first a few common points must be made.

5. Discounted cash flow (DCF) conventions. Note the following DCF conventions:

(*a*) *Layout.* The DCF layout (*see* **8**) usually incorporates columns headed "Year"; "NCF" (net cash flow); "Discount Factor" (conversion rate); "*P.V.*" (present value).

(*b*) *End-of-year convention.* By convention all cash flows are deemed to occur at the end of the year. In reality, of course, many flows run continuously throughout the year, but the error following the application of the convention is relatively insignificant. (However, if the appropriate tables are available, using a mid-year convention for appropriate flows does give a more accurate answer than the end-of-year convention.)

(*c*) *Year* 0. If the end-of-year convention is applied to the initial outlay, then the cash flow involved will be shown as occurring at the end of year 1. However, the outlay is usually such a large amount that the error resulting would be too large to ignore. Since the outlay actually occurs at the beginning of year 1, and as this is equivalent to the end of the previous year, year 0, then all initial outlays are shown as occurring in year 0. Note that since all cash flows are discounted back to the beginning of the project, then year 0 is that moment and hence the present value of £1 in year 0 is £1.

6. Selecting the interest rate. In any DCF method it is necessary to consider what interest rate is appropriate to the decision. Selection of a rate depends very much on how the final result will be interpreted. Students are warned that there is some controversy over this point, but if they regard the cost of capital to the company (V, **7**) as an appropriate rate they will find their choice will probably be accepted.

7. Illustrative figures. For the rest of this chapter the following simple figures relating to two projects will be used for illustrative purposes:

		Project A	*Project B*
Initial outlay		£10,000	£10,000
Net cash flows: Year	1.	310	7,000
	2.	1,000	2,000
	3.	1,000	2,000
	4.	4,000	1,000
	5.	10,000	730

(The large flow in the final year of project A can be regarded as the realisation of an asset having a high residual value.)

The cost of capital will be taken as 10%.

8. Net present value method: computation. Under the net present value method the cash flows of a project are discounted at the selected rate and the sum of all the present values gives the *net present value* (*NPV*) of the project ("net" because the outlay is deducted from the discounted positive net cash flows resulting from the investment).

EXAMPLE

Year	*Project A*			*Project B*		
	NCF	*Discount Factor**	*PV*	*NCF*	*Discount Factor**	*PV*
0.	£−10,000	£1·000	£−10,000	£−10,000	£1·000	£−10,000
1.	+ 310	0·909	+ 282	+ 7,000	0·909	+ 6,363
2.	+ 1,000	0·826	+ 826	+ 2,000	0·826	+ 1,652
3.	+ 1,000	0·751	+ 751	+ 2,000	0·751	+ 1,502
4.	+ 4,000	0·683	+ 2,732	+ 1,000	0·683	+ 683
5.	+ 10,000	0·621	+ 6,210	+ 730	0·621	+ 453
Net present value (NPV)			£+ 801			£+ 653

* Present value of future £ at 10% (*see* Appendix I).

9. Net present value method: interpretation. Our computation above shows that project A has a net present value of £801 (positive). Just what does this mean? One way to look at it is to say that should the project be financed by an overdraft type of loan at 10%, then if the initial outlay *together with the £801 NPV* (*i.e.* £10,801) was borrowed now and £10,000 of this invested in the project while the £801 was distributed as profit *now*, then the net cash flows of subsequent years would be just sufficient to pay off the whole of the loan together with the interest on the reducing balance. (The student should test this to his own satisfaction—working through the figures in this way will consolidate his grasp of the concept.) Alternatively, we can regard the £801 as the *present value of the ultimate profit that will accrue from the whole project* if we borrow £10,000 at 10% (reducing-balance).

However, for decision-making purposes it is really only necessary to note whether the NPV is positive or not. If it is positive our interpretation is that the return on cash invested in the project is above that of the selected rate. Conversely, if it is negative the return is below the selected rate.

10. Discounted yield method: computation. Under the discounted yield method (also known as the *Rate of Internal Return*) a trial and error procedure is adopted to ascertain what interest rate must be employed in order to make the NPV of the project zero. This means arbitrarily choosing a rate, discounting the project at this rate and then examining the NPV to see if it is zero. If not a new rate must be chosen and the procedure repeated (if the NPV is positive it means the rate chosen was too low, and vice versa). Ultimately, the rate that gives a NPV figure of zero is found and this is termed the *discounted yield*. It is then compared with the predetermined minimum rate (*i.e.* the rate discussed in **6**), which is often called the *cut-off rate*, and a decision made on the basis of this comparison.

EXAMPLE
(Project A only)

Year	NCF	*1st trial:* 10%		*2nd trial:* 14%		*3rd trial:* 12%	
		Discount Factor	*PV*	*Discount Factor*	*PV*	*Discount Factor*	*PV*
0.	− 10,000	£1·000	£−10,000	£1·000	£−10,000	£1·000	£−10,000
1.	+ 310	0·909	+ 282	0·877	+ 272	0·893	+ 277
2.	+ 1,000	0·826	+ 826	0·769	+ 769	0·797	+ 797
3.	+ 1,000	0·751	+ 751	0·675	+ 675	0·712	+ 712
4.	+ 4,000	0·683	+ 2,732	0·592	+ 2,368	0·636	+ 2,544
5.	+ 10,000	0·621	+ 6,210	0·519	+ 5,190	0·567	+ 5,670
NPV		£	+ 801	£	− 726	£	0
Conclusion:		Rate too low		Rate too high		Rate correct: 12%	

11. Discounted yield method: interpretation. What does the yield of 12% on project A mean?

Using the same approach as in the NPV interpretation (*see* **9**) we can say that if the outlay figure of £10,000 had been borrowed at 12%, reducing-balance, then the project would have shown neither profit nor loss. However, since in this illustrative case our selected rate is 10%, our cost of capital, then the project will be profitable—and the degree of profitability can be gauged by the fact that after paying the cost of capital we obtain a "net profit" of 2% on the cash invested.

12. Yield method relative, not absolute. If the discounted yield for project B is computed it will be found to be 14%, *i.e.* higher than the 12% of project A. Since the NPV method showed A to have the higher NPV (£801 as against £653: *see* **8**) it may seem surprising that B should have the better yield. However, B's higher yield is due to the fact that large cash flows inwards occur early in its life, so the high cash outlay is only tied up for a short period. Conversely, A's outlay is tied up for some time. Thus a higher rate is earned by B.

Note, though, that quick repayment does not necessarily mean high profits. In this example, for instance, since the cost of capital is only 10%, it is more profitable to earn 12% over a longer period than 14% over a short period. This the NPV method shows. One should always appreciate, therefore, that the yield is a measure of *rate* of return and not of overall profit, *i.e.* it is relative and not absolute.

13. Late negative cash flows. At this point students should be warned that the yield method may give very misleading results if there are late negative cash flows in a project. A procedure does exist to deal with this sort of situation but it is rather beyond the scope of this book. Consequently, students must be cautious of using the yield method in such circumstances.

14. Exclusive projects. Sometimes proposed projects are what is termed *exclusive*, *i.e.* only one of a group can be selected. This may be because there is physically only enough room for one of the possible projects, or it may be because the market could only carry one such project. Machine replacement decisions also clearly involve exclusive projects.

15. Evaluation of exclusive projects using yield. If projects are exclusive it is important *not* to base a decision on a comparison of yields (although a comparison of net present values is in order). Clearly, if the cost of capital is 10%, it is better to outlay £2000 to earn £2300 in one year's time (yield of 15%) than to outlay £20 to earn £24 in one year's time (yield of 20%). This, of course, is because the yield is relative while profit is absolute and it is better to obtain a relatively lower yield on a very large sum than a higher yield on a very small sum. The correct procedure to evaluate exclusive projects, then, is as follows:

(*a*) First, find the yield on the *relative* cash flows. In other words, take the more expensive project and using the relative cash flow technique (*see* X, **7**) compute how much extra the outlay will be and also how much extra the subsequent net cash flows will be. Then find the yield. This yield figure will indicate whether or not the extra outlay is warranted by the extra net cash flows, *i.e.* if this yield is above the cut-off rate, then it pays to invest the extra money in the dearer project. Conversely, if the yield is below the cut-off rate, the cheaper project is preferable.

(*b*) Secondly, having found out which is the better alternative, compute the yield of this alternative in the normal way to see *if it is worth having at all.* For example, it is obviously better to invest £500 to get £501 in a year than £1000 to get £1001, but nevertheless it is not worth investing the £500 at all if only £501 will be returned at the end of the year.

16. Net present value v. discounted yield. As there are two techniques for evaluating capital projects students will wish to know which is best. Both, of course, give the correct result if used and interpreted properly. However, despite its greater complexity the *yield method* does seem to be the better of the two. The advantages and disadvantages of the yield method as compared to the NPV can be summarised as follows:

(*a*) *Advantages of yield method:*

(*i*) Being relative, the yield shows the rate of return per £ per annum—it is measure of intensity of capital use. This means that if the capital for investment is limited, then the maximum profit is obtained by investing it in a succession of high-rate projects. And a situation where capital is limited is more common than a situation where it is unlimited.

(*ii*) By comparing yield with cost of capital a measure of return for risk is obtained. For example, a risky project may have a yield of 18% against a cost of capital of 10%. In this case the management can see they are obtaining the extra 8% for the risk, and a decision can be made as to whether this extra 8% is sufficient return for the risks to be taken. The NPV method results in no such measure: for example, a NPV of £1000 on a project requiring £10,000 may be very good if the capital is at risk for only one month. If, however, it was at risk for 50 years then the £1000 may look a very small reward.

(*b*) *Disadvantages of yield method:*

(*i*) The yield method is rather more difficult to use.

(*ii*) It must be used very cautiously if there are late negative cash flows.

(*iii*) It must be used carefully when evaluating exclusive projects, *i.e.* yields must not be directly compared.

17. Diminishing importance of future cash flows. Students should appreciate that cash flows relating to the more distant periods are relatively of much less value than the early cash flows, *e.g.* £1 at 10% in 40 years has a present value of only £0.022. This means that inaccuracies in forecasting future cash flows become of less and less importance and indeed, beyond a certain time (depending on the interest rate) such flows are so insignificant as to be not worth considering.

OTHER CAPITAL PROJECT EVALUATION TECHNIQUES

It is now generally accepted that a DCF technique is needed to enable correct capital projects decisions to be made. However, other techniques are also sometimes used and in this section the two more important ones are described.

18. Payback period technique. In this technique the *time that must elapse* before the net cash flows from a project result in the entire initial outlay being repaid is found. This time figure is called the *payback period*, and users of the technique look for short payback periods when making capital project decisions. Taking the figures in **7** above as an example, it can be seen that the payback period for project B is $2\frac{1}{2}$ years, while that for A is over four years.

The main objections to this technique are:

(*a*) It takes no consideration of cash flows after the end of the payback period. As we saw in our example, project A is the more profitable because of the cash flow in year 5 even though its payback period is nearly twice that of B.

(*b*) It ignores the timing of receipts. Thus a project C having flows of £1000, £8000 and £2000 in years 1, 2 and 3 has the same payback period as project B but the larger, earlier flows of B make it really the more profitable project.

The main advantage claimed for the technique is that if there is considerable uncertainty about the future, then an early replacement of the initial outlay by the end of a period in which events are *relatively* predictable means that the chance of at least regaining one's money is reasonably high. In the converse situation a loss is a serious possibility and may represent too grave a risk, even though a distinctly improved profit situation would result should events run as planned.

19. Average annual return technique. In this technique projects are evaluated according to the average return earned per annum as a percentage of the outlay.

(*a*) *Application.* In our illustrative projects this technique gives the following figures:

	Project A	*Project B*
Total net cash flows (5 years)	£16,310	£12,730
Average return per annum	£3,262	£2,546
Outlay	£10,000	£10,000
∴ Average annual return	32·6%	25·5%

(*b*) *Weaknesses.* This technique both ignores the timing of receipts and also is subject to distortion if the life pattern is at all unusual: for example, if project A ran on one more year with a flow in that year of a mere £4, then the average return per annum would fall to £2719 or 27·2%. (In passing it may be said that management accountants should always be wary of using averages—they often mislead.)

(*c*) *Depreciation.* Accountants, however, often go further than this bare computation given in (*a*) insomuch that they argue that if the asset is subject to depreciation, the depreciation must be deducted from the returns. Also since depreciation is a repayment of the initial outlay, then over the whole life of the project on average only about half of the initial outlay is invested. Consequently, they halve the outlay when computing the return. In our example, then, these adjustments lead to the following results:

	Project A	*Project B*
Total net cash flows	£16,310	£12,730
Total depreciation	£10,000	£10,000
Net return (5 years)	£6,310	£2,730
Average return	£1,262	£546
Average investment (½ outlay)	£5,000	£5,000
∴ Average annual return	25·2%	10·9%

COMPOUNDING FORMULAE

In this section are listed the main formulae associated with compounding. Essentially the concept is to set up a fund with or without an initial starting sum (or principal) and make, or not make, equal periodic payments into or out of the fund. The formulae indicate the relationship between these amounts, the interest rate, and time.

20. Symbols. These are:

S = Amount in fund at end.
P = Initial starting sum or principal.

p = Payment made each period that *increases* the fund. (If payment is *out* of fund, then p is negative.)
r = Interest rate per period (as a decimal).
n = Number of periods.

21. Basic formula. Using the above symbols:

$$S = (1 + r)^n \left(P + \frac{p}{r}\right) - \frac{p}{r}$$

22. Derivatives from basic formula. There are five of these:

(*a*) *Future value of present £.* Let P = £1 and $p = 0$ (*i.e.* £1 invested for n periods at r interest with no periodic payments in or out of fund). Then:

$$S = (1 + r)^n \left(1 + \frac{0}{r}\right) - \frac{0}{r} = (1 + r)^n$$

(*b*) *Present value of future £.* Let S = £1 and $p = 0$ (*i.e.* £1 is in the fund at the end). Then:

$$1 = (1 + r)^n \left(P + \frac{0}{r}\right) - \frac{0}{r} = (1 + r)^n P$$

$$\therefore P = \frac{1}{(1 + r)^n}$$

(*c*) *Future value of a £1 annuity.* Let $P = 0$ and p = £1 (*i.e.* at the end of each period £1 will be paid into the fund). Then: S (what fund will amount to after n periods)

$$= (1 + r)^n \left(0 + \frac{1}{r}\right) - \frac{1}{r} = \frac{(1 + r)^n - 1}{r}$$

(*d*) *Present value of a £1 annuity.* Let $P = 0$ and p = £1. Now the amount one would pay now for promise of a £1 annuity for n periods = Future value of £1 annuity discounted back to the present.

$$\therefore \text{PV of £1 annuity} = \frac{(1 + r)^n - 1}{r} \times \frac{1}{(1 + r)^n}$$

$$= \frac{(1 + r)^n - 1}{r(1 + r)^n}$$

(*e*) *Present value of a £1 annuity for perpetuity.*

$$\text{PV} = \frac{1}{r}$$

23. Nominal and effective rates. Note that compound interest at 12% per annum is *not* equal to 1% per month, since compounding monthly results in interest being added to the principal *monthly*, and so in later months interest is paid on the interest of earlier months. Thus 1% compound interest per month amounts to more than 12% per annum. Note the following terms in this connection:

Nominal rate (r') is the stated annual rate regardless of compounding periods (*e.g.* "12% per annum" even though compounding done monthly).

Effective rate (r) is the true rate (*e.g.* what interest is effectively paid annually as a result of compounding monthly).

The following formula converts one rate to the other:

$$r = \left(1 + \frac{r'}{m}\right)^m - 1$$

where m = number of compounding periods per annum.

24. Continuous compounding. Where compounding proceeds continuously from moment to moment the effective rate is given by the formula:

$$r = e^{r'} - 1$$

where $e = 2.71828$.

PROGRESS TEST 11

Principles

1. What is meant by the expression "present value of the future £"? **(3)**
2. What conventions underlie the use of the DCF technique? **(5)**
3. Distinguish between the net present value and the discounted yield methods as regards both computation and interpretation **(8–11)**
4. (*a*) What are exclusive projects? **(14)**
   (*b*) How should one evaluate exclusive projects if the discounted yield method is to be employed? **(15)**
5. What is meant by "payback period" and what are the disadvantages of the payback technique? **(18)**
6. What is meant by the "average annual return technique"? **(19)**

Practice

7. A company has the choice of continuing making a product on its existing machine or obtaining one of two alternative machines in lieu. Statistics relating to the machines are as follows:

Machine:	*Present*	*A*	*B*
Book value	£40,000	—	—
Re-sale value now	£85,000	—	—
Purchase price	—	£100,000	£110,000
Fixed costs p.a. (including depreciation)	£12,000	£27,000	£33,000
Variable running costs per unit (including labour)	£1·50	£0·75	£1·25
Units produced per hour	4	4	6

Additional data is as follows:

Selling price of product	£6 each
Material cost of product	£1 each
Production hours p.a.	2000 hours
Life of all machines (as from today)	5 years
Residual value of all machines	Nil

Depreciation was calculated by straight-line method using book value or purchase price. The Sales Manager believes that the production from the present machine or machine A can all be sold without further expenditure, but that an extra £2000 p.a. will need to be spent on advertising to move the extra production given by machine B.

(*a*) On the assumption that £10,000 will need to be spent in three years' time on machine overhaul no matter which machine is employed, use the NPV method to evaluate all three projects at 10%.

(*b*) On the assumption that no overhaul will be required, estimate by the yield method the return from each project.

Tables

Present value of the future £—10%:

Year	1	2	3	4	5
PV	0·909	0·826	0·751	0·683	0·621

Present value of a £1 annuity for five years:

Rate	8%	10%	12%	14%	16%	18%	20%
PV	3·993	3·791	3·605	3·433	3·274	3·127	2·991

CHAPTER XII

DECISION-MAKING: CONCLUSION

SELECTING THE APPROPRIATE DECISION-MAKING TECHNIQUE

IN this Part a number of different decision-making techniques have been outlined and the student may well be asking himself how he can tell which one should be selected for a specific problem. There is, unfortunately, no simple answer, but this section should help him to make his selection with a certain amount of confidence.

1. General principles of selection. First it must again be emphasised that the fundamental idea in decision-making work is to examine *differences* between alternatives—or between undertaking a project and not undertaking it.

Applying this idea, the following points become clear:

(*a*) If the alternatives under consideration *have no effect on the fixed costs*, then the break-even or marginal cost technique is indicated. Generally speaking, the *break-even technique* is limited to single-product situations and the *marginal cost technique* to decisions involving the selection of different products or contracts.

(*b*) If *fixed costs are affected* then either the *differential cost* or the *cash flow technique* should be used. The actual choice between the two is often only a matter of preference, though probably cash flow will be somewhat easier to apply as long as the essential qualification of the technique, that all other things are equal, holds good in the given situation.

NOTE: If the circumstances are such that the actual timing of cash flows is important from an interest point of view, then it is *imperative* that one of the *discounted cash flow* techniques is used.

2. Solution independent of technique. It is important to appreciate (and perhaps may be of some relief to a worried student) that no matter which technique is selected, if it is used correctly the correct solution will emerge. (This is true for techniques other than the DCF techniques which must, of course, be used if interest is significant.) Different techniques simply approach the one correct solution from different angles—the solution itself is independent of the technique.

To demonstrate the validity of this last point the following very simple problem will be solved using the marginal cost, differential cost and cash flow techniques.

EXAMPLE

A factory has the choice of producing A, B or C. It has a total fixed cost of £25,000 per year, a total capacity of 40,000 hours and can always sell whatever it produces.
Product details are as follows:

	A	*B*	*C*
Selling price per unit	£2	£10	£20
Marginal cost per unit	£1	£5	£16
Hours per unit	2	4	5

(*a*) *Using marginal cost technique:*

	A	*B*	*C*
Selling price	£2	£10	£20
Marginal cost	£1	£5	£16
Contribution	£1	£5	£
Contribution per unit of key factor (hr)	£0·50	£1·25	£0·80

Decision: Produce B.

(*b*) *Using differential cost technique:*

	A	*B*	*C*
Potential production (units)	20,000	10,000	8,000
Sales	£40,000	£100,000	£160,000
Total marginal cost	20,000	50,000	128,000
Net differential income*	£20,000	£50,000	£32,000

Decision: Produce B.

* As fixed costs do not alter they are not entered into the differential cost analysis. As a result in this particular problem the net differential income is the same as the contribution.

(c) *Using cash flow technique:*

		A	*B*	*C*
Cash In:	Sales	£+40,000	£+100,000	£+160,000
Cash Out:	Marginal costs	−20,000	− 50,000	−128,000
	Fixed costs	−25,000	− 25,000	− 25,000
	Net cash flow	£− 5,000	£+ 25,000	£+ 7,000

Decision: Produce B.

3. Combining techniques. Techniques are essentially tools for solving problems and just as a skilled tradesman will often combine tools to make a product, so the skilled management accountant will combine techniques. For example, when employing the cash flow technique he may well ignore flows common to all alternatives (*e.g.* fixed cost flows) so that his "net cash flow" is in effect a differential net cash flow. The same solution emerges, of course, as would if a "pure" technique were used, but time and effort is saved and the sooner the student learns the trick of combining techniques the sooner he, too, will similarly save time and effort.

4. Conclusion. Applying decision-making techniques is admittedly not always easy. However, if the student bears in mind the fundamental differential principle then his own commonsense should enable him to pick his way through the figures successfully. Briefly, this principle lays down that *when comparing alternatives it is:*

(a) *Necessary to introduce any and every factor that differs between alternatives and which will have an effect on the profit of the enterprise* (*e.g.* changes in fixed costs; changes in contribution; interest); and

(b) *Permissible to ignore every factor that remains the same whichever alternative is selected.*

Beyond this there are no firm rules; the only ultimate guide is a sound appreciation of just what is required in the circumstances surrounding the whole of the decision-making situation.

DECISION-MAKING AND TAXATION

At all times the management accountant should bear in mind the tax implications of every project considered. The law in Britain in this respect is subject to continuous change, but at the time of writing the tax factors discussed in this section are currently of importance in decision-making.

5. Development areas. In order to attract industry into relatively depressed areas that firms would otherwise avoid, the British government has designated certain geographical areas as "Development Areas" and given enterprises operating in such areas special tax and other concessions. The management accountant, then, must always note just where a particular project is to be undertaken, and if it is in a development area to take into account the appropriate concessions.

6. Investment grants. Probably the major factor that the management accountant must consider is the possibility of capital expenditure qualifying for an *investment grant*. Such a grant is in effect a tax-free cash payment by the government to the enterprise. Currently most plant and machinery bought for industrial purposes qualifies for an investment grant of 25% (45% in development areas), if it is brand new, so if a piece of equipment costs £1000 (installed) then the government will make a tax-free payment to the enterprise of £250 (£450 development areas). Such a payment is normally received within nine months after the expenditure is made. Note that if the equipment is re-sold within three years part or all of the grant is repayable.

7. Initial depreciation allowance. If an investment grant is payable in respect of a piece of equipment then an initial depreciation allowance is *not* given. On the other hand, if no investment grant is payable, either because the equipment was not scheduled for a grant or because it was not bought brand new, then an initial depreciation allowance is given. Currently this runs at 30% for most industrial equipment and at 15% for industrial buildings.

8. Annual depreciation allowances. Each year an allowance is granted in respect of each asset for the year's depreciation. Note the following points regarding this annual depreciation allowance:

(*a*) The allowance is a scheduled percentage—normally either 15% or 20% or 25% for plant and machinery—of the reducing value of the asset.

(*b*) In respect of investment grants:

(*i*) If an investment grant *has* been claimed, the allowance for the first year is based on the net initial cost *after deduction of the investment grant.*

(*ii*) If an investment grant has *not* been claimed, the allowance for the first year is based on the whole of the initial cost, *i.e.* without reference to the initial depreciation allowance. Thus a machine costing £1000, not qualifying for an investment grant, and with an annual allowance of 15% will have a total allowance for the first year of 30% + 15% = 45%, *i.e.* £450. The second year's allowance will, of course, simply be 15% of (£1000 − £450), *i.e.* 15% of £550.

(*c*) Annual allowances can be claimed every year until such time as the asset is disposed of or has been written off.

9. Balancing allowances and charges. When an asset is disposed of the difference between its written-down or book value (as computed for tax purposes) and its net realised value is found. If the written-down value exceeds the realised value the difference is treated as an allowance (called a *balancing allowance*) for the year. Conversely, if the written-down value is below the realised value the difference (called a *balancing charge*) is treated as taxable income.

10. Tax and the time factor. When considering the effects of tax in decision-making it should be appreciated that tax is paid (or saved) in *the year following* the earning of the income (or the incurrence of the expenditure). This fact will, of course, materially affect a discounted cash flow analysis.

11. Evaluation involving tax. The following worked example should illustrate most of the points involved in a DCF analysis that considers the tax factors:

EXAMPLE

An enterprise has an existing machine with a book (written-down) value of £6250 and annual cash running costs (mainly labour) of £2000. Consideration is being given to trading in the machine for its book value and buying a brand new automatic machine, having annual cash running costs of only £400, for £15,625. Both machines will produce an annual income of £4400 and both will have to be retired in four years' time when the residual values will be £2000 and £7400 for the existing and the new machine respectively. Given that the investment grant is 20%, the initial allowance 30%, the annual allowance 20% and that corporation tax is at 40%, prepare DCF evaluations for both projects using a 10% discount factor.

Solution:

Existing Machine:*

(1) *Year*	(2) *Book Value*	(3) *Tax Allowance*	(4) *Net Income*	(5) *Taxable Income*	(6) *Tax Payable*	(7) *Net Cash Flow*	(8) *Discount Factor*	(9) *Present Value*
0.						£−6,250 (a)	1·000	£−6,250
1.	£6,250	£1,250	£+2,400	£1,150	£ 0	+2,400	0·909	+2,182
2.	5,000	1,000	+2,400	1,400	−460	+1,940	0·826	+1,602
3.	4,000	800	+2,400	1,600	−560	+1,840	0·751	+1,382
4.	3,200	1,200 (b)	+2,400	1,200	−640	+1,760 +2,000 (c)	0·683	+2,568
5.					−480	−480	0·621	− 298
							Net Present Value	+£1,186

New Machine:*

Yr.	*Book Value*	*Tax Allowance*	*Net Income*	*Taxable Income*	*Tax Payable*	*Net Cash Flow*	*Discount Factor*	*Present Value*
0.						£−15,625 (d)	1·000	£−15,625
1.	£12,500 (e)	£2,500	£+4,000	£1,500	£+3,125 (f)	+ 7,125	0·909	+ 6,477
2.	10,000	2,000	+4,000	2,000	− 600	+ 3,400	0·826	+ 2,808
3.	8,000	1,600	+4,000	2,400	− 800	+ 3,200	0·751	+ 2,403
4.	6,400	−1,000 (b)	+4,000	5,000	− 960	+ 3,040 + 7,400(c)	0·683	+ 7,131
5.					−2,000	− 2,000	0·621	− 1,242
							Net Present Value	+£1,952

* Column details:

Column 2—Book value of machine at beginning of year.
Column 3—20% of Column 2.
Column 4—Annual income less annual cash running costs.
Column 5—Column 4 − Column 3.
Column 6—40% of Column 5 payable one year later.
Column 7—Column 4 + Column 6 (note Column 6 is usually negative).
Column 8—Discount factors at 10%.
Column 9—Column 7 × Column 8.

Notes:

(*a*) By keeping existing machine enterprise is sacrificing trade-in value. Therefore keeping machine is equivalent to investing this sum.
(*b*) Book value less realised value.
(*c*) Cash received from sale of asset.
(*d*) Cash purchase price.
(*e*) Value after deduction of grant.
(*f*) Investment grant paid.

Finally, note that:

(*i*) the initial allowance is not actually applicable in this evaluation;
(*ii*) if the taxable income had been negative in any year a *positive* tax payable figure would have been shown since the loss incurred by the project would have reduced the taxable income of the whole enterprise and hence the tax consequently saved can be regarded as a payment to the project.

DECISION-MAKING PRINCIPLES

In this section are summarised all the main principles involved in decision-making work.

12. Importance of the future. It is vital and fundamental to recognise that all decisions relate to the *future*, never to the past. This means that the only facts which are relevant are those which *will* occur, and there is no relevance in those which did occur at a previous date. This does not mean that past experience is worthless, but only that its value is restricted to its use in predicting future events.

13. The "clean sheet" approach. From the previous principle it follows that all past costs and figures should be ignored. Only those costs which *will* be incurred and that income which *will* be received should be computed. In other words, start with a "clean sheet" in decision-making work and forget the past.

14. Sunk costs. Since sunk costs are costs incurred in the past they must be completely ignored.

15. Common costs and common income. Since decision-making is essentially the choosing between two or more alternatives, any cost or income which is common to the alternatives may safely be omitted from the calculation.

NOTE: A common cost or income is one which will be incurred, or earned, whichever alternative is chosen, and the amount involved will be the same whatever choice is made.

Although the correct inclusion of common costs will not alter the decision based on a cost study, such costs may be handled incorrectly, thereby giving rise to erroneous figures in the study. They are therefore best excluded. However, if desired, common costs may be added at the bottom of the statement in order that the overall profit or cost-per-unit figure may be calculated.

16. Cash flow technique. Since the cash flow technique adopts the "clean sheet" approach as regards cash, and since all costs and income must ultimately be reflected in the cash flows, then this technique is particularly suitable for many decision-making calculations. In using this technique, however, care must be taken that any costs and incomes which lie beyond the time-span of the calculation are allowed for in the final figures.

It should be noted that if pure cash flow is adopted, then almost certainly some common costs will be included. This conflicts with the previous principle (**15**). However, this difficulty can be overcome, if desired, by adopting the relative cash flow technique.

17. Discounted cash flow. If it is considered necessary to discount the cash flows then some common costs may need to be included if the timing of such costs differ between the different alternatives.

18. Time-span. It is advisable to compute figures over as long a period of time as is practicable so that potential errors in connection with normal period costing cannot be made. This may give large working figures, but if activity varies from one period to another, large figures are preferable to the complexities involved in attempting normal period costing.

19. Existing conditions. If one of the alternatives being considered involves the use of existing equipment or any loss of an existing advantage, then:

(*a*) if an asset, charge to the alternative requiring the use of the asset the price it would fetch if sold, *i.e.* at opportunity cost;

(*b*) if an advantage, then charge the cash loss which would be sustained by giving up the advantage. (*E.g.* assume adopting alternative X will result in the loss of bulk discounts. Charge X with value of lost discounts for purpose of making decision.) It is under this heading that consideration should be given to the contribution per unit of key factor.

20. Fixed and variable costs. Segregate fixed and variable costs. This will enable:

(*a*) fixed costs which are common to be eliminated; and

(*b*) fixed costs which apply specifically to individual alternatives to be kept distinct from the variable costs. This will avoid the danger of involving the fixed costs in calculations relating to activity.

21. Return on capital. The return on capital should normally be computed as a standard procedure, though care should be taken that its significance should be clearly explained in any report relating to the decision.

22. Standard alternatives. It should be remembered that there are almost always two standard alternatives with which any new plan can be compared. They are:

(*a*) do nothing (*i.e.* carry on as currently engaged);
(*b*) straight investment of funds required for the plan in an outside investment.

This means in the case of (*a*) a comparison of the consequences following from the operation of the plan and continued current operations, and in the case of (*b*) a comparison of the return on capital with outside investment possibilities.

It should be noted that *at any time* a comparison can be initiated between (*a*) and (*b*) for any project, *i.e.* a comparison between carrying on as currently engaged, and liquidation of current operations with subsequent investment elsewhere of the funds released.

23. Taxation. Always consider the tax effects of each alternative.

24. Decisions involving multi-alternatives. When the number of alternatives to be considered is large, it is often advisable to split the alternatives into very small groups. Each group is then considered in turn, and the best alternative singled out. Subsequent comparisons between these preferred alternatives will indicate the best one to adopt.

Such a course is advisable because the factors which are relevant to a decision differ, depending on what alternatives are being compared. To try and compare all alternatives simultaneously will involve so many factors that the comparison will be very complicated. Initial rejection of inferior alternatives within given groups very much lessens the complexity of the final comparison.

25. Purpose of investigation. Always bear in mind *the use to which the figures will be put.* (This is a fundamental management accounting rule.) Do not include any figures which may mislead, *e.g.* a cost-per-unit figure based on full capacity when full capacity cannot be attained.

26. Irrelevance of book values. Remember that book values are *never* relevant in decision-making. Only current and future actual economic values must be used.

27. Presentation. Always present figures in a comparative form. This enables managers to see how, why and where differences between alternatives arise and gives them insight into, and confidence in, the final conclusions.

28. Conclusion. Always bear in mind that the object of presenting decision-making data to management is to enable managers to determine which is the best course to set for the business. Under some circumstances all courses are unwelcome but it is still management's task to find the least unwelcome, and the management accountant must assist in this task.

This may be stated in another way by saying that in decision-making the management accountant is concerned with *profitability*, not profit. It is essential that this distinction is absolutely clear to the modern accountant.

Above all, the emphasis on the future must never be forgotten. Today's decisions are based on tomorrow's opportunities—not yesterday's errors.

PROGRESS TEST 12

Principles

1. What circumstances guide a management accountant in his selection of a decision-making technique? (**1**)
2. What is the fundamental differential principle that should be borne in mind in decision-making? (**4**)
3. In allowing for taxation factors in decision-making:
   (*a*) Is an investment grant taxable? (**6**)
   (*b*) When is an investment grant received? (**6**)
   (*c*) Can one claim an initial depreciation allowance *and*:
      (*i*) an investment grant? (**7**)
      (*ii*) a depreciation allowance for the first year? (**8**)
   (*d*) Are depreciation allowances based on total equipment cost or should investment grants be deducted first? (**8**)
   (*e*) What is a balancing charge? (**9**)
4. What are the main decision-making principles? (**12–28**)

Practice

5. Research in a departmental store established that there were three primary selling areas in the store: the "Front Counters," the "Main Store" and the "Basement." An article would sell twice as fast if placed in the Main Store as it would if it were placed in the Basement and three times as fast if it were placed on the Front Counters. Each area is divided into selling counters, and counter statistics can be shown as follows:

Area	*No. of counters*	*Relative turnover*
Basement	6	Standard
Main Store	10	2 × Standard
Front Counters	4	3 × Standard

Each counter carries one product, and products can be sold on more than one counter, though sales on the additional counters have been found to have the following pattern:

Turnover in relation to sales on the 1st counter: turnover on 2nd counter = one-half sales; 3rd counter = one-third sales; 4th = one-quarter; and 5th = one-fifth.

The fixed costs of the store are £4000 per month, and it is company policy to carry all products A to J.

Given the following product statistics, determine which products should be sold in each area and the maximum potential monthly profit:

Product	*Selling Price (New pence)*	P/V *ratio* %	*Standard Monthly Turnover (units)*
A	200	25	336
B	40	25	1320
C	80	25	1020
D	125	30	320
E	20	25	3840
F	$12\frac{1}{2}$	20	12,000
G	100	25	576
H	400	50	30
I	100	30	600
J	50	30	1040

6. A furniture company manufactures one type of lounge suite exclusively. This suite contains the following seven components: one settee, two armchairs, four armless chairs. These components can either be manufactured by the company or sub-contracted, and the relevant data relating to the components is as follows:

	Settee	*Armchair*	*Armless chair*
Direct material cost per component	£20	£10	£11
Direct labour hours per component	10	5	1
Sub-contract price per component	£50	£20	£15

Suite sales are currently running at 8000 per period, each suite selling for £150. Though the company would like to manufacture all its own components, a capacity limit of 50,000 direct labour hours obliges the company to sub-contract some components.

Cost studies have shown that variable overheads vary with direct labour hours worked and are incurred at a rate of 40p per hour. Fixed costs are £60,000 per period and labour costs 60p per hour.

(*a*) Which components, and how many, should be manufactured by the company?

(*b*) What is the maximum profit that could be earned:

(*i*) at current sales?

(*ii*) if sales were unlimited?

(*c*) If the selling price has to be reduced to £139 per suite, what is the maximum profit the company can obtain?

7. A company, about to replace an existing machine, can purchase either a brand-new replacement for £25,600 or a second-hand one for £20,480. In actual fact the second-hand one is in very good condition and it is believed that the income and running costs (including maintenance) will be the same whichever machine is purchased. The replacement machine will be retired some time during the sixth year and whichever machine is purchased the residual value is expected to be £1000. The company must decide which machine to acquire, but the decision is made somewhat more complicated by the fact that if the brand-new machine is purchased the existing machine can be traded-in for £2000 more than it would otherwise be possible to obtain. Given that the investment grant is 20%, the initial depreciation allowance is 30%, the annual depreciation allowance is 25% and corporation tax 40%, employ a DCF analysis using a 20% interest rate to assist management to make a decision.

PART FOUR

CONTROL

We now turn our attention to the management accountant's contribution to managerial economic control. It is important that the student should realise that the concept of control is a fundamental one and so the concept of control accounting is one that differs from all other accountancy concepts. Control accounting, therefore, is not merely a matter of passing accounting data to management, though in many books there is a tendency for cost control to be discussed mainly in terms of formulae and book-keeping procedures. In actual fact, cost control is a *management* function in which the management accountant gives important assistance. If, therefore, he is to maximise his contribution he must fully appreciate the basic concept of control and view all his work in this light. In this Part this concept is kept well to the forefront, so that by the end the student should be able to carry out his accounting work in relation to any management control situation in such a way that his contribution to management is made in the most effective manner possible.

This Part, then, begins with a chapter on the theory of control (XIII), and having shown that control involves first making plans, then comparing actual performance with planned, and finally taking action to correct divergencies, it continues with a chapter on cost planning (XIV). Next there follows a chapter (XV, Variance Analysis) dealing with the comparison of actual cost performance with planned—this work being management accountant's specific contribution as a member of the management team to the achievement of effective cost control. The third control requirement—the taking of action to correct divergencies—is not discussed as such, since the management accountant himself has no authority to issue instructions to non-accounting personnel. However, since correct action can only be taken on the basis of the information given to management by the management accountant, a chapter on the reporting of such information is included (XVI).

This Part finally concludes by looking at a rather special but vitally important sector of cost control, namely the control of capital expenditure (XVII).

CHAPTER XIII

COSTING FOR CONTROL

THE first task in studying cost control is to examine the fundamental principles upon which such control work is based. This, then, is the object of this first chapter.

THE BASIS OF CONTROL

1. Control fundamentals. Control is *compelling events to conform to plan.* The essentials of control are three:

(*a*) *Plan.*
(*b*) *Comparison*—of actual with plan.
(*c*) *Action*—to rectify divergencies.

If any one of these essentials is missing *there is no control.*

2. The control loop. All control is dynamic, and this aspect can be depicted in the form of the loop shown in Fig. 15. The controller in this diagram issues instructions to the operative who endeavours to carry them out. Feedback information is received indicating the actual consequences of the operative's actions. This information enables actual events to be compared with those planned, and on a basis of the divergencies revealed, the controller issues fresh instructions to the operative. This initiates a new cycle round the loop.

A feature of control is the continuing repetition of such cycles until the plan is either achieved or abandoned.

3. Control requirements. For control to be attained it is necessary that:

(*a*) All four control loop elements are present.
(*b*) Each element is functioning efficiently.

Evaluation of any control situation may be carried out in terms of these two requirements.

4. Degree of control. We often refer to control as being "tight" or "loose." This aspect of control depends on:

(*a*) *Cycle time.* The shorter the control-loop cycle time, the tighter the control. This is because the sooner one corrects divergencies, the less chance there is of the actual events reaching a point where it will be too late to carry out corrections.

(*b*) *Degree of detail in explanation of divergencies.* The more detailed the explanation of divergencies the tighter the control. This is simply because the more informed the controller is regarding divergencies, the better his instructions for their correction.

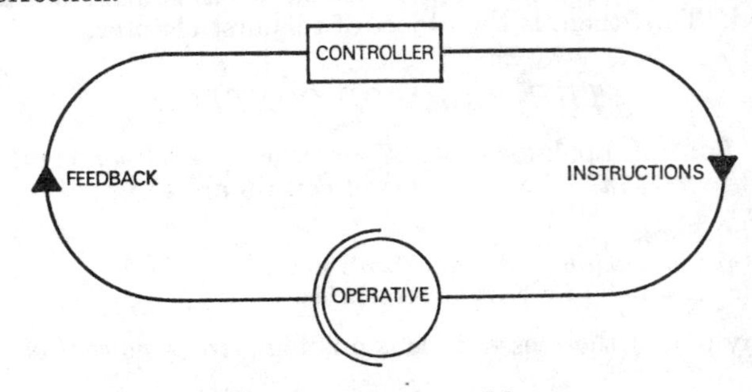

FIG. 15.—*The control loop*

Short cycle times and detailed explanations of divergencies are, therefore, both *vital* for tight control, and accountants must bear this in mind at all times.

5. Scope of theory. The above theory applies to any control situation—industrial, psychological, mechanical, social, and so on. In this book we shall be concerned with its application to cost control.

THEORY OF COST CONTROL

6. Scope of cost control. In all control work it is very important to appreciate just what factor is ultimately to be controlled. In the field of managerial economics this factor is obviously profit. The management accountant, therefore, is concerned with *profit control*. However, because management historically began this form of control by controlling costs, the technique has come to be called *cost* control. To avoid confusion with current terminology the conventional forms of expression will be used in this book. Students, therefore, should appreciate that the adjective "cost" in this context may also refer to sales and profit.

7. Cost control. Applying the theory outlined in the previous section it can be seen that if we wish to control costs we must:

(*a*) Plan the cost.
(*b*) Compare planned with actual costs.
(*c*) Take action to correct divergencies.

Tightness of control will be maintained firstly by making the comparisons at appropriate short intervals of time, and secondly by explaining the causes of the divergencies in sufficient detail to enable the correct action to be taken.

These points are briefly discussed below (**8–10**).

8. Cost plans. It should be noted that cost plans can be prepared on two different bases:

(*a*) The costs relating to a *period of time* can be planned.
(*b*) The costs relating to a *cost unit* can be planned.

The former plan is, of course, a *budget* and the latter is known as a *standard cost*. Cost planning is discussed in the next chapter (XIV).

9. Comparison of planned with actual costs: variances. When a *planned* cost is compared with an appropriate *actual* cost the difference is termed a *variance*. The following points should be noted regarding the definition of a variance:

(*a*) It is a *money* figure. This means, for instance, that the difference between a planned and an actual *quantity* of materials is *not* a variance.

(*b*) It is a *cost* (or sales value or profit) difference. It is never simply a difference between two *prices*.

(*c*) It measures the *effect on profit*. If the difference between actual and plan is such that the planned profit is increased, it is termed a *favourable variance*. If, conversely, the effect is to reduce the planned profit it is termed an *adverse variance*.

10. Tightness of cost control. There are two points to observe:

(*a*) *Cycle time*. Currently a cycle time of one month is normally regarded as appropriate for most cost control work.

However, in the foreseeable future there may well be a demand for a shorter cycle time.

(*b*) *Explanation of divergencies.* A systematic explanation of all divergencies arising is called a *variance analysis.* This topic is covered in Chapter XV. Here, however, it should be pointed out that the system employed should allow for a considerable degree of analysis if the occasion calls for it, even though the analysis in normal periods may be in much less detail.

COST CONTROL AS A MANAGEMENT TECHNIQUE

It is vitally important to appreciate that cost control is essentially a *management technique*, not an accounting technique. The accountant is certainly responsible for the work involved in making the comparisons, but management are responsible for the planning and action functions, and this section looks at the management aspect of cost control.

11. Planning is by managers. In the last analysis all cost plans are plans relating to the use and disposal of economic resources and the prices of such resources. Only managers responsible for the use and disposal of economic resources are qualified to decide what the planned quantities must be, and only managers experienced in trading in the resources are qualified to determine the planned prices. Of course, these managers will not make their decisions in isolation—a co-ordinated approach will be used so that the final plans, embodying the ultimate management objectives, are the result of management team-work. The function of the management accountant in this process is to assist these managers in making their plans.

12. Control is through managers. So far we have discussed cost control only from an overall viewpoint. Now we must introduce a principle of cost control that is fundamental to its successful operation in practice—namely that *cost control can only be attained through managers* (or, to be more specific, persons carrying out a management function).

As we have seen, action to correct divergencies is an essential element of control. Now such action can only be taken by managers. If the actual cost of operating a process is exceeding the planned cost, then only action taken by the person in charge of that process can enable control to be kept. It is obvious, then, that effective control depends upon each manager being advised of both *his actual costs and his planned costs.* Without these, control cannot be really effective.

13. Controllable and uncontrollable costs. As control is maintained through the action of managers, it is clearly very important that we distinguish between those costs that a specific manager can be held responsible for by virtue of his authority and those he cannot. For instance, a foreman can be held responsible for the cost of power in his own department but not for the power costs of another department. Costs a person can be held responsible for are termed *controllable costs* and, conversely, costs the person cannot be held responsible for are termed *uncontrollable costs*. Similarly, variances relating to controllable and uncontrollable costs are referred to as controllable and uncontrollable variances respectively.

NOTE: It is important to appreciate that the classification of a cost as controllable or uncontrollable depends wholly upon which manager is involved. If the foreman of department A is involved, departmental costs of A are controllable by him, but those of B are uncontrollable. If the foreman of B is involved then the classifications are reversed—A costs are uncontrollable and B costs controllable.

14. Allowances. Control theory lays down that cost control depends on comparing planned and actual costs and taking action to correct divergencies. However, an individual can only be held responsible for, and take action in respect of, his controllable costs. Now it often happens that a cost of a factor under the control of an individual is affected by the performance of another individual so that the original planned cost becomes virtually meaningless. For example, the original plan may have specified that planned direct production costs in a department should be £1000, based on processing 500 units at £2 each. However, if the preceding department send through only 300 units for processing, then it would clearly be ridiculous to compare actual processing costs with the planned £1000. It is fairly obvious in this case that the appropriate figure for comparison is 300 × £2 = £600.

It follows, therefore, that the original planned figure is often of no relevance for control of an individual's costs, and a new figure needs to be computed on a basis of actual performance elsewhere in the enterprise. Such a new figure is termed an *allowance* and it is with this allowance that the actual cost figure must be compared—never with the original planned figure.

15. Procedure using allowances. This concept of *comparing an individual's allowance with his actual figure* is basic to all cost control and is very much the key to the successful solution of cost control examination questions. The full procedure can be stated formally as follows:

To assess an individual's cost performance, first find his allowance by computing what cost he should have incurred after making allowances for all factors outside his control, and then compare this allowance with his actual achievement.

The thoughtful student will quickly find that if he applies this procedure intelligently to cost control problems, many solutions will be more quickly obtained than by more mechanical procedures and, of greater importance, the significance of such solutions will be much clearer.

PROGRESS TEST 13

Principles

1. Define control. (**1**)
2. What three essential elements are necessary for control? (**1**)
3. Distinguish between a budget and a standard cost. (**8**)
4. Why cannot cost control be simply an accounting technique? (**11, 12**)
5. What is a controllable cost? (**13**)
6. What is an allowance? (**14**)

Practice

7. It is planned that a foreman having an automatic process under his control should process 20,000 articles in one month. Each article requires 2 units of fuel at £0·25 per unit for processing. There is also a standing rental of £12,000 p.a. for the use of the process.

In a particular month only 14,000 articles were ultimately given to the foreman for processing, and £7400 was incurred in fuel costs.

For the particular month and foreman in question, show:

(*a*) Budget for the month.
(*b*) Allowances for the month.
(*c*) Variances for the month.

State also which costs are controllable.

CHAPTER XIV

COST PLANNING

COST planning involves the preparation of flexible budgets and standard costs. In order to show the student how these plans are integrated, a diagrammatic representation of the interconnections is shown in Fig. 16, based on a comprehensive set of illustrative figures (*see* **16**).

FLEXIBLE BUDGETS

In Chapter IV the preparation of planning budgets was discussed. Here we are now concerned with *control* budgets, often referred to as flexible budgets, and this section outlines the concept of such budgets.

1. Limitations of fixed budgets. The budgets discussed in IV are called *fixed budgets*, as the amounts detailed therein relate solely to the planned level of activity (and are therefore "fixed" in this respect). However, if the actual activity is not as planned, then obviously the budgeted costs must be amended to allow for the activity difference and to indicate what costs *should* have been incurred in view of the actual activity. A fixed budget cannot be so amended and is therefore of little value for control.

2. Flexible budgets. Amendment of the original budget is, however, possible if the budgeted costs are segregated into their fixed and variable components, for then it is a relatively simple task to compute just what costs should have been incurred for any given level of activity. A budget so prepared is termed a *flexible budget*. An example of such a budget is given in Fig. 16 and it should be noted that:

(*a*) Flexible budgets are usually restricted to overheads. Direct costs are controlled more easily by means of standard costs (*see* **5–13** below).

(*b*) To aid later computations of allowance the variable component is usually converted into a rate per unit of activity.

(*c*) A flexible budget cannot really be fully completed until

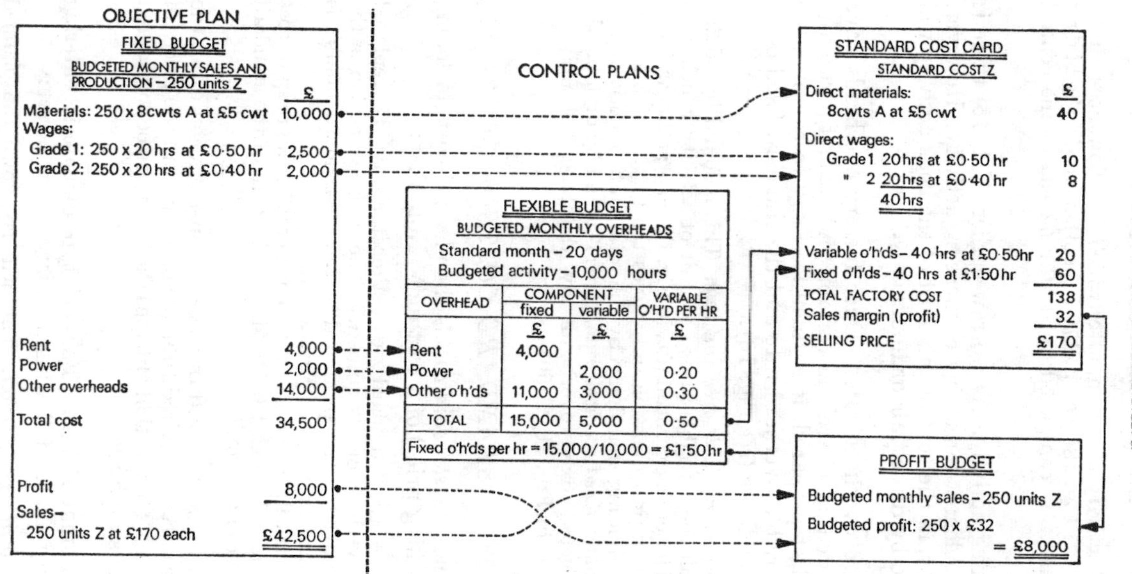

OBJECTIVE PLAN
FIXED BUDGET
BUDGETED MONTHLY SALES AND PRODUCTION – 250 units Z
£
Materials: 250 x 8cwts A at £5 cwt 10,000
Wages:
Grade 1: 250 x 20 hrs at £0·50 hr 2,500
Grade 2: 250 x 20 hrs at £0·40 hr 2,000
Rent 4,000
Power 2,000
Other overheads 14,000
Total cost 34,500
Profit 8,000
Sales– 250 units Z at £170 each £42,500
CONTROL PLANS
FLEXIBLE BUDGET
BUDGETED MONTHLY OVERHEADS
Standard month – 20 days
Budgeted activity – 10,000 hours
OVERHEAD
COMPONENT
fixed
variable
VARIABLE O'H'D PER HR
£ £ £
Rent 4,000
Power 2,000 0·20
Other o'h'ds 11,000 3,000 0·30
TOTAL 15,000 5,000 0·50
Fixed o'h'ds per hr = 15,000/10,000 = £1·50 hr
STANDARD COST CARD
STANDARD COST Z
£
Direct materials:
8cwts A at £5 cwt 40
Direct wages:
Grade 1 20 hrs at £0·50 hr 10
" 2 20 hrs at £0·40 hr 8
40 hrs
Variable o'h'ds – 40 hrs at £0·50hr 20
Fixed o'h'ds – 40 hrs at £1·50 hr 60
TOTAL FACTORY COST 138
Sales margin (profit) 32
SELLING PRICE £170
PROFIT BUDGET
Budgeted monthly sales – 250 units Z
Budgeted profit: 250 x £32
= £8,000

FIG. 16.—*Cost plans*

A fixed (objective) budget is first prepared, using the illustrative figures given on p. 150. After this the flexible budget, standard cost and profit budget can be prepared in that order. Note that if need be the control statements can easily be prepared direct from the initial data without any preparation of the fixed budget.

the actual activity is known, after which the allowances can be computed (*see* Fig. 18(*a*) on p. 170). In other words, the budget cannot finally be completed until *after the end* of the control period.

3. Measuring activity. As we saw earlier (VII, **16**) there is always a problem when trying to measure activity. However, for simplicity, in the text of this Part of the book activity will be measured by direct labour hours only.

4. Standard overhead rates. Once factory overheads have been segregated into fixed and variable and the first part of the flexible budget prepared, it is then necessary to compute the standard variable overhead rate and the standard fixed overhead rate as follows (*see* Fig. 16):

(*a*) *Standard variable overhead rate.* This is found by adding together all the variable rates per unit of activity which were computed for each overhead (*i.e.* in Fig. 16, 0·50); (alternatively, if an examination question only gives the total variable overheads, by dividing that figure by the total units of activity).

(*b*) *Standard fixed overhead rate.* This is found by dividing the total budgeted fixed overheads by the budgeted units of activity (*i.e.* in Fig. 16, £1·50).

STANDARD COSTS

5. Definition. A *standard cost* is the planned cost (including profit and selling price) of a cost unit. Note that:

(*a*) The word "standard" can almost always be replaced mentally by the word "planned." (The main exception is the term "standard hours produced" where "standard hours" is used as a measurement of production.)

(*b*) We can talk about the "standard cost" of a group of cost units, this standard cost being simply the sum of the standard costs of all the cost units.

A standard cost is based on careful consideration of all the economic resources required to make one unit and the prices of such resources. This section outlines the factors to be considered when setting standards.

6. Standard material cost. For each type of material entering into the cost unit the following standards must be set:

(*a*) *Standard specification.* This will lay down the planned specification (quality, etc.) of the material. It will be set primarily by the Design Department.

(*b*) *Standard usage.* This will relate to the *overall* material requirements for the unit, *i.e.* not just the material in the finished unit but also making allowances for items such as off-cuts and waste inevitable in manufacturing the unit. The standard will be set primarily by the Works Manager.

(*c*) *Standard price.* This will be the planned purchase price of the material and set primarily by the Buyer.

Then: *Standard material cost* = *Standard usage* × *Standard price.*

7. Standard wage cost. The labour to be used at each stage of manufacture must be determined and the following standards set:

(*a*) *Standard grade.* This will be the planned grade of labour to be used and will be set by the Works Manager.

(*b*) *Standard hours.* This will be the planned time per unit for each grade of labour at each stage of manufacture. It will be set primarily by the Work Study Department on behalf of the Works Manager.

(*c*) *Standard wage rate.* This will be the planned wage rate for each grade of labour and set primarily by the Personnel Manager.

Then: *Standard wage cost* = *Standard hours* × *Standard wage rate.*

8. Standard direct expenses. If there are any direct expenses involved in the manufacture of the unit these must be planned.

9. Standard overheads. The standard variable overheads and the standard fixed overheads for each cost unit can be found by multiplying the planned units of activity per cost unit by the overhead rates discussed in **4**.

10. Standard factory cost. If the foregoing standard costs are added (**6–9**), the standard *factory* cost of the cost unit is found. This standard factory cost figure will be used when valuing finished goods stocks.

11. Sales standards. So far we have only considered manufacturing standards. Standards relating to selling must now be discussed:

(*a*) *Standard selling and distribution costs.* These standards will give the planned selling and distribution costs of the cost unit. They will be set primarily by the Sales and Distribution

Managers respectively. (Since these costs are excluded from nearly all examination questions they are excluded, for simplicity's sake, from the illustrative figures used in this and in the next chapter.)

(*b*) *Standard selling price.* This is the planned selling price of the unit. It is, of course, a vitally important standard and though probably set on the advice of the Sales Manager, normally it will ultimately be fixed by the Managing Director.

(*c*) *Standard sales margin.* This planned sales margin for the unit emerges after the standard factory cost, standard selling and distribution costs and the standard selling price have been taken into account. If standard absorption costing is in operation it is equivalent to the *standard profit*, while if standard marginal costing is used it is equivalent to the *standard contribution.*

12. Standard cost card. All the above standards should be recorded on a *standard cost card.* Such a card, which is very similar to a job card, is made out for each cost unit manufactured and forms a complete record of all the standard costs relating to that unit. In practice, it should be laid out in such a way that the standard cost of the unit when only partly completed can be quickly found. This is important for valuing work-in-progress.

NOTE: When solving standard cost problems the standard cost card is an invaluable source of data. If a question does not give a standard cost card, the student is strongly advised to prepare his own before attempting to calculate variances.

13. Revision of standards. If some economic factor alters permanently (*e.g.* if the unions negotiate an increased wages rate), then the question arises as to whether or not the standard cost should be revised.

In theory as soon as a plan is shown to be definitely unachievable a revision should be made. If top management have accepted the fact that there has been a permanent change in an economic factor, then it is pointless computing variances based on the old standard for individual managers. One cannot control by using outdated plans. However, in practice, revising a standard cost involves considerable work and sometimes leads to serious confusion. For instance, the revision of one single minor raw material cost standard means a careful revision of:

(*a*) All standard cost cards of products using the material.

(*b*) All price lists detailing standard prices of the material *and* products.

(*c*) All valuations of stores, work-in-progress and finished goods stocks.

For this reason standard cost revisions are usually made only at year-ends. Where factors alter during the year, then in order to maintain the control value of standards, the *effect* of the revision is allowed for in management statements, although the revision is not taken into the standard costs.

PROFIT BUDGETS

14. Importance of budgeted profit. As we have seen (XIII, **6**) the ultimate factor that management are trying to control is profit. A fundamental figure, then, in cost planning is the budgeted profit.

15. Preparation of profit budget. Normally profit budgets are prepared in one of two ways. One way is to collect all the budgeted figures into a fixed budget and compute the resulting profit. The other way is simply to multiply the budgeted sales quantities by the standard sales margins of the cost units (deducting the budgeted fixed overheads if standard marginal costing is being used). This, of course, gives the budgeted profit.

Both these methods are illustrated in Fig. 16, using the basic illustrative data given in the next paragraph.

16. Illustrative figures for cost planning. The following basic data is used in Fig. 16 and in the next chapter for illustration.

Planned monthly figures:

Length of month	20 days
Direct labour hours	10,000
Rent	£4000 (fixed)
Power	£2000 (variable)
Other overheads	£14,000 (£11,000 fixed)

(Variable overheads vary with direct labour hours)

Production	250 units of Z

Production requirements for 1 unit of Z:

Material—8 cwt A at £5 per cwt
Labour—20 hours Grade 1 at £0·50 per hour
20 hours Grade 2 at £0·40 per hour

Sales	250 units of Z at £170 per unit

PROGRESS TEST 14

Principles

1. What is the primary limitation of a fixed budget for control work? (**1**)

2. What is a flexible budget? (**2**)

3. What is a standard cost? (**5**)

4. What factors should be taken into account when setting:

(*a*) a standard material cost? (**6**)
(*b*) a standard wage cost? (**7**)

5. Which departments are involved in setting which standards? (**6, 7** and **11**)

6. What is a standard sales margin? (**11**)

7. What is the value of a standard cost card? (**12**)

8. Should standards be revised? (**13**)

CHAPTER XV

VARIANCE ANALYSIS

In the last chapter we looked at cost planning. In this we look at the technique used for comparing actual figures with planned, the second requirement for effective control.

INTRODUCTION TO VARIANCE ANALYSIS

1. Illustrative figures. In order to illustrate the technique of variance analysis the same figures will be used in this chapter as were given in the previous chapter (XIV, **16** and Fig. 16). In addition the following figures relating to actual performance will be used:

Actual figures for month M:

Production	220 units of Z
Sales	200 units of Z for £34,200
Rent	£4000
Power	£1950
Other overheads	£15,000
Purchases	2500 cwt of A for £13,120
Materials used in production	1900 cwt of A
Wages: Grade 1	£2810 (5000 hours)
Grade 2	£1620 (4000 hours)
Length of month	19 days

2. Profit variance. As was explained in XIII, **6**, the factor management is ultimately aiming to control is profit. It follows, therefore, that the first comparison that should be made is that between the planned (budgeted) profit and the actual profit—and the difference between these two figures is called the *profit variance.* The computation of the profit variance for month M of our illustration is shown below, and can be seen to be £6540 *Adverse* (A).

(*a*) *Actual profit for month M* (*see* 1):

Sales (200 units)			£34,200
Costs:	Purchases A, 2500 cwt	£13,120	
	Less Closing stock A: 600 cwt at £5 cwt	3,000	
	Issues to production	10,120	
	Direct wages: Grade 1	2,810	
	Grade 2	1,620	
	Rent	4,000	
	Power	1,950	
	Other overheads	15,000	
	Total costs	35,500	
	Less closing stock Z: 20 units at £138 each	2,760	
	Cost of sales		32,740
	Actual profit		£1,460

(*b*) *Profit variance:*

Budgeted monthly profit (*see* profit budget in Fig. 16)	£8,000
Actual profit for month M (*see* (*a*) above)	1,460
Profit variance	£6,540 (A)

3. Variance analysis. Having measured the profit variance it is obviously necessary for management to know just which factors caused the variance to arise. This means the profit variance must be analysed to show the factors responsible for the variance and the extent to which they affected the profit. Such an analysis is called a *variance analysis* and the technique of variance analysis is the subject of this chapter.

4. The "allowance" technique. Variances can often be computed by means of simple formulae (Chapters XIX and XX in *Cost Accountancy*, W. M. Harper, Macdonald & Evans). However, in this book we are more concerned with the *concept* of variance analysis rather than the detailed formulae, for if the concept is firmly grasped then all variance problems, no matter how unusual, can be solved. To demonstrate this concept an approach using the allowances discussed earlier in

XIII, **14** will be employed. Essentially this involves taking each factor in turn, computing the allowance in view of the actual performances relating to other factors, and then comparing this allowance with the actual figure achieved.

At this point students should carefully note and always remember that *a variance is based on the difference between an actual figure and an "allowance"*—and never a budgeted figure, although on many occasions the allowance and the budgeted figure may well be the same amounts.

5. The effect of stock changes. When using the allowance approach students sometimes become worried when they come to see, for example, that the material variance is subdivided into one variance (price) based on the *quantity purchased* and a second variance based on the *quantity used in production.* They feel that they are not really adding like to like and that something will go wrong in the analysis. However, they need have no fears, for *provided that stocks are always valued at standard* the analysis will work out correctly and will balance. (In some systems both variances are based on quantities used in production but this is very poor control procedure, and should be avoided by the student if possible.)

A similar situation arises when production does not match sales: production variances and sales margin variances are based on different quantities. Again, however, this does not matter, provided that units placed into and withdrawn from finished goods stock are valued at standard.

STANDARD ABSORPTION COST VARIANCE ANALYSIS

The cost plans in the previous chapter were based on the technique of absorption costing. In this section the analysis of variances arising under this technique are discussed, and a chart showing the main analysis classifications and subclassifications involved is given in Fig. 17. The alternative form of analysis, standard *marginal* cost variance analysis, is discussed in the next section.

6. Overhead expenditure variance. This variance is that part of the profit variance that arises from actual overhead expenditure being other than planned. It is arrived at by the

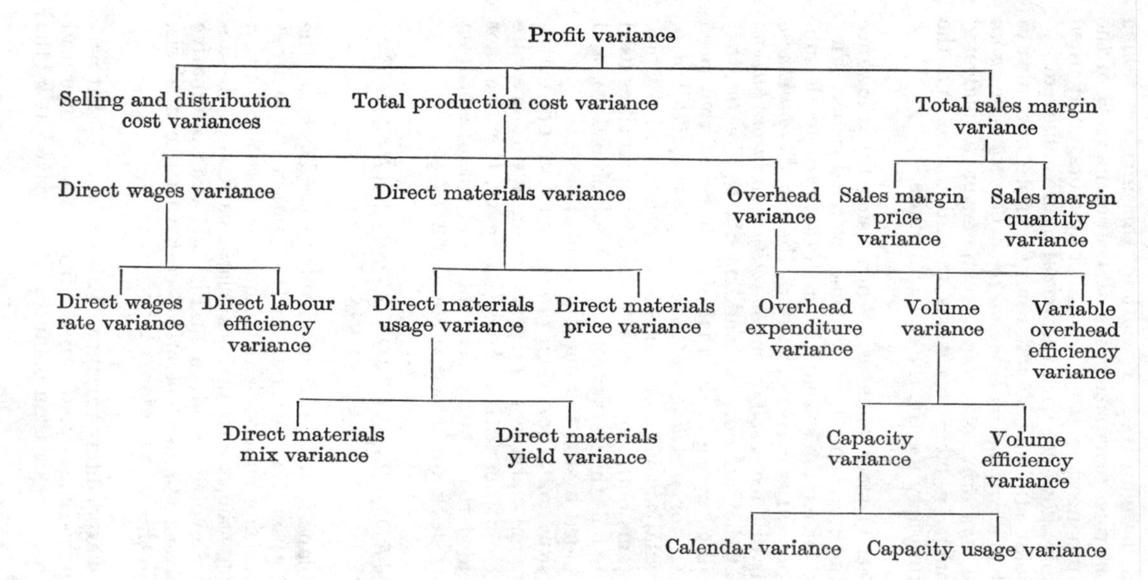

FIG. 17.—*Chart of cost variances (absorption costing)*

This chart shows the profit variance and all its sub-variances, as they are dealt with in Chapter XV. Note that the analysis is mathematically consistent, *i.e.* where a variance subdivides into two or more variances the sum of these latter variances equals the original variance.

completion of the flexible budget procedure discussed in the previous chapter (XIV). Clearly, once we know the actual activity for a month, we can easily compute the allowance for each overhead item by multiplying the variable cost per unit of activity by the actual units of activity achieved and adding the fixed component (*see* the flexible budget in Fig. 16 in the previous chapter). Knowing our allowance (*i.e.* what we *should* have spent in view of actual activity) it only remains to compare this with the actual expenditure and record the difference as the overhead expenditure variance. An example of the computation of this variance using our illustrative figures is shown in Fig. 18(*a*). The manager responsible for any given overhead will, of course, be responsible for the variance.

7. Material price variance. The *material price variance* is that part of the profit variance that is due to actual material prices differing from planned, and is primarily the responsibility of the buyer. The buyer's allowance is easily determined—simply multiply the actual quantities purchased by the standard prices. This is obviously what the purchase cost should have been, so any difference between this and the actual cost must be due to a difference in price and therefore is the material price variance.

EXAMPLE (using our illustrative figures)

Buyer's actual quantities purchased: 2500 cwt		
So allowance = 2500 × £5	=	£12,500
Actual purchase cost		£13,120
∴ *Material price variance*	=	£620 (A)

(This and subsequent variances (**7–17**) are summarised in Fig. 18 (*b*).)

8. Material usage variance. The *material usage variance* is that part of the profit variance that is due to the actual material usage differing from planned and is primarily the responsibility of the Works Manager. The allowed usage is computed by multiplying the actual number of units produced by the standard usage per unit. If the difference between the actual usage and the allowed usage is then multiplied by the standard price, the usage variance is given.

EXAMPLE

Actual units produced:	220 units of Z
Standard usage per Z	8 cwt of A
So allowed usage = 220 × 8	= 1760 cwt A
Actual usage of A	1900 cwt
Excess material usage	= 140 cwt
∴ *Material usage variance* = 140 × £5	= £700 (A)

NOTE: Multiply by *standard* price, not actual price. Actual prices are not really needed in variance analysis (though if an examination question gives an actual price, you can, if you wish, find the price variance by multiplying the difference between the actual and standard prices by the actual quantity involved).

9. Analysis of the material usage variance. Although in our illustration the material usage variance cannot be further analysed, in some instances further analysis into a *mix variance* and a *yield variance* is possible.

(*a*) *Material mix variance*. This variance is that part of the profit variance that is due to the actual mix (proportions) of materials mixed together differing from the planned mix. It can obviously only arise where materials are mixed together. To compute the mix allowance take the total *actual input*, divide it into the standard proportions, multiply each resulting material figure by that material's standard price, and then add the products. The mix variance is then found by subtracting from this total the actual cost of the input (valuing actual materials used at *standard* price, of course, since if actual prices were used the resulting variance would include both the mix and the price variances).

(*b*) *Yield variance*. This variance is that part of the profit variance that is due to the actual yield differing from planned yield. It obviously can only arise where there is a normal loss in process. Where such a loss occurs, a planned percentage loss is deducted from 100% to give a standard percentage yield. To find the allowed yield it is only necessary to multiply the actual input by the standard yield. The yield variance is then found by comparing the actual yield with the allowed yield and valuing the difference at *the standard cost per unit of output*.

EXAMPLE

Using the data given below find the mix and yield variances.

Standard cost:

14 gallons of P at £5 per gallon	£70
11 gallons of Q at £4 per gallon	44
25 gallons	114
5 gallons (20% standard loss)	—
20 gallons (80% standard yield)	£114

Standard cost per gallon of output $= \frac{£114}{20} = £5{\cdot}70$

Actuals:

Input: 3000 gallons of P
2000 gallons of Q
Output: 3900 gallons

Solution:

(*a*) *Mix variance*

Allowed cost of mix, 5000 gallons in the proportion of 14:11

2800 gallons of P at £5 per gallon	£14,000
2200 gallons of Q at £4 per gallon	8,800
5000	£22,800

Actual cost of mix:

3000 gallons of P at £5 per gallon	£15,000
2000 gallons of Q at £4 per gallon	8,000
5000	£23,000

∴ *Mix variance* = £23,000 − £22,800 = £200 (A)

(*b*) *Yield variance*

Allowed yield: 80% of 5000 =	4000 gallons
Actual yield	3900 gallons
Excess loss	100 gallons

∴ *Yield variance* = 100 × £5·70 = £570 (A)

NOTE: The usage variance can be computed as follows:

Allowed cost for actual output: 3900 × £5·70 =	£22,230
Actual cost (*see* above)	£23,000
Material usage variance	£770 (A)

which exactly equals the sum of the mix and yield variances.

10. Wage rate variance. The *wage rate variance* is that part of the profit variance that is due to the actual wage rate differing from planned. It is usually the responsibility of the Personnel Manager although if a different grade of labour than planned is used by a production manager on a job, then he, of course, will be responsible.

A wage rate is, in effect, the price for labour, and the variance, therefore, is found in the same way as a price variance. First the allowance is computed, by multiplying the actual hours worked by the standard rate. Then the difference between this and the actual wages paid is the wage rate variance.

EXAMPLE

	Grade 1	*Grade 2*
Actual hours worked	5000	4000
Standard rate	£0·50	£0·40
Allowed wages	£2500	£1600
Actual wages paid	£2810	£1620
Wage rate variance	£310 (A)	£20 (A)

11. Labour efficiency variance. The *labour efficiency variance* is that part of the profit variance that is due to the actual labour efficiency differing from planned, and is primarily the responsibility of the Works Manager. In effect it is the excess wages paid because of inefficiency (or wages saved because of above-planned efficiency). Since the time taken on a task relative to that planned is a measure of efficiency, then this variance can be based on the comparison of actual with planned times and can be regarded simply as a usage variance. Therefore, to find the allowed time it is only necessary to multiply the actual number of units produced by the standard hours per unit. The difference between this allowance and the actual hours taken, multiplied by the standard wage rate, gives the labour efficiency variance.

EXAMPLE

	Grade 1	*Grade 2*
Actual production (units)	220	220
Standard hours per unit	20	20
Allowed time (hours	4400	4400
Actual time taken (hours)	5000	4000
Difference (hours)	600 over	400 under
Standard wage rate per hour	£0·50	£0·40
∴ *Labour efficiency variance*	£300 (A)	£160 (F)

12. Volume variance. The *volume variance* is that part of the profit variance that is due to the actual volume of production differing from planned, and is primarily the responsibility of the Works Manager. It arises solely in connection with fixed overheads and is quite simply the over or under recovery of fixed overheads arising from actual production not being as planned. In standard absorption costing each unit of production carries a standard fixed overhead charge, and since fixed overheads are fixed and do not alter with changes in production, then if there is any difference between the allowed production (which here is the same as the budgeted production) and the actual production, then there is a volume variance (under or over recovery) equal to the difference multiplied by the fixed overhead charge per unit of production.

EXAMPLE

Allowed (budgeted) production, Z	250 units
Actual production, Z	220 units
Under production	30 units
Standard fixed overhead per unit	£60
∴ *Volume variance* = 30 × £60 =	£1800 (A)

13. Capacity variance. The *capacity variance* is that part of the profit variance that is due to the actual capacity differing from planned. Capacity is normally measured in hours, and this variance essentially explains how much of the volume variance arose because the factory worked more or less hours than planned and hence was able to produce more or less units than planned. Under normal circumstances the allowed capacity will be the same as the budgeted capacity, although if a particular manager made a decision that affected the capacity, he would be charged (or credited with) the resulting under (or over) recovery of fixed overheads. To find the capacity variance, therefore, it is only necessary to compare the budgeted working hours with the actual hours and multiply by the fixed overhead rate per hour.

EXAMPLE

Allowed (budgeted) working hours	10,000
Actual hours worked	9,000
Difference (hours)	1,000
Standard fixed overhead rate per hour	£1·50
∴ *Capacity variance* = 1000 × £1·50 =	£1,500 (A)

It should be appreciated that the capacity variance can easily be analysed into sub-variances indicating the effect of any factor affecting capacity (*e.g.* idle time, breakdowns, strikes, absenteeism) by simply multiplying the hours involved by the fixed overhead rate.

14. Calendar variance. In some standard cost systems the total budgeted working hours for the *year* is divided by twelve to give the average monthly working hours, a figure termed the *standard month*. Where such a system is in use, therefore, part of the explanation of the capacity variance lies in the fact that the actual possible working hours in the specific month concerned differed from the standard month (allowed hours) because there were more or less working days in the month than average—because of calendar factors. The under or over recovery of fixed overheads that results from this is termed the *calendar variance* and is computed by simply multiplying the hours gained or lost by the fixed overhead rate.

EXAMPLE

Standard month	20 days
Actual month	19 days
Difference	1 day

Planned hours per days $= \frac{10,000}{20} = 500$

∴ *Calendar variance* = 1 × 500 × £1·50 = £750 (A)

NOTE

(*i*) If the calendar variance is deducted from the capacity variance, the remaining balance is called the *capacity usage variance* (*see* Fig. 17).
(*ii*) Calendar variances will always cancel out over the year, and can, in fact, be computed for the whole year in advance.
(*iii*) A calendar variance is not a true control variance. One cannot compel an actual month to equal an average month.

15. Fixed overhead efficiency variance. The *fixed overhead efficiency variance* is that part of the profit variance that arises in respect of fixed overheads and is due to the actual efficiency differing from planned. Since ultimately fixed overheads can only be recovered on finished production, hours worked in excess of those allowed for the actual production achieved fail to recover any overheads. The fixed overhead efficiency variance can be found, then, by multiplying the difference between the allowed hours for production and the actual hours taken by the fixed overhead rate.

EXAMPLE

Actual production, Z	220 units
Standard hours per unit (total)	40
Allowed time for production	8800 hours
Actual time taken (total)	9000 hours
Excess	200 hours
Standard overhead rate per hour	£1·50

∴ *Fixed overhead efficiency variance* = 200 × £1·50 = £300 (A)

16. Variable overhead efficiency variance. The *variable overhead efficiency variance* is that part of the profit variance that arises in respect of variable overhead resources and is due to actual efficiency differing from planned.

When preparing a standard cost it is necessary to plan the number of units of activity that will be needed to produce the cost unit. (In our illustration activity is measured by working hours and, as can be seen from the standard cost card in Fig. 16 (p. 151), 40 hours of activity are required to make one Z.) If now, through the efficient use of the variable overhead resources, cost units are produced for less than the planned units of activity, then the saved activity units will not need to be purchased. The profit, then, will be increased by this saving—and conversely, reduced by the cost of excess activity units required should there be inefficient working. To compute the variable overhead efficiency variance, therefore, we must compare the allowed units of activity for the actual production achieved with the actual units of activity consumed and multiply the difference by the rate per unit of activity.

EXAMPLE

Actual production, Z	220 units
Standard units of activity per Z	40 hours
Allowed units of activity	8800 hours
Actual units of activity	9000 hours
Excess units of activity	200 hours
Standard rate per unit of activity (*i.e.* per hour)	£0·50

∴ *Variable overhead efficiency variance* = 200 × £0·50 = £100 (A)

17. Sales margin variances. We now come to sales margin variances which are, of course, primarily the responsibility of the Sales Manager. The two main variances arising in this part of the analysis are as follows:

(*a*) *Sales margin quantity variance.* This variance is that part of the profit variance that is due to the actual sales quantity differing from planned. Clearly, the Sales Manager is under instructions to sell the budgeted sales quantities, and so the allowed quantity is the same as the budgeted. Now if the actual quantity sold differs from this allowance, then for every unit remaining unsold the possible profit will be reduced by that unit's sales margin, and vice versa. To compute the sales margin quantity variance, then, compare the allowed (budgeted) sales quantity with the actual and multiply the difference by the standard sales margin.

EXAMPLE

Allowed (budgeted) sales quantity, Z	250 units
Actual quantity sold, Z	200 units
Difference	50 units

∴ *Sales margin quantity variance* = 50 × £32 = £1600 (A)

(*b*) *Sales margin price variance.* This variance is that part of the profit variance that is due to the actual selling price differing from planned. It is identical in concept to the material price variance. Therefore, to find the Sales Manager's allowance in respect of selling prices it is only necessary to multiply the *actual* quantities sold by their standard selling prices. Since any sum above or below this allowance that the Sales Manager obtains must increase or decrease the profit by just that amount, the sales margin price variance is simply the difference between the actual sales and the allowance.

EXAMPLE

Allowed sales value of actual quantities sold = 200 × £170 =	£34,000
Actual sales value	34,200
∴ *Sales margin price variance* =	£200 (F)

STANDARD MARGINAL COST VARIANCE ANALYSIS

There are reasons for believing that the conventional form of variance analysis given in the previous section is misleading as regards volume (*see* **12**) and sales margin quantity (*see* **17**) variances. In this section the alternative form of analysis—marginal cost variance analysis—is outlined.

18. Differences between absorption and marginal cost variance analysis. Marginal cost variance analysis differs from

(a) Flexible Budget—Overhead Expenditure Variances

Actual activity for month M: 9000 hours.

Overhead	Allowance				Actual Cost	Overhead Expenditure Variance
	Variable cost per hour	Allowed variable cost	Allowed fixed cost	Total allowance		
	£	£	£	£	£	£
Rent	—	—	4,000	4,000	4,000	—
Power	0·20	1,800	—	1,800	1,950	150 (A)
Other overheads	0·30	2,700	11,000	13,700	15,000	1,300 (A)
Total	0·50	4,500	15,000	19,500	20,950	1,450 (A)

(b) Other variances

Factor	Allowance	Actual	Variance (£)	Manager concerned
Material price	2,500 cwt at £5 = £12,500	£13,120	620 (A)	Buyer
Wage rate: Grade 1	5,000 hr. at £0·50 = £2500	£2,810	310 (A)	Personnel Manager
Grade 2	4,000 hr. at £0·40 = £1600	£1,620	20 (A)	
Material usage	220 units × 8 cwt = 1760 cwt	1900 cwt	140 at £5 = 700 (A)	Works Manager
Labour efficiency: Grade 1	220 units × 20 hr = 4400 hr	5000 hr	600 at £0·50 = 300 (A)	
Grade 2	220 units × 20 hr = 4400 hr	4000 hr	400 at £0·40 = 160 (F)	
Fixed overhead efficiency	220 units × 40 hr = 8800 hr	9000 hr	200 at £1·50 = 300 (A)	
Variable overhead efficiency	220 units × 40 hr = 8800 hr	9000 hr	200 at £0·50 = 100 (A)	
Capacity usage	19 days × 500 hr per day = 9500 hr.	9000 hr	500 at £1·50 = 750 (A)	
Sales margin quantity	250 units (as budgeted)	200 units	50 at £32 = 1,600 (A)	Sales Manager
Sales margin price	200 units at £170 = £34,000	£34,200	200 (F)	
Calendar	20 − 19 = 1 day = 500 hr		500 at £1·50 = 750 (A)	Adjustment only
Total overhead expenditure variances (see (a))			1450 (A)	
Profit variance			F 6,540 (A)	Managing Director

FIG. 18.—*Variance analysis*

This is a summary of the sub-variances computed in the text, (**6–17**) for illustrative month M. (Only the ultimate sub-variances are shown).

absorption cost variance analysis insomuch that in marginal cost variance analysis:

(*a*) A *contribution quantity variance* takes the place of the volume variance (and hence the capacity, calendar and fixed overhead efficiency variances) and the sales margin quantity variance.

(*b*) The sales margin price variance is referred to as the *contribution price variance*.

(*c*) Finished goods are valued at standard marginal cost.

Apart from these differences the analyses are identical.

19. Basic features of standard marginal costing. The basic features of standard marginal costing are as follows:

(*a*) Direct materials, wages and expenses, together with variable overheads, are set out on a standard cost card as usual.

(*b*) A *standard contribution* is added to the standard marginal cost to give the standard selling price. This contribution is, of course, the standard sales margin.

(*c*) Budgets are prepared for:

(*i*) Fixed costs.
(*ii*) Sales volume.

(*d*) In the variance analysis a *contribution price variance* and a *contribution quantity variance* are calculated in exactly the same way as the sales margin price and quantity variances discussed in **17**. All other variances (other than the volume and associated variances which disappear) are as before.

20. Standard marginal costing illustrated. The illustrative figures of the previous section can again be used to demonstrate a marginal cost variance analysis. Since much of the analysis and procedure remains unchanged, only the differences will be discussed and these are as follows:

(*a*) *Standard marginal cost.* Fixed overheads will, of course, be excluded from the standard cost and so the standard marginal cost will appear as shown on the standard marginal cost card in Fig. 19.

(*b*) *Actual profit.* As finished goods are valued at marginal cost, the closing stock value for the 20 units of Z shown in 2(*a*) must be amended. The new actual profit, therefore, will be computed as follows:

Total costs (as 2(*a*))	£35,500
Less Closing Stock: 20 Z at £78 each	1,560
Cost of sales	£33,940

∴ *Actual profit* = £34,200 (sales) − £33,940 = £260

(*c*) *Profit variance.* The profit variance in this case will be as follows:

Budgeted monthly profit (as before)	£8,000
Actual profit for month M (as above)	260
Profit variance	£7,740 (A)

(*d*) *Contribution quantity variance:*

Allowed (budgeted) sales quantity, Z	250 units
Actual quantity sold, Z	200 units
Difference	50 units
Standard contribution per unit	£92

∴ *Contribution quantity variance* = 50 × £92 = £4,600 (A)

STANDARD MARGINAL COST

(Z − 1 unit)

Direct materials: 8 cwt A at £5 cwt		£40
Direct wages: Grade 1	20 hr at £0·50 hr	10
Grade 2	20 hr at £0·40 hr	8
	40 hr	
Variable overheads: 40 hr at £0·05 hr		20
Total factory marginal cost		78
Contribution (sales margin)		92
	Selling Price	£170

FIG. 19.—*Standard marginal cost card*

Fixed overheads are excluded from the standard cost.

(e) *Eliminated variances.* Note that the following variances in Fig. 18(b) are eliminated:

Fixed overhead efficiency	£300 (A)
Capacity usage	750 (A)
Calendar	750 (A)
Sales margin quantity	1,600 (A)
	£3,400 (A)

(f) *Contribution price variance.* Note that the *sales margin* price variance of £200 (F) is now renamed the *contribution* price variance.

(g) *Remaining variances.* These are unaffected, as the following calculations will make clear:

(i) Marginal cost profit variance—

(c) above	£7,740 (A)
Absorption cost profit variance 2(b)	6,540 (A)
Increase in profit variance	£1,200 (A)

(ii)

Contribution quantity variance (d) now added into analysis	£4,600 (A)
Variances eliminated (e)	3,400 (A)
Increase in variances in analysis	£1,200 (A)

Since the change in the profit variance has been fully accounted for, all remaining variances in the analysis in Fig. 18 are, therefore, unchanged.

PROGRESS TEST 15

Principles

1. What is a variance analysis? (3)
2. Is it true that a variance is found by comparing an actual figure with a budgeted figure? (4)
3. Define the following variances:

(a) Profit. (2)
(b) Overhead expenditure. (6)
(c) Material price. (7)
(d) Material usage. (8)
(e) Wage rate. (10)
(f) Labour efficiency. (11)
(g) Volume. (12)
(h) Capacity. (13)

(*i*) Capacity usage. **(14)**
(*j*) Fixed overhead efficiency. **(15)**
(*k*) Variable overhead efficiency. **(16)**
(*l*) Sales margin quantity. **(17)**
(*m*) Sales margin price. **(17)**

4. Into what main sub-variances can a material usage variance sometimes be analysed? **(9)**

5. What is a standard month? **(14)**

6. How is a sales margin price variance computed? **(17(*b*))**

7. How does a standard *marginal* cost variance analysis differ from a standard *absorption* cost variance analysis? **(18)**

Practice

The student is warned that the following question is not a straight-forward variance analysis. It has been designed so that thought must be given to the underlying principles of cost control in management accounting. It also reflects the more practical situation where various factors interact, so that the resulting analysis is much more complex than most textbook examples. However, if the student tackles this question quietly and thoughtfully and then compares his analysis with the suggested answer, it should help to bring the whole concept of cost control into focus. (The student who would prefer a more conventional problem is referred to *Cost Accountancy*, W. M. Harper, Macdonald & Evans.)

8. Cybernet Limited manufactures a single product, Cyberloops, out of Cybersheet. It is organisationally divided into one production centre and four service centres. The activity measures relating to these service centres and their standard and budgeted costs are as follows:

Service	*Unit of activity*	*Standard Variable Cost per unit of activity*	*Budgeted Fixed Costs per month*
Test	Test hours	£4	£600
Administration	Direct labour hours	40p	£5000
Stores	Stores points*	£2	£400
Selling	Units sold	£4	£1000

* Stores variable costs have been found to vary in proportion to the number of stores points incurred, points being awarded in respect of various activities as follows:

Cybersheet issued	= 1 point per 5 ft.
Spoiled Cyberloops received for disposal	= 1 point per unit
Guillotine set-up costs for cutting Cybersheet	= 25 points per batch

The company normally works 10,000 direct labour hours per month (with no overtime) manufacturing Cyberloops in batches of 50 units, each unit having the following standard marginal cost:

Direct materials: 5 ft Cybersheet at 60p per ft		£3
Direct labour: 20 hours at 50p per hr		10
Factory variable overheads:		
Test: ½-test-hour at £4 per hr	£2	
Administration: 20 direct labour hours at 40p hr	8	
Stores: 1½ points* at £2 point	3	13
Factory marginal cost		26
Selling variable overheads: 1 unit at £4 per unit		4
Total marginal cost		30
Contribution		20
Standard selling price per unit		£50

* Each unit: 5 ft Cybersheet issued = 1 point

$\frac{1}{50}$ of the 25 guillotine points per batch = ½ point

1½ points

At the Management Planning Committee Meeting held at the end of April to prepare plans for May, the Sales Manager was given a sales budget of 500 Cyberloops. He accepted the budget and then requested that the finished goods stock be increased by 100 Cyberloops (from 200 to 300) by the end of May, as he believed that sales during the summer would be well above the normal 500 level and he felt that it would be as well to have extra stock in hand early in the season. The Works Manager, Mr Wood, pointed out that the production of a total of 600 Cyberloops would necessitate working 2000 hours above normal capacity. After discussion the Committee decided to comply with the Sales Manager's request, plan for 600 units' production and obtain the extra hours by overtime working. (All overtime working in Cybernet is at time-and-a-half.)

The Chief Storekeeper then requested that stocks of the raw material, Cybersheet, be reduced from a current level of 4000 feet to 2000 feet since he believed that there was a serious risk of deterioration if the material remained in stock too long in the increasingly warmer weather. The Buyer quickly pointed out that in the event of such a stores run-down his purchases for the month would fall below the quantity discount level they were currently receiving and which, in fact, was taken credit for in the standard price of 60p per foot. The Committee, however, after ascertaining the quantity discount was 4%, accepted this consequential loss in the interest of reduced risk of stock damage through deterioration.

May proved to be a bad month. Actual sales only reached 450 Cyberloops for a value of £21,810. The Chief Storekeeper's fears were proved and 400 feet of stored Cybersheet was found to be unusable and scrapped. Worse, a faulty production set-up resulted in the whole of the first batch of 50 Cyberloops being rejected on test (*i.e.* after all factory costs had been incurred) and these spoiled units were ultimately disposed of through stores and sold at a mere £2·50 per unit. A replacement batch was quickly put in hand but inevitably this meant 1000 more overtime hours were needed. Also a further 1000 hours' overtime was found to be necessary as 1000 normal working hours had been lost through absenteeism. In the final event 13,500 hours were paid for for a total wage bill of £7875—the actual hourly rate being held constant throughout at standard.

Other figures were not so bad. The Buyer purchased 1000 feet of Cybersheet for £625 and the service centre costs were:

Test (315 actual test hours)	£1,820
Administration	£10,500
Stores	£2,450
Selling	£2,790

The final closing stocks were:

Cybersheet	1400 feet
Cyberloops	350 units

Compute the relevant variances for May.

CHAPTER XVI

REPORTING FOR CONTROL

Now that we have discussed the comparison of actual cost with planned we can consider the final essential factor of control—namely, action to correct divergencies. Action, as we have seen, is wholly a management function, but clearly in cost control action can only be taken on a basis of cost reports which are prepared by the management accountant. This chapter, then, deals with cost control reports. (The technique of reporting generally is discussed in Appendix II.)

RESPONSIBILITY ACCOUNTING

1. The irrelevance of product cost. It is very important to appreciate that in control-reporting *the product cost is totally irrelevant.* Cost control involves compelling actual costs to conform to planned costs and this can only be achieved by taking action at the point where actual and plan diverge. The product cost, however, is only the sum of the costs of a large number of otherwise unconnected economic factors entering into the making of the product. The difference, therefore, between the actual product cost and the planned product cost is simply the net difference of many diverse variances and gives no indication whatsoever as to the point at which action should be taken. A product cost variance, therefore, rarely has any control use.

2. The relevance of cost responsibility. In XIII, **12**, it was shown that all control is through managers. It is, therefore, necessary to orientate the variance analysis so that it is quite clear which manager is responsible for any given variance. (Strictly speaking, in fact, analysis of variances to managers should precede analysis along the lines of classification detailed in the previous chapter, though in practice it is usually possible to prepare a single analysis incorporating both aspects, *e.g.* a price variance is almost always the Buyer's variance.) Now since a variance cannot be analysed to a manager unless he had been previously made responsible for the factor causing the variance, it is essential in cost control that individual costs, or the factors affecting costs, are first made the responsibility of specific managers.

3. Budget centres. To enable variances to be unambiguously analysed to individual managers it is necessary to subdivide the whole organisation into centres which are very similar to cost centres except that they relate to the areas of responsibility (and authority) of managers rather than being simply locations. Such centres are called *budget centres.* Thus a whole department, if under the control of a single foreman, would be a budget centre, and so would an office under a specified office manager.

In connection with budget centres note that:

(*a*) Centres group to form bigger centres. Thus all the factory centres will form a single factory budget centre under the control of the Factory Manager.

(*b*) Occasionally costs charged to a cost centre may be charged to a budget centre that does *not* take in that cost centre. For example, paid leave specifically granted by the Personnel Manager to a shop-floor employee may be charged in the *accounts* to the shop-floor as an overhead, but it would be charged for *control* to the Personnel Officer budget centre, since the Personnel Manager was responsible for sanctioning the cost.

4. Responsibility accounting. Clearly, cost control requires a system of accounting that is designed to present managers with control information relating to their individual fields of responsibility. The employment of such a system is called *responsibility accounting.* The principles of responsibility accounting can be summarised as follows:

(*a*) *All data are analysed in terms of budget centres.* Variance analyses and reports are all drawn up on a basis of these centres. Needless to say, an organisation chart and manual are invaluable in setting up such a system.

(*b*) *Only controllable costs and their associated variances are charged to budget centres.*

(*c*) *Every cost must be charged to someone,* even if that person's responsibility extends only to explaining the cause of the variance (*e.g.* local government rates are hardly controllable, but somebody should be responsible for ensuring that overpayments due to incorrect assessment are not inadvertently made).

When a manager is responsible for a field that includes the fields of a number of his subordinates (*e.g.* a Works Manager), then the subordinates have their own individual statements while he has a statement that summarises their performances and also includes data applicable to him alone (*e.g.* costs relating to the Works Manager's office).

5. Principle of immediate and full variance reporting. Variance analysis is not a book-keeping exercise; it is a management control technique. Consequently a variance must be reported immediately and in full, regardless of whether or not such reporting fits in with a neat book-keeping routine. Thus the accountant may, in his book-keeping, apportion rates equally over the twelve months. Nevertheless, when the rates assessment is known if it is different from that planned, the variance must be shown *in full in the period the assessment became known*. There must be no apportionment of the variance over months, nor even a delay of the reporting until the amount is paid. For effective control managers must know all divergencies in full and as soon as possible.

PSYCHOLOGY AND CONTROL

It has been continually emphasised that control is through managers, and since managers are ordinary human beings it is obviously logical that consideration be given to the psychological aspects involved in control. Already in Chapter I the need for the management accountant to have an understanding of the technique of management has been shown. In control work such understanding is essential. In this connection the points discussed below should be noted in particular.

6. Budgets and standards must be accepted. It is a fundamental principle of good control that the person responsible for maintaining control must *accept the plan*; that is, he must believe it is attainable and agree to be held responsible for those factors within his control in the event of failure. Budgets and standards, therefore, should never be imposed on anyone. If they are, failure is highly probable because the person concerned will:

(*a*) be indifferent to failure, since he will argue he cannot be held responsible for something he said could not succeed from the beginning;

(*b*) have a vested interest, in fact, in failure, since success of the plan will prove that his original objections were not valid.

One excellent way of obtaining a man's acceptance of budgets and standards is to allow him to set them himself. Modification resulting from other people's plans is, of course, inevitable, but if such modifications are tactfully made, acceptance is not usually withheld.

7. Management by exception. Once a plan has been made, management's primary task is to correct divergencies from that plan. It is unnecessary—indeed, it is unwise—for them to concern themselves with matters that are going according to plan. In order, therefore, to direct their attention to matters that need their time and efforts, the concept of *management by exception* has been evolved. Under this concept only those matters which are not going according to plan are reported to managers. When events are going exactly as planned no reports are made.

It can be seen that the variance analysis technique is wholly in line with the concept of management by exception since emphasis is laid on divergencies from plan. If there are no divergencies there are no variances, and if there are divergencies then the variance analysis indicates exactly where the divergence occurred and its importance (in value). Managers are therefore encouraged to tackle such divergencies in order of importance rather than spend their time on unnecessary or trivial matters.

8. Praise and blame. Students sometimes wonder to what extent a variance analysis should be used to apportion praise and blame. It must be strongly emphasised at this point that *it is not part of the management accountant's work to give praise or blame in any form whatsoever.* Praise and blame lie wholly and exclusively with a manager's immediate superiors. The management accountant must always regard his function as that of providing a constructive service to individual managers and his reports should be framed with this object solely in mind.

REPORTS FOR TOP MANAGEMENT

9. Role of top management in cost control. Before any trading period begins top management will have made extensive plans culminating in a *budgeted profit* for the period. By the end of the period they will have expected actual events to have conformed to those plans, particularly in respect of the profit. Their first interest will centre on the difference between the actual and budgeted profit and the reasons for it.

Top management, however, will not be so much concerned with the details that went wrong as in identifying the broad areas where things went particularly badly (or well) and especially identifying *which manager is to be held accountable.* They will then look to such a manager for explanations as to the causes of the variances and consider in what way they can assist the manager in bringing his costs under control.

10. Profit control statement. For top management, therefore, it is logical to present a *profit control statement* that is headed with the budgeted profit which they planned before the period began and have been attempting to control throughout the period. Below this budgeted profit should be listed all the major variances in such a way that the manager concerned is identified. By appropriately adding and subtracting the different variances the statement can be concluded by giving the actual profit for the period. In Fig. 20 such a statement is shown, using our previous illustrative figures (XIV and XV).

It should be noted that some managements prefer the statement to start with budgeted *sales.* This is doubtful practice since management's interest should be primarily in profits (sales *margins*) rather than sales. Moreover, it involves the need to include the standard cost of actual sales, an additional step which otherwise need not be taken.

REPORTS FOR INDIVIDUAL MANAGERS

11. Role of individual managers in control. It is the responsibility of individual managers to ensure that the actual costs under their control conform to plan. Such managers, then, will need all the information that they can profitably use relating to the importance of divergencies and point of occurrence. Having this information they must then decide upon the action to be taken and, if called upon, also advise top management as to the underlying causes of the divergencies and the steps they are taking to correct them.

PROFIT CONTROL STATEMENT

For period..........Month M..........

Budgeted profit for period			£8,000
Sales Manager—Sales margin variances			
Favourable:	Price	£200	
Adverse:	Quantity	1,600	− 1,400
	Actual sales profit		6,600
Works Manager—Production variances			
Favourable:	Labour efficiency, Grade 2	160	160
			6,760
Adverse:	Labour efficiency, Grade 1	300	
	Material usage	700	
	Variable overhead efficiency	100	
	Fixed overhead efficiency	300	
	Overhead expenditure	1,450	
	Capacity usage	750	− 3,600
			3,160
Buyer—Purchasing variances			
Adverse:	Material price	620	− 620
			2,540
Personnel Manager—Wage rate variances			
Adverse:	Wage rate, Grade 1	310	
	Wage rate, Grade 2	20	− 330
			2,210
Adjustments			
Adverse:	Calendar variance	750	− 750
Actual profit for period			£1,460

FIG. 20.—*Profit control statement*

Note that the manager concerned with each group of variances is clearly identified.

12. Control ratios. In addition to variances, management often find *control ratios* of assistance in their control work. The most important of these, and their methods of calculation, are as follows:

$$(a)\ \textit{Efficiency ratio} = \frac{\textit{Allowed hours}}{\textit{Actual hours worked}} \times 100$$

$$(b)\ \textit{Capacity ratio} = \frac{\textit{Actual hours worked}}{\textit{Budgeted hours}} \times 100$$

$$(c)\ \textit{Activity ratio} = \frac{\textit{Allowed hours}}{\textit{Budgeted hours}} \times 100$$

13. Departmental operating statements. The basic document for all control reports to managers is the *departmental operating statement*. This is a comprehensive statement of the operating performance of a departmental manager for a specific period. (Note that in this context the term "departmental manager" refers to any person who has responsibility for a budget centre.) An example of a departmental operating statement is given in Fig. 21, once again using our illustrative figures as a framework (though our illustration is so simple that there is in effect only one production department, while in practice there would be many).

Note the following points regarding such statements:

(*a*) The *name* of the person responsible is given. Action can only be taken by a person, not by a department or a product, and so the statement names the controlling person. Indeed, every figure on the statement relates to his performance specifically.

(*b*) The *period reported on* and the *date reported* are both vital pieces of information and must be clearly stated.

(*c*) The main body of the statement contains:

(*i*) Production data.
(*ii*) Control ratios.
(*iii*) Material usage.
(*iv*) Labour usage.
(*v*) Controllable overhead expenditure.
(Often some non-controllable data are shown. This type of information, while not strictly necessary, does help the manager to envisage the over-all situation in which he operates.)
(*vi*) Efficiency measures.
(*vii*) A summary providing a commentary on overall performance and on any specific factors relevant to departmental operations.

(*d*) *Variances* are clearly shown, individually and in total.

(*e*) *Reasons for variances* are given. These reasons will, of course, frequently be given by the manager himself. However, they should be inserted so that there is both a complete record

DEPARTMENTAL OPERATING STATEMENT

Department..............Factory.. Production ....220 units Z ....
Manager.................P. S. Elderman .... Working hours........... 9000 ....
Position ....Works Manager.................................. Budgeted hours (for actual month) ....9500 ....
Period ....Month M ....
Control ratios:
Activity..............93%.............. Efficiency..........98%.............. Capacity..............95%..............
(Note: Overspending +; Saving −; All costs and variances in £s.)

Direct Materials:

Code	Unit	Allowed quantity	Actual quantity	Difference	Standard price	Usage variance	Reason
A	cwt	1760	1900	+140	£5	+700	Defective weighing machine
Total						£+700	

Direct Labour:

Grade	Allowed hours	Actual hours	Difference	Standard rate	Efficiency variance	Reason
1	4400	5000	+600	£0·50	+300	Badly planned training scheme resulted in excess of highly skilled labour which subsequently had to be used on low-skilled but unfamiliar work for which they lacked specific training.
2	4400	4000	−400	£0·40	−160	
Total	8800	9000	+200		£+140	

Controllable Overheads—Expenditure:

Overhead	Allowed expenditure	Actual expenditure	Expenditure variance	Reason
Rent	4,000	4,000	—	—
Power	1,800	1,950	+ 150	Excessive idling
Other overheads	13,700	15,000	+1300	Increase in factory administative salaries.
Total	£19,500	£20,950	£+1450	

Controllable Overheads—Efficiency (Actual hours.........9000)

Efficiency classification	Allowed hours	Difference	Overhead rate	Variance	Reason
Variable overheads	8800	+200	£0·50	+100	Same as Labour efficiency variances
Fixed overheads	8800	+200	£1·50	+300	(Same as Labour efficiency variances)
Capacity usage	9500	+500	£1·50	+750	80% Absenteeism 20% Idle time
Total				£+1150	

Variance Summary:

Factor	Variance
Direct Materials (Usage)	+ 700
Direct Labour (Efficiency)	+ 140
Overhead Expenditure	+ 1450
Overhead Efficiency	+ 400
Capacity Usage	+ 750
Total	£+3440

Comments: A rather disastrous month—factory variances have cut the Company's budgeted profit by nearly one-half. The high overhead expenditure variance of £1300 due to the increase in factory administrative salaries suggests a look at the possibility of mechanising some of the routine factory administration. For the record:

(*a*) The weighing machine has now been repaired.
(*b*) It has been agreed to allow natural wastage to reduce the excessively large skilled labour force.
(*c*) Absenteeism: see the Personnel Manager's report of the 3rd of this month.

Date...........8th month N............ *Signed*.....J. Marshall........
Management Accountant

FIG. 21.—*Departmental operating statement*

of the period's performance and in addition a brief summary should top management wish to peruse any manager's statement.

14. Further variance analysis. Once a manager has received his departmental operating statement he can consider the action he must take. However, it will frequently happen that the underlying real cause of a variance can only be identified after further analysis. The management accountant, therefore, must be prepared to make further *ad hoc* detailed analyses at points selected by the manager. Although time-consuming, this is often not difficult to do; for example, a wage rate variance can be broken down to *each individual employee* by comparing their individual actual wages with their allowed wages (found, of course, by multiplying their actual hours of work by their standard wage rates), and in a similar manner the material price variance can be broken down for the Buyer into the variances arising on *each single invoice* by comparing the invoice cost with the allowed cost. The further analysis of the capacity variance is often particularly required at this point (both in practice and in examinations), such analysis being in terms of idle time, strikes, break-downs, absenteeism, lateness —the amounts involved being computed quite easily by multiplying the hours involved by the fixed overhead rate per hour (or by a contribution rate, if standard marginal costing is employed).

15. Control accounting as a service to management. Nowhere is the role of management accounting as a service to management more clearly evident than in control work. In this field the management accountant's sole object should be to assist managers from the managing director down to the most junior foreman in the control of their costs. Every report made should be designed to aid personally the individual whose name heads the report, and should that individual require further details, then reporting such details should rank a high priority in the work of the accounting department. It is again emphasised that the management accountant is *not* there to call managers to task, he is there to be of service to the managers. He must never forget that he himself cannot make one penny profit—all he can do is to supply information to managers who, acting on that information, make the profits. His value to the organisation, therefore, can only be measured by the help he gives its members, each and every one of them.

PROGRESS TEST 16

Principles

1. What is the control value of comparing actual product cost with planned? (1)
2. What is a budget centre? (3)
3. Outline the principles of responsibility accounting (4)
4. What is the principle of immediate and full variance reporting? (5)
5. Why should a manager be asked to accept a plan? (6)
6. Explain the concept of management by exception. (7)
7. What considerations underlie the preparation of reports:
   (*a*) to top management (9, 10)
   (*b*) to individual managers? (11)
8. What are the more important control ratios and how are they calculated? (12)
9. What information should appear on a departmental operating statement? (13)

Practice

10. In respect of the data given in Question 8 of Progress Test 15:
    (*a*) Prepare a Profit Statement for May for the Management Planning Committee.
    (*b*) Prepare a Departmental Operating Statement for May for the manager of the production centre (Mr M. Underwood).

NOTE: The student is advised to refer to the suggested answer to Question 8, Progress Test 15, given in Appendix III, before attempting this question.

CHAPTER XVII

CONTROL OF CAPITAL EXPENDITURE

So far we have only discussed profit control. Although the principles are unchanged, the control of capital expenditure is sufficiently important in its own right to warrant a few words of discussion.

BUDGETING CAPITAL EXPENDITURE

1. Capital expenditure budget. The capital expenditure plan will, of course, be the planned capital expenditure over a period of time, *i.e.* a budget. Such a budget will take into account expenditure required both to replace worn out or depleted assets and to acquire additional assets needed for future enterprise growth. The planning horizon in this situation lies many years in the future and in fact advances in step with the passing years. The budget period, therefore, will be one of many years and each year an additional year should be added to this budget period, so that capital expenditure is always planned for a constant number of years ahead.

2. Capital expenditure budget committee. The capital expenditure budget is important enough to require its own committee though it will, of course, form a subcommittee of the main budget committee referred to previously (IV, **27**). This committee will be the capital expenditure budget committee.

3. Capital expenditure budget classifications. The capital expenditure budget will not initially detail every expenditure, for at the time of making the budget the exact form of expenditure will not be known; for example, the budget may specify that £50,000 may be spent in a given year on asset replacement, but it is very doubtful if the exact assets to be replaced will be known at the time the budget is prepared. Even in the case of a major project it will not always be known just what work will be done in any given year. This means then that the budget will lay down expenditure in classifications rather than identified projects (*e.g.* press shop machine replacements; maintenance shop extension; new product equipment), and these classifications will be the formal content of the capital expenditure budget.

CONTROLLING CAPITAL EXPENDITURE

4. Need for capital expenditure authorisation. Since the capital expenditure budget does not detail expenditure it is essential that before any individual projects relating to capital items are started, the expenditure is specifically authorised. If this is not done far more cost may be incurred than was budgeted or even than can be financed. The student should appreciate that simply starting a project can commit the enterprise to heavy future expenditure that it may not be possible to cut back—a half-finished factory fully paid for is a worse proposition than a fully finished factory heavily mortgaged. Indeed the maxim "Don't start anything you can't finish" was never more true than in this context.

5. Capital expenditure authorisation: procedure. When any manager wishes to incur capital expenditure he should first complete a formal request incorporating the following details:

(*a*) Project details (and number if available).

(*b*) Whether the expenditure is in respect of a project already started or whether it is a new project.

(*c*) Amount of expenditure for which authorisation now is required.

(*d*) Estimated cash flow throughout the period of authorisation. (An important aspect of the work of the capital expenditure budget committee will be to watch the cash position, and the authorisation of capital expenditure will naturally only be given if, and in respect of the moment when, finance is available.)

(*e*) Subsequent total expenditure for which authorisation will be required (*i.e.* estimate to complete).

(*f*) Capital expenditure budget classification.

(*g*) Confirmation or amendment of earlier budgeted figures and assumptions in respect of the project. Of particular importance here is the expected future return. (In the case of a project not previously planned, the estimated future return must be stated.)

(*h*) The amount of internal work involved. (If a department in the factory is temporarily slack, work can be carried out in that department at marginal cost only. This will reduce the capital expenditure otherwise required and make the project more attractive.)

(*i*) The reason why the manager believes the expenditure should be authorised. This will usually simply be a matter of referring to the original capital budget which carries the initial broad authorisation. However, for projects not specifically envisaged in the original budget reasons for the expenditure must naturally be given, *e.g.* necessary for safety; to avoid risk of major breakdown; new opportunity to obtain high return on investment; cost savings required to meet increased competition.

This formal request will then go before the capital expenditure budget committee along with all other similar requests and ultimately will be returned authorised, deferred or rejected.

6. Comparison of actual capital expenditure with planned. Once a project has been authorised and given a project number the budgeted costs will be carefully detailed by the accounts department. Next both *commitments* (in the form of purchase contracts and manufacturing sub-contracts) and actual expenditure will be recorded against the project. A control statement similar to that shown in Fig. 22 will be raised for the project and periodically updated, copies being submitted to the manager-in-charge, the capital expenditure budget committee and other interested persons. The manager-in-charge will, of course, also be given a detailed variance analysis.

7. Capital expenditure control: action. On receipt of his capital expenditure control statement the manager-in-charge will naturally take steps to bring his actual expenditure into line with the budget. However, in addition the capital expenditure budget committee will need to consider all control statements submitted to it and be prepared to call a halt to any project if the estimate to complete appears excessive, *i.e.*if further expenditure appears uneconomic.

In the event of a halt being called, a decision will need to be made as to whether the project should be scrapped or just temporarily halted until the committee is able to earmark the extra funds needed to complete. Scrapping a project is likely to be a very expensive matter and, indeed, usually indicates an

CAPITAL EXPENDITURE CONTROL STATEMENT

Project .... New Press Dept.—1st stage .... Project No, ... 3406/A ....

Authority No. .... 617/66 .... Date commenced .... 1/1/68 ....

Manager in Charge .... C. F. Bowden .... Estimated date of completion .... 30/6/68 ....

BUDGET:

Reference No: .... CEB 914 .... Total Expenditure Authorised .... £50,000 ....

AUTHORISED REVISIONS:

Date	10/4/68					
Budget Committee Reference	174/68					
New Total	£57,200					

Date	Actual Expenditure	Current Commitments	Additional Expenditure to Complete	Variance* (Adv/*Fav*)	Reason for change in Variance
1968	£	£	£	£	
Jan 31	200	5,100	44,700	—	No variances as yet
Feb. 29	7,300	15,700	30,000	3,000	All-round increases
March 31	14,800	23,400	19,000	7,200	See report 1/4/68
April 10		Authorised Revision			
April 30	25,300	20,100	11,000	*800*	Improved labour efficiency
May 31	42,100	8,200	6,500	*400*	Miscellaneous minor items
June 30	55,500	1,900	1,300	1,500	Unanticipated drainage difficulties
July 31	59,400	—	—	2,200	See final report 10/7/68

* Authorised expenditure — sum of previous three columns.

FIG. 22.—*Capital expenditure control statement*

When a project is a large one (as in this example), expenditure will be authorised in sections. In such a case a separate control statement should be raised for each section and the project number carry a suffix to show which section is being controlled by the statement.

initial serious budgeting error. In practice it is often found that the value of the completed project consistently exceeds the estimate to complete and therefore no matter how much was spent earlier, it is nearly always more economic to continue a project than to abandon it. This, of course, heavily underlines the need for sound estimating before a project is started, otherwise considerable sums of money can be irrecoverably lost.

PROGRESS TEST 17

1. What are capital expenditure budget classifications? (**3**)
2. Why is it necessary to authorise individual capital expenditure projects? (**4**)
3. Outline a procedure for authorising capital expenditure projects. (**5**)
4. In what respect can the fact that part of a capital project involves internal work affect the likelihood of authorisation? (**5**(*g*))
5. What information would you expect to find on a capital expenditure control statement? (**6** and Fig. 22)
6. What action can be taken to control capital expenditure? (**7**)

PART FIVE

PERFORMANCE EVALUATION

One of the most difficult tasks facing the management accountant is the evaluation of performance, more usually that of his own organisation, but sometimes that of another company. Traditionally, of course, the Profit and Loss Account with its net profit figure was the main medium through which this function was carried out. However, for modern analysis the net profit figure is both crude and suspect—crude because it gives no indication as to just which detailed aspects of performance went well and which went badly, and suspect because there is a distinct doubt regarding the validity of the assumptions on which it is based. Clearly a net profit is very much affected by the charge made for depreciation and the valuation of stock, yet neither of these can be determined with certainty. To add to the confusion the assessment of both figures is subjected to the complicating effect of inflation. We start this Part of the book, therefore, by looking at inflation and depreciation (XVIII) and stock valuation (XIX).

Performance is not, of course, measured by profit alone. A profitable policy that leads the company to insolvency should earn no praise at all. Assets and liabilities must be subject to the same attention as profit, and performance must be evaluated in terms of these factors also. In Chapter XX then, the technique of balance sheet analysis in the evaluation of performance is discussed.

Finally, performance is often relative, *i.e.* dependent upon what could be achieved in the actual circumstances existing. Clearly, it is not enough just to make a profit during a boom period, the profit should be a "good" profit. What is good and bad at any individual time can often only be measured by comparing one's own performance with that of others. The last chapter of this Part then, briefly examines interfirm comparison.

CHAPTER XVIII

INFLATION AND DEPRECIATION

INFLATION

UNDERLYING many problems relating to the evaluation of economic performance is the disturbing influence of inflation. This topic is both complex and also still subject to much controversy. In spite of this, or because of it, examiners tend to avoid setting questions in this field, and so here we will only comment briefly on the subject.

1. What is a "£"? We said earlier that money can be used as a measure of economic performance (*see* I, **16**) and since the pound is a basic unit of money, we measure economic performance in pounds. This is all very straightforward until we ask, what is a "pound"? It most certainly is not a bank note, since that (if we accept the printed statement thereon) is simply a promise to pay a pound. A moment's thought (or a short course in economics) tells us that a "pound" is really *a unit of purchasing power*. It gives us the power to purchase goods.

Unfortunately we have still not progressed very far since the next question is, what goods, and in what quantities? To this question there is no clear answer; one can only say those goods one wants and in those quantities other people will supply in exchange for one's pound. And neither the goods one desires, nor the quantities others are prepared to supply, remain constant. The pound, then, is *not* a permanent, objective measure of any kind.

2. Unsuitability of money as a measure of performance. Clearly, the pound suffers from a double instability: not only may its value be halved, for instance, by the simple act of other people refusing to supply more than half what they previously supplied in exchange for it, but also, because our desires for particular goods may change, it means the underlying nature of the pound in effect is subject to change. If we draw an analogy from the realm of distance measurement, then the first form of instability—the halving of the value of the pound—can be likened to having a measuring tape made of elastic so that a given rod of iron one day measures one foot, but the next day measures two feet. If we now introduce the second form of instability—changing from one kind of goods to another—we can have a situation in which we stretch the elastic differently according to what we are measuring so that one day a foot of rope is longer than a foot of cloth, and the next day the foot of cloth is the longer, though at the same time both are shorter than they were the previous day. The confusion that would arise in such circumstances is understandable: the confusion that arises from using a monetary unit with just these qualities is inevitable.

3. Inflation a fact of life. Students will not need to be told that, apart from occasional periods, inflation seems to be with us continuously. It is a process that has operated throughout history, and events of the twentieth century have confirmed even more dramatically its existence as a fact of life.

4. Inflation and the management accountant. Though management accountants can usually ignore the effect of inflation on day-to-day figures and also often in many of the reports that they make to management, nevertheless in a really searching evaluation of management performance the management accountant must always give due consideration to inflation. This, of course, is of particular importance when the time-span involved runs into many years.

5. Basic approach to adjusting figures for inflation. Since a pound now has not the same purchasing power as a pound in the past, these pounds are not of equal value. In effect, they are different currencies and should not therefore be added together.

Here the student may notice a similarity to the position discussed in XI where future pounds were declared to be unequal to present pounds. Fundamentally the concepts there are the same as those involved here, though the following important differences should be noted:

(*a*) In XI the value of the pound was variable with time because we wished to allow for the effect of *interest on in-*

vestment. Here we wish to allow for the effect of *inflation* on the value of the pound.

(*b*) There we were concerned with decision-making, which involves *future* figures and hence future pounds. Here we are concerned with performance evaluation, which involves *past* (historical) figures and hence past pounds.

However, despite these differences the idea of converting pounds of other periods into present-day pound values remains the same: in other words, in order to adjust for inflation we will convert pound figures relating to an earlier period into present-day pounds by assessing how many pounds would be needed *now* to equal the purchasing power of the earlier pounds in the earlier period. These converted values could be termed "present values," but to avoid confusion with discounted cash flow terminology we will refer to them as "current values." We are, therefore, concerned in ascertaining the current value of past £s.

6. The current value of the past £. There are two views as to how the current value of the past £ should be assessed which lead to two methods of adjusting for inflation: the "replacement" and the "general purchasing power" methods.

(*a*) *The replacement method.* Here it is argued that the current value of the past £ should be based upon the change in the purchasing power of the pound *in relation to the item being valued.* Thus, if buildings are being valued, the change in the purchasing power of the pound relative to buildings will be examined, so if £15,000 was needed now to buy what £10,000 had bought in the past period, then the current value of the past £ would be 150.

This method is based on the view that there can be no economic surplus (profit) made until either the physical assets with which the enterprise began the period have been replaced or sufficient pounds set aside to enable this to be done. Here profit is judged to be the surplus that is left after ensuring that the enterprise is at the same *physical* level as that from which it started (or can be raised to that level).

NOTE: When dealing with inflation index numbers are conventionally used and so this convention is followed here. Students who wish to learn about index numbers are referred to Chapter XXII in *Statistics*, W. M. Harper, Macdonald & Evans.

(*b*) *The general purchasing power method.* In this method it is argued that the current value of the past £ should be based upon the change in the *general purchasing power of the pound.* Thus if the index number that measures the overall purchasing power of the pound rises by 50% then the current value of the past £ would be 150.

This method is based on the view that a pound is a unit of *general* purchasing power. If the price of an asset does *not* go up during an inflationary rise, then it is considered that a loss has been made in respect of this asset. For example, if the asset price was £1000 at the beginning and end of the period and the current value of the past £ at the end of the period was 150, then it would be argued that the current value of the asset at the beginning was £1000 × 1·5 = £1500. Since its current value (ignoring depreciation) is still only £1000, then a loss of £500 has been suffered. Note that from this viewpoint profit is considered to be the excess value remaining, after ensuring that the purchasing power of the enterprise owners' investment at the beginning of the period is still intact at the end.

7. Determining the current value of the past £. Under neither method of assessment is the determination of the actual current value figure simple. In each case index numbers are used, but in both cases there are complications.

(*a*) *Replacement method.* In theory, using this method it is only necessary to look up in suppliers' price-lists the current price of the asset being valued. Unfortunately, in practice it often happens that an equivalent asset no longer exists in the same form as the one originally purchased—design changes are always being made to general-purpose equipment while it is wellnigh impossible to discover the current price of a special-purpose building that was built some years ago. The problem is solved to some extent by preparing price index numbers relating to broad categories of assets, though care is needed in this sort of work.

(*b*) *General purchasing power method.* An index number claiming to measure changes in general purchasing power always runs into controversies as to what items should be included in the index and what weights should be given these items. In this situation one is really left with one's own judgment alone.

8. Index numbers and the base year. Usually in these computations the "past year" is the base year, *e.g.* if the price in the past year was £1000 and the price in the current year was £2500, then the index number would be $\frac{2500}{1000} \times 100 = 250$.

If, however, the *current* year is given as the base year (so that in our example here the past year index number is $\frac{100}{250} \times 100 = 40$) then the current value of the past year is in effect the reciprocal of the index number multiplied by 10,000 (*i.e.* $\frac{1}{40} \times 10{,}000 = 250$, as before).

9. Application of the current values. In theory, the current values of the past £ are applied to all the relevant items in the accounts. However, the procedure is so complex that as yet it is hardly regarded as a practical operation and until accountants begin to use thorough-going conversions, students are advised to leave the topic at this point. There is, however, a need to make conversions in one section of the accounts—namely in relation to fixed assets—and this will be examined in the next section on depreciation.

10. Conclusion. We may therefore conclude this section by saying that although a rigorous procedure to convert all performance statements into current values is probably unwarranted in most accounting situations, the management accountant must clearly bear both views relating to inflation adjustment in mind. If, for instance, the price of an asset rose in absence of a fall in the general purchasing power of the pound, then failure to retain pounds in the business to cover the higher replacement price of the asset would mean that fewer units of this type of asset could be purchased at each replacement stage, and so the profit-earning potential would progressively diminish although the capital value in pounds and in general purchasing power would remain unchanged. (This, of course, assumes no new capital introductions.)

On the other hand, if there were a fall in the general purchasing power of the pound over a period during which the price of the asset remained unaltered, then to regard the almost certainly higher profit figures as representing higher real profit would be wrong. Clearly, if such higher profit only purchases the same as what the previous profit had purchased, there is no improvement in this respect—and, indeed, the failure of the asset to rise with the fall of the purchasing power would indicate that there has, in fact, been a loss to the owners since their asset represents a lower purchasing value than before.

DEPRECIATION

Another topic of complexity is that of depreciation. This, and the associated topic of obsolescence will now be discussed.

11. Depreciation. *Depreciation* is the loss in value of an asset due to wear and tear and deterioration. Usually the loss in value is due primarily to wear and tear, but an unused asset will lose value on account of deterioration.

12. Obsolescence. *Obsolescence* is the loss in value of an asset due to its supersession, *i.e.* the loss due to the development of a technically superior asset. There are degrees of obsolescence, since it is rare that the technical improvement is so dramatic that an existing asset is reduced to scrap value only.

The major problem with obsolescence is predicting its occurrence. Unfortunately it often occurs with very little warning (though past experience may give some guide to the type of equipment likely to become rapidly obsolete, *e.g.* computers, aircraft). This means, of course, that it is rarely possible to make any regular and realistic allowance for the future obsolescence of existing assets. To avoid being caught out some businessmen write down their equipment to scrap value as quickly as possible.

13. Depreciation and obsolescence. As obsolescence involves loss of asset value, it is often considered to be a part of depreciation, which is then defined as "loss of value due to effluxion of time," but as the loss of value is due to quite another reason than wear and tear and the circumstances are so very different, it is considered advisable to keep the two concepts quite separate.

14. Depreciation and obsolescence charges. The costs of asset depreciation and obsolescence are clearly chargeable to all production that makes use of such assets. Methods of making such charges fall into two groups:

(*a*) Methods based on the passing of *time*.
(*b*) Methods based on *production*.

Obsolescence charges should naturally be made on the basis of time, since an unused asset can be rendered just as obsolete as a well-used asset if a new development should emerge. However, as we have said, the life an asset will possess before becoming obsolete is rarely known, and such charges are, therefore, usually only inspired guesses (though *see* **20** for a possible solution to this problem).

On the other hand, depreciation charges can often be based on production, since wear and tear usually depends more on use than time.

NOTE: The traditional use of time as a basis for depreciation depended partially on the assumption that asset use would be constant (a rather doubtful assumption today, in view of modern machine diversification) and partially on the desire to incorporate some sort of charge for possible obsolescence.

It should be appreciated that charges are not made for *both* depreciation and obsolescence. The selection depends upon whether the asset will be obsolete before it is worn out, or vice versa. If this cannot be gauged, then the asset should be written down each year by an amount that reduces the asset value to one the management regard as realistic. This may result in fluctuating charges, but these are preferable to unnecessarily fast, or slow, asset write-downs.

15. Life of an asset. When discussing depreciation, reference is often made to the "life" of an asset. This life is often assumed to be its potential physical life. This is not always true; assets may well be used by the enterprise for a period less than their normal physical life (*e.g.* when bought for use on a particular contract only). To avoid error, therefore, the life of an asset should be regarded as *the length of time such an asset will be used.* It may be measured in years, production hours or units of production.

16. Revision of asset life. As time passes the original estimate of asset life may well be seen to be erroneous. In such a case the asset life should be revised and depreciation amounts adjusted accordingly. Although this may well cause some alteration of previously accepted figures, it is better to admit an error and minimise its effects than to ignore the error and allow some future period to carry large and inappropriate losses or gains.

NOTE: When revision is carried out:

(*i*) The problem of whether or not to charge depreciation where an asset is fully written-down disappears (since it cannot become fully written-down until its life is ended).

(*ii*) Any gains or losses due to incorrect charging in previous periods should be written off to profit and loss and *not* carried forward into future periods.

17. Asset cost. The full loss of value that must be accounted for by depreciation and obsolescence charges should be computed as follows:

$$\textit{Total loss in value} = \begin{matrix}\textit{Asset}\\\textit{purchase}\\\textit{price}\end{matrix} + \begin{matrix}\textit{Purchase and}\\\textit{installation}\\\textit{charges}\end{matrix} - \left(\begin{matrix}\textit{Scrap}\\\textit{value}\end{matrix} - \begin{matrix}\textit{Dismantling}\\\textit{and removal}\\\textit{charges}\end{matrix}\right)$$

This overall charge is normally simply referred to as "asset cost." A simple worked example is given in illustration.

EXAMPLE

Data:

Purchase price	£10,300
Freight and purchase costs	£80
Installation costs	£320
Scrap value	£800
Disposal costs	£100

Method:

Asset cost is, therefore:
£10,300 + £80 + £320 − £(800 − 100) = £10,000

18. Depreciation methods. There are a variety of methods that aim at ensuring that the total depreciation of an asset over its whole life is equitably charged to accounting periods. Such methods are outlined in most accounting and costing textbooks to which the student is referred.

19. Straight-line v. reducing balance. A machine with an estimated life of ten years is bought for £1000. At the end of the first year of its life its resale price is £700. Should the depreciation charge for the year be

$$£1000 - £700 = £300; \textit{ or } \frac{£1000}{10} = £100?$$

The answer to this question depends upon which of the following views is regarded as correct—views that underly the straight-line/reducing balance controversy of the textbooks:

(a) *The reducing balance view.* Here it is held that the depreciation charge should reflect the *actual* drop in the economic value of the asset from the first day of the period to the last (a figure which in practice is approximated to by using the reducing balance method of depreciation).

(b) *The straight-line view.* This view holds that the depreciation charge should reflect the *average* drop in value of the asset per period over the whole life of the asset.

Some accountants, concerned with the preparation of final accounts that should show asset values as realistically as possible, will tend to favour the charge of £300, the reducing balance method. Other accountants, who reason that the service given by the asset in its first year will be no different from that given in subsequent years (and who will also argue that fixed assets are bought for use, not resale, so the market value is irrelevant) will favour £100, the straight-line method.

Both views are, in fact, legitimate in their appropriate contexts. If we wish to prepare a statement that shows as near as possible the *actual* current economic value of assets—*e.g.* a balance sheet—then we must show assets at their current economic value which (ignoring inflation) roughly approximates to the reducing balance values. Conversely, if we wish to prepare a statement that shows what proportion of an original asset cost should be *equitably* borne by the current and future periods, then the straight-line method would give better figures.

20. Obsolescence, an insurable risk. As indicated earlier (**14**), assessing a realistic charge for the obsolescence of an asset is almost impossible, as essentially it involves predicting the unpredictable. Unlike wear and tear which inevitably is incurred if an asset is used and is also incurred at a relatively constant rate, obsolescence may not be incurred at all. Moreover, should it be incurred then the impact falls at a single and unforeseeable moment in time. Obsolescence, therefore, is more akin to fire or accident than factors which are involved in the operation of an asset such as power, oils and depreciation. This suggests that obsolescence should be regarded in the same way as fire or accident is regarded, *i.e.* as an insurable risk. Of course, no insurance company is likely to insure an enterprise against obsolescence, but this does not stop the enterprise insuring with itself by the use of a premium that results in the cost of individual cases of obsolescence being shared equitably among all assets.

21. Insuring against the costs of obsolescence. Using this concept of self-insurance a scheme along the following lines could be employed:

(*a*) All assets are firstly classified into a few main categories according to the probability of obsolescence. Thus a computer would fall in a high-probability category while a standard electric motor would fall in a low-probability category.

(*b*) The actual probability of obsolescence within a given category is then estimated on a basis of past experience.

(*c*) Using this estimated probability, a premium rate for the category is found and applied to each individual asset in that category.

EXAMPLE

To illustrate this procedure, assume that in one of the categories on average one asset item in five becomes obsolete after only half of its expected life has expired. This means that if there were five assets having an asset cost of £1000 each, one asset would need to be written-off when its value was still £500, *i.e.* £5000 worth of assets would incur £500 obsolescence. If we now assume the expected life of these assets is ten years, then £500 cost will be incurred over a ten-year period. Clearly, the best way to recover this sum in the accounts is to make a standard percentage charge each year, based on the written-down value of the assets. Assuming depreciation is straight-line, then calling this annual charge $x\%$, it is clear that:

$x\%$ of the average written-down value of the machine $\times$ years involved $=$ £500.

Bearing in mind that four machines have lives of ten years and depreciate from £1000 to nothing, and that one machine has a life of only five years and depreciates from £1000 to a book value of £500, then:

$$(4 \times x\% \times £500 \times 10) + (1 \times x\% \times £750 \times 5) = 500$$

Solving for x, we find $x = 2{\cdot}1\%$. This means that an insurance premium rate of, say, $2\frac{1}{2}\%$ on written-down value would be charged to the operating costs of each asset in the category.

NOTE: This would *not* be used to reduce the asset value but would be regarded in exactly the same way as would a fire insurance premium.

The book-keeping in this scheme is relatively straightforward. The insurance premium is debited as an expense incurred in operating the asset, and the credit is taken to a Provision for Obsolescence Account. When an asset becomes obsolete the amount that must be written-off as a loss due to obsolescence is credited to the asset account and debited to the Provision for Obsolescence Account.

DEPRECIATION AND CHANGING PRICE LEVELS

If there is a period in which price levels change, then the depreciation charge and asset values are very much affected. This section outlines the approach management accountants must take in these circumstances.

22. Object of depreciation charge. First we must consider what the object of the depreciation charge really is. Three distinct and conceptually conflicting objectives are usually put forward, these being:

(*a*) *To recover the original asset cost over the life of the asset.* This is a book-keeping approach, the argument being that as the original payment for the asset is, in effect, only a prepayment, then all the depreciation charge amounts to is sharing this prepayment equitably between periods that benefit from the asset. From this point of view any change in price levels is clearly irrelevant.

(*b*) *To ascertain the actual economic value consumed as a result of using the asset during the period under review.* This is an economic argument based on the view that if an asset was worth £x at the beginning of the period and £y at the end, then the use of that asset has resulted in an economic loss of £ $(x - y)$, and this, then, is the appropriate depreciation charge.

EXAMPLE

Assume a machine that depreciates physically at a constant rate for ten years (after which it is worthless) is bought for £1000. At the beginning of the second year of its life, owing to changing price levels such a machine new would cost £2000. Since using the machine for one year results in the consumption of one-tenth of the machine, then the second year's depreciation charge must be one-tenth of the value of a new machine at the time of use, *i.e.* one-tenth of £2000 = £200.

In general, then the formula will be:

$$\textit{Depreciation charge for one period} = \frac{1}{\textit{Life of asset}} \times \textit{Replacement value of machine, new}$$

(c) *To ensure sufficient money is retained in the business to enable the asset to be replaced at the end of its life.* This is taking a financial viewpoint, concerned to see that *from the beginning* sufficient cash is retained to replace the asset.

If the £1000 machine discussed in the example above would cost £4000 in ten years' time, then the annual depreciation should be $\frac{4000}{10}$ = £400.

Although (*b*) and (*c*) look quite different, in actual fact they can be equated, as will be shown below. (**24**).

23. Objection to using original cost for depreciation. There is a very good reason for not using original cost for computing depreciation in management accounting, and that is that it provides no valuable information for management. Management is concerned with real economic values, not book-keeping figures and the economic cost of currently using an asset is always the opportunity cost which depends upon the replacement price, never original cost. Moreover, even when measuring *historical* profit, using depreciation based on original cost is wrong, since such a profit would be made up of revenue income and expenditure measured in *current* pounds and depreciation measured in *past* pounds. Such a profit figure is, of course, meaningless for the *management* of an enterprise though it may have some book-keeping significance.

24. Justification for using current replacement price for depreciation. If we eliminate original cost as the basis for depreciation we are still apparently left with a choice between using current replacement price or future replacement price. From the economic point of view, the loss in economic value of an asset as a result of using that asset for a period is the depreciation charge for the use of that asset. On the face of it, though, using such a charge will not enable us to place on one side sufficient money to replace the asset at the end of its life—as we saw in our example (**22** (*b*) and (*c*)) only £200 would be charged for the second year whereas £400 a year is needed for replacement at the end of the tenth year.

This, however, is a wrong conclusion for there is really no difference between the two charges. To appreciate this, consider what should be done with the money retained as a result of the depreciation charge. It can be used in many ways (*e.g.* to set up a depreciation fund), but it can be best used for buying new assets. Assume in our example that the £200, the second year's depreciation charge, was used to buy a non-depreciating asset (*e.g.* land). Remember now that the replacement price during this year was £2000, but by the end of the tenth year it was £4000, *i.e.* prices doubled. If this is so and if our non-depreciating asset shares in the price increase, then its value will also double to £400, *i.e. the exact amount necessary for one year's depreciation using the future replacement price.* Since every asset purchased with a depreciation charge will have appreciated in a similar way, then by the tenth year the total value of all assets bought out of the depreciation monies will be £4000—just what is required.

Of course, the bought assets will not be sold. What in fact will happen is that the original asset will be replaced out of the depreciation charges made on *all* the assets in the enterprise for the tenth year, as is shown in **25** below. The point to note, of course, is that if the depreciation charges for normal assets are based on *current replacement prices* and such charges invested in new assets, then the business will automatically retain sufficient money to pay for the ultimate replacement of all assets, even though these future replacement costs are not known at the time of making the charges. (Note that this principle assumes asset replacement to be relatively constant from year to year.)

25. Illustration of depreciation based on current replacement price. The above principle can be demonstrated by the following example:

EXAMPLE

Assume the business uses only one type of machine that has a total life of three years. The price of those machines new at the beginning of year 1 is £150, but the price rises by £30 on the first day of year 2, another £60 on the first day of year 3, and another £15 on the first day of year 4.

The company decides to adopt the following equipment policy:

(*a*) Buy three machines at the beginning of year 1, one of which will be two years old (A); one one year old (B); and one new (C).

(*b*) To retire the oldest machine at the end of each year and buy a new one in lieu.

If now the depreciation charge for a year is one-third the current replacement value we can obtain the following figures:

Year	PER MACHINE		TOTAL DEPRECIATION (3 machines)
	Replacement Price	*Depreciation*	
1.	£150	£50	£150
2.	£180	£60	£180
3.	£240	£80	£240
4.	£255	£85	£255

Clearly it can be seen that when A is thrown away at the end of year 1, there will be £150 retained earnings in respect of depreciation, which is just enough to buy a new machine. Similarly by the end of year 2 when B is retired there is again just enough money retained to buy a new machine.

It can be seen that this situation continues indefinitely. Therefore by making a depreciation charge based on *current prices* enough money is retained to pay the ultimate replacement price of a machine.

26. Ledger entries: at year end. Though the concept of charging profit and loss with a depreciation figure based on asset replacement prices is relatively straightforward, the ledger entries are more complex. This is because such a depreciation charge includes both a provision for depreciation amount that must be cancelled on the retirement of the asset and also a replacement reserve amount that remains as a permanent balance. The following procedure is suggested for solving this problem (and is illustrated in **28** below):

(*a*) At the year end ascertain by index numbers or other methods the *replacement price* of each asset.

(*b*) Compute the *percentage increase* in the price of each asset for that particular year.

(*c*) Multiply the written-down value of each asset at the beginning of the year (*see* (*f*)) by this percentage and debit the asset account with this product.

(*d*) Total all the debits made in (*c*) to asset accounts and credit a *Replacement Reserve Account.* This indirectly fixes that part of the depreciation charge based on replacement which is really the permanent reserve.

(*e*) Find for each asset its depreciation for the year by reference to its replacement price *at the end of the year.* The total of these depreciation figures is, of course, the depreciation charge to the Profit and Loss Account and the credit is taken to the Provision for Depreciation Account.

(*f*) Compute the new written-down value for each asset by the following formula:

New written-down value = *Old written-down value*
+ *Asset debit made in* (*c*)
− *Depreciation computed in* (*e*)

NOTE:

(*i*) Written-down values will need to be kept in memorandum form.

(*ii*) The first written-down value for a new asset is its purchase price.

(*iii*) On the balance sheet the asset should be shown as original cost plus debits made in (*c*) (and shown as "Price appreciation") less cumulative provision for depreciation.

27. Ledger entries: on retirement of an asset. When an asset is retired the following ledger entries should be made:

(*a*) Debit cash, credit asset account with realised amount.

(*b*) Charge the difference (profit or loss) between the realised amount and the written-down value to the Depreciation Account and make the double-entry in the asset account.

(*c*) Transfer the balance on the asset account to the Provision for Depreciation Account.

28. Ledger entries: illustration. The ledger entries outlined in **26** and **27** can be shown, using the following data:

(*a*) At the beginning of year 1 a machine having an estimated ten-year life with no residual value was purchased for £4000 by a business.

(*b*) By the end of year 1 the replacement price of the machine was £5000.

(*c*) By the end of year 2 the replacement price was £6000.

(*d*) Early in year 3 the machine was sold for £4000.

The *memorandum* figures for this asset would appear as follows:

Period	*Old written-down value*	*Replacement price (year end)*	*% price increase*	*To Replacement Reserve*	*Depreciation (10%)*	*New written-down value*
Year 1.	£4,000	£5,000	25%	£1,000	£500	£4,000 + 1,000 − 500 = £4,500
Year 2.	£4,500	£6,000	20%	£900	£600	£4,500 + 900 − 600 = £4,800
Year 3.	£4,800					

The *ledger accounts* would be as follows:

Asset Account

1. Cash	£4,000	3. Cash	£4,000
Replacement reserve	1,000	P/L—Loss on realisation	800*
2. Replacement reserve	900	Provision for depreciation	1,100
	£5,900		£5,900

* Difference between realised amount and written-down value (4000 − 4800)

Provision for Depreciation Account

3. Asset	£1,100	1. P/L	£500
		2. P/L	600
	£1,100		£1,100

Replacement Reserve Account

		1. Asset	£1,000
		2. Asset	900
			£1,900

The *balance sheets* for years 1 and 2 would be as follows:

Balance sheet

	Year 1	Year 2		Year 1	Year 2
			Fixed assets		
			Machine: Original cost	£4,000	£4,000
Reserves			*plus* Price appreciation	£1,000	1,900
Replacement reserve	£1,000	£1,900		5,000	5,900
			less Provision for depreciation	500	1,100
			Written-down value	4,500	4,800

PROGRESS TEST 18

Principles

1. Why is money an unsuitable measure of economic performance? **(2)**
2. How does re-evaluating money figures relating to a different period of time differ from the re-evaluations discussed with regard to decision-making involving capital projects? **(5 and XI, 1–4)**
3. (*a*) What are the two methods that can be used to convert past £s to current £s and how do the concepts of profit implied by each method differ? **(6)**
   (*b*) How can the current value of the past £ be determined under each of the two methods? **(7)**
4. Distinguish between depreciation and obsolescence. **(11, 12)**
5. Methods of charging for depreciation and obsolescence fall into two main groups. What are these groups and which group is most suitable for which expense? **(14)**
6. What is the life of an asset? **(15)**
7. What should one do if it is later found that the original estimate of the life of an asset was incorrect? **(16)**
8. How would you decide whether to use the straight-line method of depreciation or the reducing balance? **(19)**
9. (*a*) When making a depreciation charge one of three different objectives may be in mind. What are they? **(22)**
   (*b*) As a management accountant what should your views be in this respect? **(23, 24)**

CHAPTER XIX

STOCK VALUATION

Now we examine a third complication entering into performance evaluation, the valuation of stock. The problems involved in such valuations arise in respect of finished goods stock more than other kinds of stock, so this chapter will primarily concern itself with the valuation of finished goods stock.

VALUATION METHODS

1. Methods of valuing finished goods stock. The following are the main methods of valuing finished goods stock:

(*a*) Total absorption cost.
(*b*) Marginal cost.
(*c*) Replacement cost or price.
(*d*) Net realisable value.
(*e*) Standard cost.

These methods are discussed individually below (**2–6**).

2. Total absorption cost and marginal cost methods. The difference between these two methods is emphasised by their treatment of fixed costs.

(*a*) *Total absorption cost.* In this method of valuing stock all actual costs incurred in the production of the finished goods are taken into the valuation, including a share of the fixed costs of production. This is the most conventional of the methods.

(*b*) *Marginal cost.* Here stock is valued at marginal cost only —any fixed costs are rigorously excluded.

3. Total absorption cost v. marginal cost method. The controversy as to whether total absorption cost or marginal cost is the better method of valuation hinges on whether or not fixed costs should be included in the valuation figure.

(*a*) *Marginal cost* exponents argue that since fixed costs are incurred on a time basis they are not affected by production. They must, therefore, not be charged against production at all, but against the time-period to which they relate. Consequently, they must be charged in their entirety to the Profit and Loss Account for the period and not carried forward into another period as part of the valuation of stock manufactured during the period.

(*b*) *Total absorption cost* exponents, however, argue that since the stock could not have been manufactured in the absence of fixed costs (particularly, for example, factory rent and depreciation), then such costs must form part of the cost of manufactured goods. If any of these goods remain in stock at the end of the period, then logically their valuation must include some fixed costs.

Marginal cost exponents tend to counter this argument by asserting that even if the argument holds true for the bulk of production, it certainly does not hold true for that excess production which is not sold but only stocked, since only marginal costs were incurred manufacturing these extra items, *i.e.* no extra fixed costs were incurred at all. The true valuation of such excess, then, is the extra cost only, *i.e.* the marginal cost.

Needless to say, exponents of both methods are able to describe circumstances in which their own particular method is obviously correct and the other obviously wrong. Students, therefore, must form their own conclusions in respect of this controversy, though if they ultimately decide that the correct method will depend on the specific circumstances surrounding the situation (as does seem probable), they must appreciate that in borderline cases the correct valuation may be *between* the total absorption cost figure and the marginal cost figure. How such a valuation can be made must be left for the student to decide for himself.

4. Replacement cost or price method. Under this method the valuation is based on what it would cost to *replace* the stock under current economic conditions, *i.e.* if goods are manufactured what the replacement cost would be, and if goods are purchased what the replacement price would be.

This method aims at making allowances for inflation. It should be noted that its use does imply taking an unrealised profit, though correct treatment of this profit (*see* **7**) should ensure that the conventional objections are successfully met.

5. Net realisable value method. Here stock is valued at the price it would realise if sold, less any costs of realisation (*e.g.* advertising, sales commission, distribution).

This method is often used where it is otherwise impossible to value stock. This is particularly the case where joint products abound, as in the farming and butchery industries. Clearly one cannot find the cost of producing one lamb's liver, so a conventional valuation based on cost is not possible. (Again, note that an unrealised profit will probably be taken.)

6. Standard cost method. This method values stock at standard cost. It can, of course, only be used where standard costing is in operation, but there are definite advantages to using it when possible, namely:

(*a*) It is simple to apply.

(*b*) It enables comparisons to be made between stock-holding levels at different periods (and also period profits) without the distortion otherwise introduced by either temporary changes in price levels or fortuitous changes in actual costs of production.

(Again note that unrealised profits may be taken.)

A word of warning should, however, be given here. Standard costing is a *control* technique and standard costs are not therefore set with the object of using them for economic valuations. Provided, however, that the standards are up to date, it is generally safe enough to use them for such valuations.

PRINCIPLES OF STOCK VALUATION

7. Should unrealised profits be taken? More than once we have mentioned that an unrealised profit may be taken as a result of using a particular method. There are two points of view on this, either of which is correct, according to the circumstances.

(*a*) *The financial aspect.* The conventional accounting principle relating to this point emphatically asserts that such a profit must not be taken. This view arose from the convention of conservatism which aims to ensure that no cash will be paid out as dividends unless it represents certain and indisputable profit. Financially this is sensible, since a withheld dividend can always be paid later if need be, but a paid dividend can never be recalled. In other words, the principle applies to money as an *economic factor*, *i.e.* cash (*see* I, **16**(*a*)).

(*b*) *Economic performance.* However, when assessing performance we will employ money as a *measure of performance* and so the conventional accounting principle will not apply. Indeed, not to take profits, realised or otherwise, for the period in which they are earned results in that period's performance being under-stated and the performance of a later period gratuitously over-stated. This viewpoint is particularly relevant in the case of standard costing. Clearly any favourable variance (especially efficiency variances) arising during a period reflects *improved operations during that period* (relative to plan). The gain from such improvement must obviously be credited to the period in which it was made and not the period in which the final product fortuitously happened to be sold.

It should be fully appreciated that profits arise just as much from high efficiency as good salesmanship—a manufacturer, say, whose costs are only half those of his competitors would need to be a very poor business man if he were unable to show good profits on his operations.

We can conclude, then, by saying that unrealised profits must *not* be taken where the *financial* aspect is the relevant factor, but *must* be taken when *economic performance* is being evaluated.

8. The role of "evidence." If one closely examines the accountancy convention of conservation it is soon found to be arbitrary, even though the object may be praiseworthy. If it is argued that we cannot value an item at its selling price because there is no certainty that that figure will be obtained, then it surely can be argued that it is also wrong to value it at cost, since if prices are so uncertain there is no guarantee that even the cost will be recovered. Should one, to be safe, value stock at scrap price only? Clearly, this cannot be correct either since such a method of valuation would grossly distort the profit figures for the period.

A surer way of approaching stock valuation is to base it upon *evidence* rather than an indefinite principle. Provided the evidence is sound (and with the proviso that the object is not to determine dividend payments) then the resulting valuation should be accepted.

9. Types of evidence. There are basically the following three types of evidence:

(*a*) *Cost* (*total absorption*). If a manufacturer is normally competitive, then his cost of production is likely to be similar to that of other manufacturers, and so, in a period of stable prices, akin to the market price. The cost may, therefore, be evidence of the value of an item. (This type of evidence is particularly useful for production which, as such, has no market price, *e.g* half-completed work.)

(*b*) *Market price.* If prices are stable then the fact that a product is actually selling at a given price is reasonable evidence that it has that value at the point of sale. Its stock value, therefore, is the market price less costs to be incurred between stocking and the point of sale.

(*c*) *Standard cost.* This is similar to (*a*) but even better since the effect of temporary chance cost variations is eliminated. It does, however, very much depend upon the standards being up to date.

10. Importance of price stability. It should be noted that price stability (*i.e.* prices not subjected to sudden erratic changes) is basic to all valuation methods. If, in fact, prices are not stable then stock valuation quickly becomes arbitary, and indeed in these circumstances it may well be asked if there is any meaning to the terms "manufacturing profit" and "trading profit" since all profits are purely speculative under such conditions.

11. Stock valuation and inflation. Where there is inflation the falling purchasing power of the pound results in stock bought or made in an earlier period being worth more current pounds than past pounds. The effect of inflation is, of course, not so great on stocks as on fixed assets, for stock should not be held in the enterprise for anything like as long a time as fixed assets and so the gap between original cost and current value should never be so significant. However, there is some effect and probably the easiest way to take this into the ledger is to add just enough on to the original cost to bring it up to the replacement value and credit this addition to a Stock Replacement Reserve, *i.e.* the ledger entry would be: *Debit Stock, Credit Stock Replacement Reserve, with the difference between stock at original cost and stock at replacement value.*

12. Raw materials and work-in-progress. Clearly much of what has been said in respect of finished goods stock applies to raw materials and work-in-progress stock. Note, however, that market price (**9** (*b*)) cannot be used for valuing work-in-progress and that in the case of raw materials the total absorption/marginal cost controversy (**3**) is irrelevant.

PROGRESS TEST 19

1. What are the main methods of valuing stocks? (**1**)
2. Should fixed costs be included in the valuation of finished goods stock? (**3**)
3. Should unrealised profits arising from the valuation of stock ever be taken? (**7**)
4. What do you understand by the concept of stock valuation on the basis of "evidence" and what are the three basic types of such evidence? (**8, 9**)

CHAPTER XX

BALANCE SHEET ANALYSIS

INTRODUCTION

1. Need for balance sheet analysis. Performance evaluation is not measured by profit alone—it is just as important to avoid jeopardising profit *potential*. In some ways companies are like athletes who can only keep winning races if they keep fit. To win a race at the cost of permanent physical injury is rarely a satisfactory outcome, and in the same way to make a large profit at the cost of a compulsory liquidation rarely benefits anyone.

A company "keeps fit" by ensuring that, among other things, its various financial proportions are kept healthy: that, for example, debts and stocks are not excessive and that it is not vulnerable as regards liquidity. The health of a company in these respects can be evaluated by reference to many balance sheet figures and for this reason no company performance evaluation is complete without such an analysis.

2. Internal and external analysis. An analysis can be either:

(*a*) *Internal, i.e. an analysis of the company's own balance sheet.* In this type of analysis the object is to uncover either any financial poor health to be corrected as a matter of urgency (such as over-stocking), or any unhealthy trend developing. Analysis is aided here by the fact that all recorded data are available to the analyst.

(*b*) *External, i.e. an analysis of the balance sheet of another company.* This sort of analysis is usually made when an amalgamation or takeover is in mind and aims to uncover either poor financial health that suggests the immediate financial value of the company analysed is less than it appears, or unhealthy trends that may indicate some fundamental defect in the company (*e.g.* decreasing management efficiency) which may considerably reduce its long-term prospects. The data for the analysis here are very often limited to the balance sheet alone (with perhaps just the odd additional major figure, *e.g.* sales) and the analyst may have to uncover a fact that is otherwise known only to the company itself.

3. Use of ratios. Company fitness depends very much on healthy financial *proportions* rather than absolute amounts, just as a man's healthy weight depends upon his height. Consequently balance sheet analysts work almost exclusively with proportions expressed in the form of ratios.

4. There are no "ideal ratios." Students like to be told that, for example, current assets to current liabilities should be in the ratio of 2 : 1, for if such ideal ratios existed balance sheet analysis would be simple. Unfortunately there are *no* ideal ratios. Firstly, company circumstances vary—the stock turnover in a supermarket will clearly be well above that of a whisky wholesaler. Secondly, health often depends on the actual items making up the ratio, so that a poor current assets to current liabilities ratio may be satisfactory if the current assets are wholly cash balances. Thirdly, a "poor" ratio may be the result of either financial incompetence or financial wizardry, *e.g.* a book publisher with £1000 equity and £20,000 debt may have reached this position accidentally and be quite unaware of his highly precarious position, or it may be that he knew at every moment what was happening, allowed it to happen, and intends to avoid the obvious dangers by his financial skill.

This all means, therefore, that good balance sheet analysis requires a combination of commonsense and sound financial judgment, neither of which, unfortunately for students, can be reduced to a set of notes.

5. Analysis in examinations. In examinations it helps if students know in an analysis question what to look for first: poor financial health or adverse trends. Generally speaking, if only *one* balance sheet is given look first for poor financial health, while if *more than one* is given look for trends.

6. Terminology. Students should note that the terms used in this chapter are accountancy terms, and may on occasions differ from those used on the Stock Exchange or in investment journals.

BALANCE SHEET RATIOS

7. Balance sheet ratios classified. The main balance sheet ratios are listed below, together with illustrative figures.

(a) *Illustrative balance sheet figures.*

Capital: 6000 £1				
Ordinary	£6,000	Fixed assets		£13,000
Reserves	4,000	Current assets:		
Equity	10,000	Stock	£4,000	
Debentures—7½%	6,000	Debtors	2,000	
Current Liabilities	4,000	Cash	1,000	7,000
	£20,000			£20,000

Sales £7,000; Net profit (after debenture interest, before tax) £1,400; Corporation tax 40%; Dividend 10% (gross).

(b) *Solvency ratios*—indicating the extent to which a company can meet its current commitments:

Current ratio

Current assets: Current liabilities = 7000: 4000 = 1·75

Liquid ratio

Liquid assets: Current liabilities = 3000: 4000 = 0·75

Vulnerability

Cash £1000 + Debtors £2000 + Stock £1000 = 25% Stock

(c) *Equity ratios*—indicating the extent to which the company is financed by the shareholders.

Equity: Total capital employed = 10,000: 20,000 = 0·5
Equity: Equity + Long-term debt = 10,000: 16,000 = 0.625
Equity: Fixed assets = 10,000: 13,000 = 0.77

(d) *Operating ratios*—measuring operating performance in terms of sales and capital employed:

(*i*) Sales.

Capital turnover Sales: Total capital employed
= 7000: 20,000 = 0·35 = 3 years

Equity turnover Sales: Equity
= 7000: 10,000 = 0·7 = 1½ years

Current assets turnover Sales: Current assets
= 7000: 7000 = 1·0 = 1 year

Working capital turnover Sales: Working capital
= 7000: (7000 − 4000) = 2·3 = 5 months

Stock turnover Sales: Stock
= 7000: 4000 = 1·75 = 7 months

Debtors turnover Sales: Debtors
= 7000: 2000 = 3·5 = 3½ months

(*ii*) Return.

Net profit: Total capital employed = 1400: 20,000 = 7%
Net trading profit: Trading capital employed
(not illustrated; *see* **18**(*c*))

Net profit: Equity	= 1400: 10,000 = 14%
Net profit: Sales	= 1400: 7000 = 20%
Net profit: Working capital	= 1400: 3000 = 46·7%

(*e*) *Cover*—indicating the margin of safety available to the company's investors of capital.

Debenture interest cover	Net profit before interest and tax*: Debenture interest = (1400 + 450): 450 = 4 times
Dividend cover	Net profit after Corporation tax: Gross dividend = 60% of 1400: 600 = 1·4 times

The ratios are virtually self-explanatory, though points of importance are discussed below (**8–13**).

8. Current ratio (current assets : current liabilities). This is, perhaps, the most common balance sheet ratio. It indicates the level of safety involved in relying on current assets being sufficient to pay current liabilities. (Note that a company which is forced to sell *fixed* assets to pay its liabilities is reducing its production potential and so lessening the profits on which the continued existence of the company depends.) Traditionally the ratio is supposed to be about 2 : 1 though under modern conditions this is usually found to be too conservative. Too high a ratio suggests inefficient use of capital (*e.g.* excessive debtors or stock), while too low a ratio suggests lack of liquidity.

9. Vulnerability. Linked with the current ratio is the concept of *vulnerability*. Vulnerability is measured by calculating the extent to which current assets, starting with the most liquid asset, would need to be realised before the whole of the current liabilities were covered. In the example given in **7** for instance, to pay current liabilities of £4000 we would need the whole of our £1000 cash, the whole of our £2000 debtors (the next most

* Since there can be no taxable profits until all interest payments have been made, this measure relating to interest cover must take net profit *before* tax.

liquid asset) and one quarter of our £4000 stock. We would say, therefore, that our vulnerability was "25% stock," (**7** (*b*)) *i.e.* we need all the most liquid assets up to and including 25% of the stock.

10. Liquid, acid or quick ratio (Liquid assets : Current liabilities). When using this ratio a decision has to be made as to what is to constitute liquid assets. Often cash and debtors are so regarded, though if the terms of trade allow long-term credit, only immediate debtors may be included. Traditionally a ratio of 1 : 1 is looked for, but much depends upon how soon each class of liability must be paid; a tax demand payable in nine months is quite different from a worried creditor whose account was payable some two months previously.

If the company should have an unused portion of an agreed overdraft limit, the portion is sometimes regarded as cash since it is available to pay liabilities, *i.e.* the full overdraft limit is listed among the current liabilities and the unused portion listed as a cash balance in the current assets. This, of course, improves a ratio that is worse than 1 : 1.

11. Equity ratios. There are three ratios to consider:

(*a*) *Equity to total capital employed* indicates how much of the total capital being used by the company has in fact been supplied by the shareholders.

NOTE: Students should be warned that *total capital employed* is defined in various ways by various people. Basically, however, it is the balance sheet total, although most authorities exclude intangible assets and some also deduct current liabilities (*see* also **17–20**).

(*b*) *Equity to equity + long-term debt* measures the proportion of the permanent capital that is financed by shareholders.

(*c*) *Equity to fixed assets*, of course, indicates the extent to which the shareholders have financed the fixed assets.

12. Operating ratios. These can be classed as:

(*a*) *Sales.* These ratios help to measure the efficiency of the use of capital, since the less capital needed per £ of sales the more effectively and intensely capital is being employed.

(*b*) *Stock and debtors.* These ratios help to assess whether stock is too high or whether debtors are taking too long to pay.

The example in **7** above shows that it would take seven months at current rate of sales to "sell" all the stocks, though whether this is good or bad depends, of course, on the type of business. Similarly the debtors on average are taking $3\frac{1}{2}$ months to pay, and again whether or not this is excessive depends on the business and its terms of trade.

13. Cover. Cover measures how many times a payment to investors could be made out of profits or other specified form of return. It is computed by the following formula:

$$\textit{Cover} = \frac{\textit{Amount available to pay investors after deducting prior charges}}{\textit{Amount for payment}}$$

"Prior charges" are payments that must first be made before the investors can receive their payment.

Clearly, the more times a payment is covered the higher the chance of continued payments.

14. "Window dressing." Students should be warned that a company may deliberately arrange its affairs so that the balance sheet gives better-than-average ratios. A common method of doing this is to select a financial year end that comes at the slackest moment in a seasonal trade. At such time stocks, debtors and creditors are abnormally low, while cash is high. Solvency ratios, therefore, look better than at any other time of the year. This is termed "window dressing" and balance sheet analysts should allow for this.

It should be pointed out, however, that there are other more honourable reasons for ending a company year in the slack season, for at that time there is both less pressure of work on all personnel and also smaller quantities of stock to be taken. Both these factors facilitate preparing final accounts at this time.

15. Other ratios. There are, of course, many other ratios that can be computed if they are thought to be relevant to the industry or the particular analysis; for example, work-in-progress turnover in a civil engineering company would measure the extent to which capital was tied up in long-term contract work. In an examination students should be ready to devise such ratios if the circumstances warrant them.

RETURN ON CAPITAL IN BALANCE SHEET ANALYSIS

16. Basic formula. As explained in I, **18** the return on capital measures the creation of economic wealth relative to the economic wealth tied up in the process, and so the basic formula can be expressed as follows:

$$\textit{Return on capital} = \frac{\textit{Profit}}{\textit{Capital employed}}$$

17. Defining profit and capital employed. This formula will give a variety of results depending upon how "profit" and "capital employed" are defined. Essentially the appropriate definitions depend upon the *interpretation* that will be put on the return on capital figure.

18. Interpretation and status. Often this interpretation is influenced by the status of the person interested in the figure. Note how people with the following status will probably interpret return:

(*a*) *Investor—Net profit after tax: Capital invested.* The investor will probably be primarily concerned with what he receives as dividend and growth (*i.e.* net profit) relative to the amount he originally invested.

(*b*) *Managing director—Net profit after tax: Equity.* The managing director will probably feel his performance should be judged on a basis of profit earned *after* tax (since minimising tax is part of his job) relative to total equity entrusted to him by the shareholders—to whom he is, of course, primarily responsible.

(*c*) *General manager—Trading profit before tax: Total trading assets employed.* Here we are making a rather theoretical distinction between a managing director and a general manager, but for illustrative purposes it is perhaps in order to view the general manager as someone being particularly interested in assessing the creation of economic wealth from trading relative to the assets tied up in the process of creating that wealth, while the managing director looks first to his responsibility of serving the shareholders. In practice, of course, they are often the same person.

(*d*) *Departmental manager—Departmental profit (before tax): Departmental assets employed.* The departmental manager will take the same point of view as the general manager, but restrict measurement to items under his own control.

19. Interpretation and purpose. When evaluating performance one has the choice of valuing assets at original cost, replacement cost or realisable value. In balance sheet analysis the choice depends upon the *purpose* of the analysis, more specifically, upon whether one wants to know if the company is doing as well as it ought, or if it is doing so badly that it would pay to liquidate it. The former purpose uses replacement cost and the latter realisable value, the reasons being as follows:

(*a*) *Replacement cost.* A company cannot be judged to be doing as well as it ought to unless all the economic resources consumed and employed are valued in the same currency as sales, *i.e.* in current pounds. This means asset values must be based on replacement cost. If it is found that the company is not doing as well as it should, then further investment in the company in the form of extra capital or retained profits should cease unless particularly warranted by a specific project.

(*b*) *Realisable value.* If the situation is so bad that liquidation is being considered, then realisable values must be used. Using these values it is possible to compute how much cash would be released by liquidation, and if the return currently earned by the company on this amount is below that which could be obtained by re-investing the cash, then clearly it pays to liquidate the company. If above, it pays to keep it in existence.

The occasions when valuation at *original cost* is the valid choice are so rare that the method does not warrant discussion. Current performance cannot be assessed on a basis of past and out-of-date values.

20. Additional points for consideration. In respect of return on capital note also that:

(*a*) *Assets should be taken at their depreciated value.* The capital tied up in an asset is its economic value at the time of the analysis, not the original cost nor the full replacement cost of a brand new asset.

(*b*) *If profit is compared with total capital employed, then interest must be added back.* If the *total* capital employed is to be used as the denominator of the return-on-capital formula (16), then obviously it must be compared with the *total* return to all the contributors of capital, *i.e.* lenders as well as shareholders.

(c) *To find the trading return on capital, non-trading assets should be excluded from the capital employed figures.* This also means that non-trading profit (or loss) should similarly be removed from the profit figure.

MAKING THE ANALYSIS

Now that all the ratios have been considered we can turn to the actual analysis procedure.

21. General procedure. Balance sheet analysis is unfortunately a matter of flair rather than routine. This means that the only advice one can give the student is to review all data thoughtfully, and if anything appears a little unusual then probe at that point. However, generally speaking most analyses do seem to involve the following five steps:

(a) Decide whether the more significant conclusions will emerge from assessing financial strength or from ascertaining trends (*see* **5**).

(b) Compute what one feels will be the most revealing ratios.

(c) Probe intelligently where anything appears a little unusual or is somewhat inconsistent with the rest of the data.

(d) Compute the *true* return on capital, *i.e.* a return based on the results of the analysis and not on the initial unanalysed balance sheet figures (*e.g.* after revaluation of assets).

(e) Consider the surrounding circumstances in conjunction with the analysis and reach conclusions.

22. Overtrading. A common type of financial weakness is *overtrading*, a financial state that arises when a company attempts to conduct a larger volume of trade than it is financially equipped to do.

(a) The *symptoms* of overtrading include:

(i) Excessive creditors' figure.
(ii) High debtors' turnover.
(iii) Overdraft consistently at the limit.
(iv) High equity turnover.
(v) High stock turnover, which is also often coupled with high stock to equity ratio.
(vi) Fixed assets on hire-purchase or fully mortgaged.
(vii) Relatively high overtime working and excessively generous cash discounts to debtors.

(b) The *dangers* of overtrading must be stressed. There is a chronic shortage of cash and the situation can only usually continue until creditors lose patience and begin to resort to legal action to obtain their money. If every fixed asset is fully mortgaged then not only can no more money be raised on mortgage, but also selling fixed assets will only release a small amount of cash, as the bulk of the proceeds must go to clear the mortgage on those assets. Moreover, such fixed assets will prove to be vital to the enterprise's continued existence, otherwise they would have already been sold to raise money. Consequently, compulsory liquidation is virtually inevitable.

Students should appreciate that almost invariably high profits are earned when overtrading, the lure of such profits usually being the reason for such a situation. But making a profit is not the only requirement for business success—financial health is equally important. Indeed, more businesses have probably failed as a result of financial weakness than of weakness in trading.

23. Undertrading. Undertrading is the opposite of overtrading, *i.e.* being financially equipped to conduct a much larger volume of trade than is actually being achieved. In an analysis a low return on capital often indicates undertrading, but if in fact very good profits are being made this figure may appear quite satisfactory. Indeed, all ratios will almost certainly appear "sound," but although the company may never be in any financial trouble, its performance must still be judged poor since its use of capital employed will in reality be very inefficient. It is important, therefore, to be able to detect undertrading, and the usual sympton is a *very high current ratio* with investments probably representing excessive reserve funds.

24. Valuing shares. If the purpose of the analysis is to determine the value of the company shares for a business merger or takeover, then such a valuation forms an additional step in the analysis.

There are two different bases on which shares can be valued:

(a) *Earning basis.* Here the value depends upon what you would be prepared to pay to buy the *future return* that the company will earn *under your management.* Usually there is an accepted normal percentage return for businesses in the particular industry concerned, so that the value of a share in a given business can be found from the following formula:

$$\textit{Share value (earnings basis)} = \frac{\textit{Expected return (£s)} \times 100}{\textit{Normal percentage return for industry} \times \textit{Number of issued shares}}$$

EXAMPLE

If 20% before corporation tax is the normal percentage return for the type of business given in **7**, and the net profit before tax is expected to be maintained at £1400, then:

$$\text{Share value (earnings basis)} = \frac{£1400 \times 100}{20 \times 6000} = £1{\cdot}17$$

(*b*) *Assets basis.* Here the value depends upon the break-up value of the assets less all debts, *i.e.* the formula is:

$$\textit{Share value (assets basis)} = \frac{\textit{Break-up value of assets} - \textit{All debts}}{\textit{Number of issued shares}}$$

EXAMPLE

If the value of current assets in **7** are considered to be equal to their balance sheet values, while the fixed assets are considered to have a break-up value of only £8000, then:
Share value (assets basis) =

$$\frac{£(7000 + 8000) - (6000 + 4000)}{6000} = £0{\cdot}83$$

Note that having valued the shares on both bases, the *higher* value is clearly the appropriate one to serve as a guide to fixing an actual share price, since the person acquiring the company can elect to run or break-up the business as he wishes.

In practice, of course, the final share price will depend on negotiation. Moreover, the existence of preference shares or other obligations will complicate the valuations. In such situations the student must be guided by his commonsense, bearing in mind that at all times he must approach the topic from the viewpoint of the practical businessman.

25. Non-monetary items. It is vitally important that students should realise that a balance sheet only details items *that can be measured in money terms*. It cannot show among the assets high staff morale nor among the liabilities a reputation for late deliveries. In the case of a small business it is also unable to record the value of the owners, whose particular character and know-how may be ideal for that particular business or whose private contacts may be uniquely suitable for that trade. Yet these factors may be crucial to the success of the business, and although they are not in the balance sheet consideration must be given to them when drawing final conclusions from the analysis.

26. Analysing for trends. Throughout this chapter the emphasis has been on analysing for financial health. When we turn to consider analysing for trends we find there is very little that can be said. Initially much the same approach needs to be taken as in financial health analysis (although as there will be more than one balance sheet firmer conclusions regarding the underlying financial strength are often possible, since temporary situations can be identified). The main ratios will, of course, be computed for each balance sheet, trends noted, and conclusions drawn accordingly.

Sometimes there are hidden trends that an intelligent analysis reveals, but unfortunately such analysing calls for even more flair than that required for analysing for health. However, if there are sudden balance sheet ratio changes or puzzling trends in any ratios, then these will indicate where to probe. Laying bare the *real* situation as against the apparent situation calls for a combination of imagination and logical deduction which, regrettably, cannot be taught by a book. In this respect the student is very much on his own.

PROGRESS TEST 20

Principles

1. Why is there a need for balance sheet analysis? **(1, 2)**
2. What are:

   (*a*) Solvency ratios?
   (*b*) Equity ratios?
   (*c*) Operating ratios?
   (*d*) Cover? **(7)**

3. What do you know about:

   (*a*) Current ratio? **(8)**
   (*b*) Liquid ratio? **(10)**

4. What is the formula for cover? **(13)**
5. What is "window dressing? **(14)**

6. In what ways can "profit" and "capital employed" be interpreted? **(18)**

7. When evaluating performance under what circumstances should one value assets at:

(*a*) Historical cost?
(*b*) Replacement cost?
(*c*) Realisable value? **(19)**

8. What are the following and how are they recognised:

(*a*) Overtrading? **(22)**
(*b*) Undertrading? **(23)**

9. On what two different bases can shares be valued, and which basis should be selected for a given share valuation? **(24)**

10. Are non-monetary items an important consideration in balance sheet analysis? **(25)**

Practice

11. The executors of H. Nelson, boat-builder, who was tragically drowned on his thirtieth birthday while testing a new boat design, wish to sell both his and his wife's holdings in his company, Dreamboats Ltd. Mr and Mrs Nelson were the sole shareholders, and though Dreamboats is a successful company, Mrs Nelson has no desire to carry on with a business that took her husband from her.

On the day after the tragedy the following balance sheet of Dreamboats Ltd was prepared:

Authorised capital (£1 ordinary)	£100,000
Issued capital (£1 ordinary)	20,000
Reserves	5,000
Loan—Mrs Nelson	10,000
Provision for taxation (1 year at 50%)	10,000
Creditors	25,000
Overdraft	10,000
	£80,000
Fixed assets (less depreciation)	£70,000
Stocks	6,000
Debtors	4,000
	£80,000

Last year, for the fifth year running, Dreamboats obtained sales of over £60,000 from light sailing dinghies. This gave a profit before corporation tax of 100% on issued capital.

You have been asked to consider purchasing the business. How much per share would you be prepared to offer?

(Assume that in this type of business 20% gross return on invested capital is considered normal.)

CHAPTER XXI

INTERFIRM COMPARISON*

PRINCIPLES OF I.F.C.

1. Value of I.F.C. It is not enough that a company knows it is making a profit: it also needs to know if it is making as much profit as it could. While theoretical studies may point to perfect maximisation of profit, it is accepted that perfection is impossible in practice and businessmen require a more practical test. Such a test exists in the comparison of the company's performance with similar companies. If, as a result of such a comparison, it can be seen that Company A has a better performance than Company B, then the management of B know that an improvement is possible *in practice* and therefore that it is worth their time and effort to determine how such an improvement can be made.

2. Psychological effect of comparison. The psychological effect of comparison must never be under-estimated. Managers accept that quality of management is measured by performance; to discover that other managers have achieved a better performance stimulates a manager more, possibly, than anything else. It is, after all, a reflection on his competence. Some managers, of course, defensively put forward the argument, "My business is different," and although it is true that wholly unqualified comparison is unfair, the very fact that there exists a suggestion of inferior performance keeps a manager alert to the possibility of making improvements. Such an environment is much more healthy and fertile than one of complacency.

3. Requirements of effective comparison. It is not sufficient merely to know that another company has an overall better performance. If management are to employ their efforts to match such performance effectively they also need to know in just which areas of performance the other company is ahead of

* Usually referred to by the initials I.F.C.

them. A company may waste considerable management time investigating those matters in which it is doing well (e.g. labour efficiency, selling) before discovering that, say, material is being uneconomically used. A good comparison scheme then will not only compare overall performance but also performance in as many facets of the business as is practical.

4. Main forms of comparison. The following are among the main measures of comparison:

(*a*) Return on capital.
(*b*) Percentage profit on sales.
(*c*) Capital turnover (*i.e.* sales/capital employed).
(*d*) Percentage to sales of:

(*i*) production cost;
(*ii*) selling and distribution cost; and
(*iii*) administration cost.

(*e*) Ratio of sales to:

(*i*) current assets;
(*ii*) fixed assets.

(*f*) Ratio of:

(*i*) current assets to current liabilities;
(*ii*) liquid assets to current liabilities.

(*g*) Technical measures, *e.g.* direct labour hours per £ sales; material cost per unit produced.

5. Initial requirements for an I.F.C. scheme. Before an I.F.C. scheme can be expected to operate successfully the following requirements must be met:

(*a*) *Participants must be assured that their data will be kept confidential.* This is often the greatest problem arising when introducing a scheme. It is inevitable that the people involved in compiling the comparison reports will often be working with confidential data. As the participating companies will usually be competitors the importance of confidentiality is obvious. A solution to this problem is discussed in **6** below, though it should be noted that where the participants are all subsidiary companies under a holding company this problem does not arise and the introduction of I.F.C. therefore is very much easier.

(*b*) *The participants must form a relatively homogenous group.* Inter-firm comparisons can only be meaningfully made between companies engaged in similar work. If such a group of companies does not exist—if, for example, you are the sole manufacturer of waterproof socks for cold-footed ducks—then apart possibly from the general measure of return on capital there can be no valid I.F.C.

(c) *There must be a uniform costing system.* Unless all data is classified in a uniform manner, comparisons will be distorted. If, for example, one participant classifies the Works Manager's salary as administration overheads and another participant classifies it as factory overheads, then comparison between participants where this cost is involved will be misleading. Distortion will similarly arise if participants use different methods of computing depreciation. To avoid these difficulties uniform costing must be employed. (Uniform costing is discussed in Chapter XXIII of *Cost Accountancy*, W. M. Harper, Macdonald & Evans.)

6. Solution to problem of confidentiality. The problem of confidentiality can be solved in the following way:

(a) A neutral body can be set up to collect the data and prepare reports. This body would be charged with maintaining full secrecy. Often such a neutral body can be formed within a trade association.

(b) Ratios only should be published in the reports, never the absolute figures. This helps prevent identification of companies in the report from the size of the figures (*e.g.* the biggest participant would otherwise be identifiable simply from the biggest figures).

(c) If ratios would still enable participants to be identified (*e.g.* the most mechanised company would normally be identifiable by the lowest direct-labour-cost-per-unit figure), then each participant could be presented with a report that showed only his own ratios as compared with averages for the group, or better still, with medians and quartiles for the group.

7. Use of ratios. Apart from maintaining secrecy, it is better to use ratios than absolute figures when comparing performance. A larger company may make more profit than a small company, but if its ratio of profit to capital employed is lower than that of the small company it is almost certainly lower in performance achievement.

CENTRE FOR INTERFIRM COMPARISON LTD

As an example of I.F.C. in practice, we will briefly examine in this section the approach made by the Centre for Interfirm

'PYRAMID' OF RATIOS FOR GENERAL MANAGEMENT

This is an example of ratios used in comparisons for general management. The ratios are meant to show those at director level.

(a) *how* the overall performance of the business – measured by return on capital – compares with other firms.

(b) *why* it differs – as indicated by carefully chosen subsidiary ratios.

In an actual comparison in any industry, the set of ratios used is modified and extended to suit the industry's particular needs – e.g. the division of costs may be different; and it is usual to give more detailed information on causes of differences in the ratios which appear at the bottom of the pyramid below.

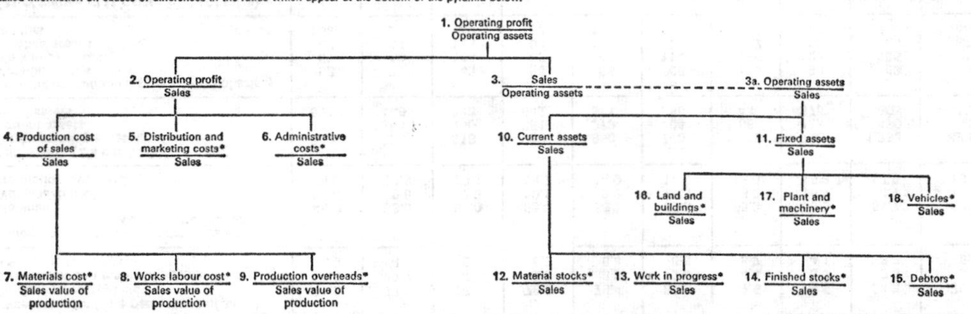

* Explanatory ratios relating to possible reasons for interfirm differences in this ratio are used in an actual comparison.

The key ratio which sums up the firm's success is its return on capital (operating profit/operating assets). This is selected as the primary ratio because it reflects the earning power of the operations of a business. A favourable ratio will indicate that a company is using its resources effectively, and will put it in a strong competitive position. A firm's operating profit/operating assets depends first of all on two other important relationships (ratios) namely that between its operating profit and its sales, and that between its sales and its operating assets.

Ratio 2 shows *what* profit margin has been earned on sales, whilst ratio 3 shows *how often* the margin has been earned on assets in the year. In fact, if you multiply ratio 2 by ratio 3 you will arrive at ratio 1.

Ratio 3 shows how many times assets have been turned over in a year. Ratio 3a expresses asset utilisation in an alternative form by showing the assets required per £1,000 of sales.

Thus the return on operating assets of a firm depends upon the relationship between its ratios 2 and 3, and this in turn depends on the relationships between its sales and its profits (and therefore its costs, shown on the left-hand side of the pyramid), and between its sales and its assets (shown on the right-hand side). By working systematically down the 'pyramid', a firm taking part in a comparison can therefore track down specific areas of business operations which are responsible for differences between its overall success (return on capital) and that of other firms.

FIG. 23.—*Interfirm comparison: pyramid of ratios for general management, devised and used by the Centre for Interfirm Comparison Ltd*

A brief example of interfirm comparison – using the pyramid of ratios for general management

This example is intended to show the way in which the pyramid ratios for a comparison are presented, and how conclusions may be drawn from them. The actual figures used are hypothetical, but are typical of the results found by the Centre for Interfirm Comparison in its work in many industries. In practice a comparison normally covers more firms, and also includes more detailed data, such as those referred to in 'What the Comparison Shows Firm 6'

RATIOS	FIRMS									
	1	2	3	4	5	6	7	8	9	MEDIAN*
1. Operating profit/Operating assets	20.2	17.9	14.3	13.3	11.3	7.9	7.4	3.9	3.1	11.3
2. Operating profit/Sales	18.2	14.9	13.1	11.9	10.9	6.1	7.6	3.1	3.8	10.9
3. Sales/Operating assets (times)	1.11	1.20	1.09	1.12	1.04	1.30	0.98	1.25	0.81	1.09
Departmental costs (as a percentage of sales)										
4. Production costs	71.3	77.1	77.4	79.6	79.4	84.2	82.5	89.5	84.3	79.6
5. Distribution and marketing costs	4.9	3.7	4.1	2.2	3.3	2.9	4.4	3.3	3.6	3.6
6. Administrative costs	5.6	4.3	5.4	6.3	6.4	6.8	5.7	4.1	8.3	5.7
Production costs (as a percentage of sales value of production)										
7. Materials cost	46.9	53.0	51.0	50.8	56.2	55.3	56.3	56.5	51.7	53.0
8. Works labour cost	10.4	9.8	7.3	10.1	9.2	12.3	8.2	16.1	14.7	10.1
9. Production overheads	14.0	14.3	19.1	18.7	14.0	16.6	18.0	16.9	17.9	16.9
Asset utilisation (£'s per £1,000 of sales)										
3a. Total operating assets	899	833	918	893	960	770	1,019	798	1,233	899
10. Current assets	328	384	400	351	379	404	589	423	430	400
11. Fixed assets	571	449	518	542	581	366	430	375	803	518
Current asset utilisation (£'s per £1,000 of sales)										
12. Material stocks	58	73	43	58	86	65	129	80	68	68
13. Work in progress	51	90	104	63	44	114	164	122	135	104
14. Finished stocks	66	94	123	63	118	77	147	60	84	84
15. Debtors	153	127	130	167	131	148	149	161	143	148
Fixed asset utilisation (£'s per £1,000 of sales)										
16. Land and buildings	240	87	102	143	156	88	47	73	299	102
17. Plant and machinery	316	343	407	389	413	267	363	289	486	363
18. Vehicles	15	19	9	10	12	11	20	13	18	13

*The median is the middle figure for each ratio

WHAT THE COMPARISON SHOWS FIRM 6

Suppose you are the managing director of firm 6 in the table opposite, what does the comparison show you?

1. First and most important, the comparison gives you for the first time an objective yardstick of your firm's overall success—as indicated by the standing of your operating profit/operating assets ratio against that of other firms.

The comparison of this primary ratio shows that your firm's overall success and effectiveness is *less* than that of the majority of the others, since your return on assets is only 7·9% against the median of 11·3%.

2. What is the cause of your low operating profit/operating assets? Comparison of ratios 2 and 3 shows that the reason is your low operating profit/sales—your figure of 6·1% is the third lowest of the figures shown. On the other hand, your turnover of assets, ratio 3, is the fastest of any firm. It therefore seems that you should first of all investigate the cost ratios which determine your operating profit/sales.

3. Looking at the departmental cost ratios, you find that your production cost, ratio 4, is high; your distribution and marketing cost, ratio 5, is below-average; and your administration cost, ratio 6, is above-average.

4. The causes of your high ratio 4 are shown by ratios 7 and 8 to be your high materials and labour costs, In the actual comparison, you have access to more detailed comparative data which throws further light on these points—it shows (*a*) that your high materials cost is related to your high materials waste ratio, and (*b*) that your high works labour cost is caused, not by high wages, etc. costs per employee, but by low volume of output per employee.

5. Turning to the asset utilisation ratios you see that your fast turnover of total operating assets (ratio 3) is expressed in a different way by ratio 3a, which shows that you have the lowest figure of total operating assets per £1000 of sales. You will see from ratio 11 that this is because you have the lowest figure of fixed assets in relation to sales. This is, in turn, mainly due to your low plant and machinery ratio (ratio 17). Incidentally, the fixed asset figures used in this comparison are based upon comparable valuations.

The more detailed data available (not shown in this table) indicate that the average age of your plant is greater than that of most other firms; and that your value of plant and machinery per works employee is below the average. The comparison therefore suggests that your low labour productivity (a major cause of your high production costs) may be due to the fact that your plant is not sufficiently up to date.

6. Your current asset utilisation ratios (ratios 12 to 15) show that most of your current asset items are about average—with the exception of your work in progress, ratio 13, which is above the average. This seems to provide another indication of the need for altering your production arrangements so as to allow a faster throughput.

FIG. 24.—*Interfirm comparison: sample report*

Comparison Ltd, a body set up in 1959 by the British Institute of Management in association with the British Productivity Council to organise interfirm comparison schemes.

8. "Pyramid" of ratios. The underlying framework of the Centre's method of making comparisons is the "pyramid" of ratios shown in Fig. 23. Comparison starts with the most fundamental ratio of all—profit to capital employed (*see* I, **18**)—which is then analysed into component ratios, *i.e.* profit to sales, and sales to capital employed. These ratios are in turn analysed, as are the resulting sub-ratios, such continuous breakdown proceeding until further detailed analysis is impossible or irrelevant. The advantage of this type of scheme is that participants can see at just which points competitors having a better return on capital are superior, and, moreover, the extent to which any factor contributes to the higher return.

9. Reporting. An example of the sort of report that is given an individual participant is shown in Fig. 24. The actual ratios detailed in any particular scheme can, of course, be tailored to the requirements of the participants, as can the length of period covered and the frequency of the reports.

10. Advantages of using the Centre. The advantages of using the Centre for I.F.C. schemes are as follows:

(*a*) The problem of confidentiality is solved as the Centre is completely neutral.

(*b*) The Centre employs experienced professional men on its staff. Continuous professional attention raises the quality of schemes to above that which would otherwise be attainable.

(*c*) The experience gained by the Centre in running many and varied schemes is of very great value in running each individual scheme. Past errors are not repeated and professional skills are improved.

PROGRESS TEST 21

Principles

1. Why is I.F.C. valuable? (**1, 2**)
2. What are the initial requirements for an I.F.C. scheme? (**5**)
3. Why are ratios used so much in I.F.C.? (**6, 7**)
4. What are the advantages of a group of companies using an organisation such as the Centre for Interfirm Comparison Ltd? (**10**)

PART SIX

DATA-PROCESSING

THE "raw material" of the management accountant is data, and in modern businesses the volume of data that must be dealt with is considerable. Part of the management accountant's task, therefore, is to see that these data are efficiently handled. To aid him in this work a variety of types of office equipment have been developed: adding machines, book-keeping machines, copying equipment, duplicating equipment, filing systems, etc. However, the most versatile and powerful of all aids are those that handle data electronically. In this part of the book we look at these types: first, the traditional punched card installation, and second, the most modern and most powerful of all data-processing devices, the computer.

CHAPTER XXII

PUNCHED CARD DATA-PROCESSING

ALTHOUGH computers are taking over more and more of the data-processing work previously done on punched card equipment some work can still be carried out more economically on such equipment. Moreover, punched card equipment is sometimes used in conjunction with computers. For these reasons (quite apart from others) punched card data-processing is briefly examined in this chapter.

BASIC PRINCIPLES

1. The underlying idea of punched card operations. The idea underlying the whole of modern punched card operations is that if a *hole* is punched in a card which is subsequently passed between a metal roller and a wire brush, then when the hole is reached the brush comes into momentary electrical contact with the roller. This is called *sensing* and with the appropriate wiring this contact will result in the flow of electric current that will operate switches controlling the workings of a complex machine. By arranging for different switches to be operated depending on the *position of the hole* in the card, a vast combination of machine responses can be controlled.

2. The punched card. Clearly in a system such as this everything depends upon the *punched card*. Modern cards are usually designed so that holes can be punched in 80 separate columns across the card and in 12 separate rows down the card (*see* Fig. 25), ten of the rows being used for the digits 0 to 9 (while the other two rows are used for 10*d*. and 11*d*.). If it is desired to punch alphabetic letters into the card then this can be done by punching two holes in a column and coding the two-hole arrangements (*e.g.* A = 12 and 1; B = 12 and 2; etc.).

3. One card per item. To ensure that data is effectively handled one card is used per "item." What constitutes an "item" depends on the system, but in payroll work, for example, a separate card is usually used per employee. Although such a card will record all sorts of information (*e.g.* clock number, hours worked, gross pay, PAYE, age, sex) a separate card will be used for each individual employee.

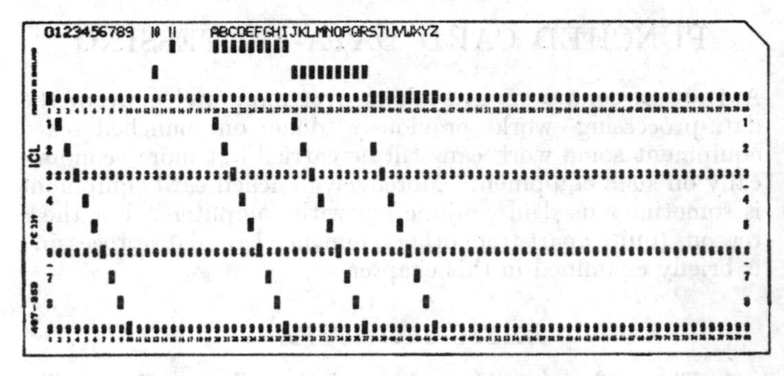

FIG. 25.—*An 80-column punched card*

4. Punched card fields. The columns on a punched card are arranged in groups called *fields*. Each field records a factor of information. For example, one field could record an employee's clock number. If no clock number exceeded four digits, then four columns would be grouped to make this field since any four digits can be punched using four columns. Obviously, with 80 columns on a whole card quite a number of different fields can be designated, and so a considerable amount of information can be punched into a single card.

It is very important to appreciate that a field designated for one set of cards need not relate to a second set. Thus in a set of cards used for payroll work the first four columns may be the clock number field, but in a set used for sales accounting the first four columns could be designated as the date field. Punched card equipment is very flexible and can be set up to deal with the particular field arrangement of any specific set of cards.

5. Punching. Clearly the first operation in punched card data-processing is punching the holes in the card. This is done on a machine called a *punch*. The punch-operator takes the document to be "punched" (*e.g.* a sales invoice) and by pressing keys similar to typewriter keys punches holes in the card according to the information on the document. In this operation the card passes under the punching head one column at a time and so the information is punched in a predetermined order according to the order of the fields on the card.

6. Verifying. It is very important that the card is punched absolutely correctly since any error at this point will be repeated in every piece of work subsequently done using that card. For this reason the punching is checked on a *verifier*. This piece of equipment is very similar to the punch except that instead of punching a hole it tests to see if a hole exists. To verify, another operator takes the punched card and the original document from the punch-operator, sets the card in the verifier, and then "re-types" the information from the original document. If the test shows there is a hole where the operator's "typing" indicates one should be, then nothing happens. If, however, there is no hole then the machine stops and the operator checks to see if she struck a wrong key or if the hole punched earlier by the punch-operator is wrongly placed (in which case a new card is punched). This procedure ensures that unless both punch and verifier operators "type" exactly the same data in exactly the same place the verifier stops. Since it is virtually impossible for both operators to punch exactly the same *wrong* information at exactly the same place, a card that has been verified can be taken as correct.

7. Sorting. A pack of cards which has been verified is a pack of cards that is known to be correct but is in no particular order. To put the cards in order (*e.g.* clock number or invoice number order) a *sorter* is used. This is a machine that simply takes a pack of cards and sorts them into numerical order (though actually it can only sort on one column at a time, so if the field is one of four columns the pack has to be put through the sorter four times before the whole pack is finally in correct order throughout).

8. Tabulating. The heart of punched card data-processing is the *tabulator*. This is a complex machine, able to sense holes in all columns simultaneously, that takes a pack of punched cards and prints information from them either on a wide roll of blank paper or on sets of pre-printed stationery (*e.g.* sales invoices). This information includes:

(*a*) Data from any part of an individual card (though the data need not appear on the tabulation in the same order as it appears on the card).
(*b*) Cross-addition and/or subtraction of figures on a card.
(*c*) Sub-totals for any group of consecutive cards (*e.g.* total sales in a given sales area).
(*d*) Grand totals for the entire pack of cards.
(*e*) Print-out in alphabetic letters of coded alphabetic data.

Tabulators are very flexible and in order to set up the tabulator to carry out the procedures required for any given task, a *plug-board* is prepared. The idea behind a plug-board is similar to that of a manual telephone exchange: using a large panel of sockets and plugs, any desired pattern of electrical connections can be wired up. This enables the operator to prepare the plug-board so that the tabulator will follow one desired series of operations out of potentially an almost infinite number.

AUXILIARY EQUIPMENT

In addition to the basic equipment discussed above there is certain auxiliary equipment that very much increases the effectiveness of a punched card data-processing unit.

9. Interpreter. An *interpreter* is a piece of equipment that simply prints on the top of a punched card the data punched in the card. Though a skilled operator can easily read the numbers punched in a card by the position of the holes, alphabetic data are not so easily read and it is often useful to have the punched letters printed on the card.

10. Gang punch. When punching a set of cards there are very frequently some data that are common to all the cards, *e.g.* the payroll date on a set of employee payroll cards. To save the punch operator's time punching these data over and over again, the whole set of cards can be loaded into a *gang punch*. This punch is set with the common data and it will then automatically punch these data into every individual card.

11. Summary punch. After a tabulation has been prepared it is often necessary to punch special cards that record the various sub-totals thrown up by the tabulation (*e.g.* a card for each sales area recording the total sales of the area). To save a punch operator's time punching those cards a special punch called a *summary punch* can be connected to the tabulator and set to punch such cards automatically as the tabulator computes the totals.

12. Collator. If two packs of cards are to be merged into one pack, all in the correct order, then this can be done on a machine called a *collator* (though note that each pack must have its cards in the correct order at the beginning).

Collating often occurs in punched card data-processing, for frequently the system adopted uses *master packs*, *i.e.* packs containing a punched card for every known item in a particular category, and carrying certain basic data relevant to the item (*e.g.* a card for every customer carrying his name, address, code number, sales area, trade discount rate; or a card for every item in stock carrying its description, code number, location, standard price, re-order level, re-order quantity, etc.). When an operator wants, for example, to price the stores issues made on a given day, she will arrange to have the issued quantities punched on new cards and then she will withdraw ("*pull*" is the technical term) the relevant master cards from the master pack and collate these with the newly punched cards. The cards will then be processed in pairs to obtain the required information, and at the end of the operation the master cards are sorted from the other cards and then collated with the master pack so as to return them to their original positions.

Apart from straightforward collating, a collator can also be used to:

(*a*) check if a set of cards is in the correct order;
(*b*) extract any designated card.

13. Calculator. So far there has been no reference to multiplication and division. Originally punched card equipment could only handle additions and subtractions, but nowadays electronic calculators can be connected to tabulators so that multiplication and division can also be carried out.

Calculators are commonly used to compute values of items. For example, if the price and quantity issued of a material is punched in two fields on a card, then the tabulator will sense this information, transfer it to the calculator, which will carry out the multiplication and transfer the value of the issue back to the tabulator. This value will then be printed on the tabulation or punched into a new field on a new card by the summary punch (along, of course, with the data from all the other fields).

14. Scope of punched card operations. Students often ask, what work can be carried out on punched card equipment? The only answer to this question is, all that it is capable of doing. Once the student appreciates the function of each piece of equipment it is wholly up to him to use his imagination to devise a series of operations that will enable him to run the punched card installation to obtain from it the information he particularly wants. The individual machines are like tools in the carpenter's tool-box, and just as the range of the carpenter's creations depends primarily on his ingenuity in using his tools, so the range of the operator's data-processing achievements depends primarily on his ingenuity in using his equipment.

PROGRESS TEST 22

Principles

1. What is a punched card? (2)
2. What is a "field"? (4)
3. Distinguish between punching and verifying. (5, 6)
4. What can a tabulator do? (8)
5. Explain the function of the following pieces of equipment:
   (*a*) Sorter. (7)
   (*b*) Interpreter. (9)
   (*c*) Gang punch. (10)
   (*d*) Summary punch. (11)
   (*e*) Collator. (12)
   (*f*) Calculator. (13)

CHAPTER XXIII

COMPUTERS: HARDWARE

DISCUSSION of computers can be conveniently dealt with in two parts—one relating to "hardware" and the other "software." *Hardware* is the term given to the actual equipment, electronic circuits and so forth used in a computer installation. *Software* relates to the systems to be used in conjunction with the hardware and also the records needed for operation, particularly programs. In this chapter we look at hardware, and in the next at software.

HOW A COMPUTER WORKS

1. Moving data by pulses. If you were to take a long piece of string, fasten one end to a post, hold the other so that the string was just taut and then pluck the string, you would see a "pulse" travel quickly down the string to the post. If the string were long enough (and you were quick enough) you would be able to pluck the string three or four times before the first pulse reached the post. You would then see a succession of pulses travelling down the string, one after the other.

It requires little imagination to appreciate that if somebody was stood by the post you could send him information by using the pulses in a form of code. Such a code may be rather long and cumbersome, but you could achieve considerable coding efficiency if you could arrange for pulses to be spaced regularly, for then the *absence* of a pulse in its expected position could give information to the receiver. Indeed, it is possible to code sixteen different pieces of information into a 4-pulse interval if desired, as is shown in Fig. 26.

In computers electrical pulses, similarly coded, are used in the same way to transfer data from one end of a wire to another. To envisage this part of computer operation, then, you simply imagine a series of pulses with gaps indicating no-pulses all travelling (at the speed of light) along the wires of a computer, the order of pulses and no-pulse gaps being coded data.

2. How to store pulses. Now an electric pulse in a wire, like a pulse in a piece of string, only exists as long as it is travelling. A problem arises, therefore, if we wish to store such a pulse.

There are a number of solutions to this problem but at the moment the most usual solution is to store it *magnetically* in the same way as a tape-recorder enables us to store sound. Imagine

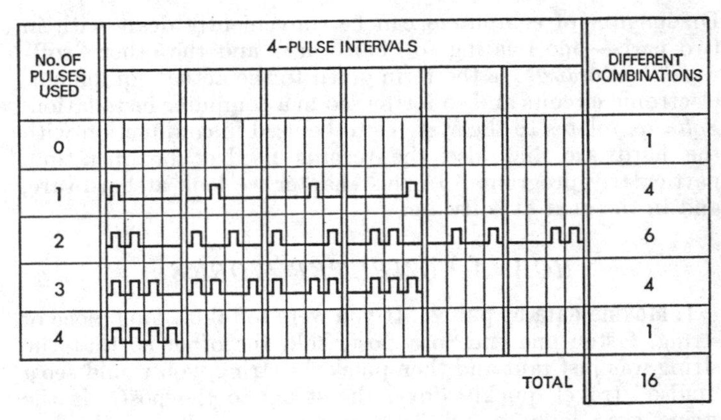

Fig. 26.—*Coding sixteen pieces of information into a 4-pulse interval*

the electrical pulses travelling along a wire at the end of which is a small coil. Immediately below the coil is a moving surface made of potentially magnetic material. Now when a pulse passes through the coil it momentarily makes the coil into a magnet, which in turn magnetises the small area of material immediately below it. There is, therefore, a magnetic "spot" at that point. As the surface is moving the spot moves on so that when a later pulse reaches the coil it causes another spot to be "written" further along the surface. In this way a pattern of transitory pulses can be converted into a pattern of magnetic spots that remains as long as we desire (*see* Fig. 27). This process is called *writing*, and the coil a *writing-head*, and is the exact equivalent of writing down information on a piece of paper.

3. How to read magnetic spots. To convert magnetic spots back into pulses so that data can be transferred to another part of the computer simply entails "playing-back" the magnetic surface, *i.e.* running the surface with the spots on it just below a small coil so that each magnetic spot induces a momentary current in the coil which then emerges in the form of an electrical pulse (*see* Fig. 27). The pattern of such pulses, of course, matches the pattern of the spots exactly. This process is called *reading*, and the coil the *reading-head*. The magnetic spots naturally remain unchanged on the surface, though they can be removed as and when desired.

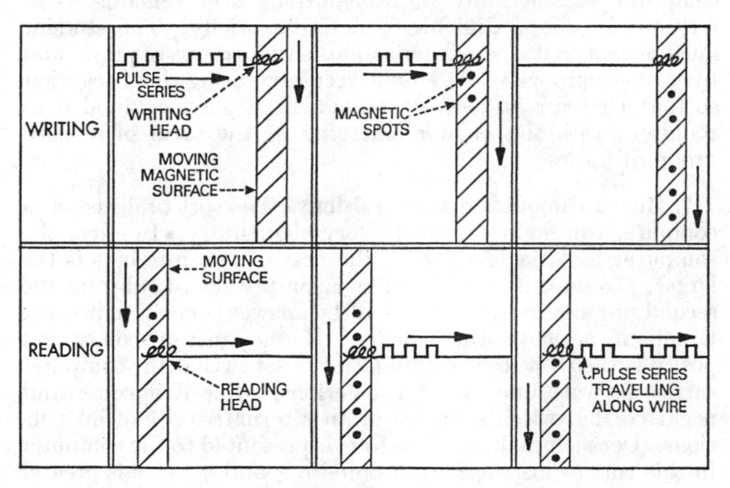

FIG. 27.—*Writing and reading coded pulses*

Both in writing and reading the pattern of pulses matches the pattern of spots exactly.

4. How to change data into pulses. So far we have assumed our data already exist in the form of coded pulses. The next point to consider is how to change ordinary data into electrical pulses.

This can be done quite easily by punching the data as groups of holes in either a *punched card* or a piece of *paper tape*, the positions of the holes reflecting the pulse code we are using. The card or tape is then passed through an *input reader*, a piece of equipment that senses where the holes are and automatically converts them into electrical pulses. These pulses then pass into the computer.

5. How to change pulses into data. We can perform the reverse operation, *i.e.* changing pulses into data, by passing the pulses into a *printer*. This machine automatically decodes groups of pulses and prints the result either as a tabulation or on to sets of continuous stationery.

6. How a computer computes. As yet we have considered only data which stay unchanged. The problem of how the computer can actually do calculations still remains. Unfortunately this is difficult to describe briefly. The student must accept that a computer can take two groups of pulses and by using appropriate electronic circuitary bring them together so that they are added, subtracted, multiplied or divided as required, with the answer emerging in the form of a third group of pulses.

7. How a computer makes decisions. The sort of decisions a computer can make are really very elementary. In effect the computer is "asked" to see if the first of two numbers is the larger. To do this the computer is simply set to subtract the second number from the first—if the answer is positive it is the larger, if negative the smaller. If the answer comes out positive, then a switch is automatically set so that the computer carries on with one set of instructions, while if it comes out negative the switch switches in an alternative set of instructions. Decision-making, therefore, is presented to the computer in this sort of instruction: "Compare x and y. If x is greater than y then take step a; if not take step b."

8. Summary: what a computer can do. A computer can really do no more than the above. Summarising, we can say that a computer can:

(*a*) Read information punched as holes in cards or tape and convert this into coded electrical pulses which can travel to any part of the computer.
(*b*) Store the pulses in the form of magnetic spots.
(*c*) Re-convert stored pulses into moving electrical pulses.
(*d*) Electronically manipulate two groups of pulses so that a mathematical operation is carried out.
(*e*) Make decisions by comparing two groups of pulses and setting switches within itself according to which group is the larger.
(*f*) De-code pulses and print out data.

COMPUTER STORAGE

A feature of the application of computers to commercial work is the very large volume of data involved. Consequently storage of data is a major consideration and this section looks at computer storage.

9. Addresses. Whenever we put data into store it is very important to know just where we have put them so that we can find them again when wanted. This means carefully designating each piece of physical space into which we can magnetically write data with a location reference number. This reference number is called the *address* of the space. When we give an address to the computer it will write data into, or read data from, that physical location. A single address will, of course, be physically large enough to contain the complete series of pulses needed to encode a single piece of information (*e.g.* an employee's clock number).

10. Magnetic tape storage. Magnetic tape storage is very similar to the "storage" of sound on an ordinary tape-recorder. Data are simply written onto a continuously moving magnetic strip. There is, of course, unlimited capacity in this form of storage since one can use as many tapes as one needs to store all the data. Tapes, incidentally, are also the cheapest type of storage. Unfortunately they suffer from the great disadvantage that the order of reading from the tape is strictly laid down; if the piece of data required is at the end of the tape then the whole tape must be run through before the data are accessible. By computer standards this takes an unacceptable length of time. However, tape storage is particularly valuable where stored data are to be fed into the computer in the stored order (*e.g.* feeding employee data into the computer for a payroll procedure in employee clock number order).

An address in tape storage designates the position along the tape of the very small strip of magnetic surface that carries a specified piece of stored data.

11. Drum or disc storage. To avoid the problem of having to run through a whole length of tape to read out a specific piece of data, such data is written on the surface of a revolving drum, or alternatively a series of rotating discs. Writing and reading heads are positioned over such a surface so that the whole area can be utilised. Addresses are small strips on this surface. Essentially, then, the time it takes to reach data in a specified address is simply the length of time it takes for the drum (or disc) to revolve until the address comes under the reading head. Since drums can revolve 50 times a second or more, the time waiting (the *access time*) is much less than with tapes. However, such storage is clearly limited by the total drum (or disc) surface area. It is also relatively much more expensive.

12. Core storage. Fast though the access time is with drum storage, it is still not fast enough for some types of operations. For these operations *core storage* is used. In this form of storage the reading and writing of data is done slightly differently, each magnetic spot being, in fact, a tiny magnetised ferrite ring. Thousands of these rings are arranged on a network of wires (to form a "core") in such a way that any individual ring can be written (magnetised) or read almost instantaneously. In such a core an address is a specified group of rings.

This type of storage certainly minimises access time, but since the equivalent of a magnetic spot is a complete ring, the total amount of data that can be stored is even more limited than in the case of drum storage. Also it is very much more expensive.

13. Punched cards and paper tape as a form of storage. In addition to these more specialised forms of storage it should be appreciated that data can be stored quite effectively on punched cards or paper tape. If a form of summary punch is attached to the computer, then any results can automatically be punched into cards or tape.

This form of storage is cheap and has unlimited capacity. It is, however, cumbersome. Transferring data back to the computer is relatively very slow with this form of storage, and the actual physical space taken up per unit of data is very much greater with cards and paper tape than with magnetic tape. However, there are occasions when such a form of storage is fully warranted.

COMPUTER EQUIPMENT

We are now in a position to look at the more basic pieces of equipment in a computer installation.

14. Central processing unit. The *central processing unit* is the heart of a computer. Everything is built around it. Essentially it contains the core store (and the drum store, too, if drum storage is used) and the circuits for the mathematical computations. To look at, it is rather like a set of metal lockers.

15. Tape-decks. A *tape-deck* is a piece of equipment used for writing and reading magnetic tapes. It looks very like an over-sized tape-recorder.

Often in commercial work we need to shuffle data from one tape to another. Most installations, therefore, have more than one tape-deck, four being a popular number.

16. Input equipment. Basically there are two forms of data input (apart from magnetic tape input): punched cards and punched paper tape. If cards are used then a *card reader* is required; if tape, then a *paper tape reader*.

17. Output equipment. Usually output is handled by a *printer* that prints information on sets of continuous stationery or long rolls of wide paper. Additional equipment can be attached to the installation so that alternatively the output information can be punched into cards or paper tape. Such a form of output will, of course, only be used for data that ultimately will be needed for feeding into the computer again. It is, in fact, a form of data storage and much cheaper, though less convenient, than magnetic tape.

18. Console. A *console* is a control desk. It comprises switches to start and stop the computer and the various pieces of equipment linked to it. It has also a display panel so that the operator can see just what the computer is doing at any given moment. Attached to the console is a typewriter which types out messages from the computer to the operator. Typical messages are facts such as that the card reader has come to the end of a pack of cards, or that a piece of information necessary for continued operation is missing. The typewriter can also be used by the operator to type special information straight into the computer.

19. Additional equipment. Apart from the basic equipment discussed above, computer installations use various pieces of additional equipment. Punches and verifiers (XXII, **5** and **6**) are clearly essential and interpreters (XXII, **9**) are also useful. Computers employed on special work will, of course, have special equipment such as television screens, etcetera.

20. On-line, off-line equipment. As already explained, the heart of a computer is the central processing unit. Any equipment which is electrically connected to this unit, either by direct wiring or through some other piece of equipment directly wired, is said to be *on-line equipment*. Equipment not so connected (*e.g.* punches and verifiers) are said to be *off-line equipment*. Some pieces of equipment may be on- or off-line depending on the installation. For example, printers, usually on-line, may in fact be off-line if their speed is unacceptably slow—the output data first being transferred to fast on-line tapes, which are then run through a tape-deck on a totally separate tape-deck/printer circuit at printer speed.

PROGRESS TEST 23

Principles

1. What, in terms of basic elements, can a computer do? (**8**)
2. How does a computer make decisions? (**7**)
3. What is an address? (**9**)
4. Distinguish between the following forms of storage:
   (*a*) Magnetic tape. (**10**)
   (*b*) Drum or disc. (**11**)
   (*c*) Core. (**12**)

5. What are the five basic pieces of equipment in a computer installation? (**14–18**)
6. Explain what is meant by the following terms:
   (*a*) Hardware. (Introduction to chapter)
   (*b*) Writing-head. (**2**)
   (*c*) Access time. (**11**)
   (*d*) On-line. (**20**)

CHAPTER XXIV

COMPUTERS: SOFTWARE

IT is one thing to have a computer, quite another to operate it. We now consider the operations side—the "software"—with which the management accountant will be closely involved.

PROGRAMS

1. The program. So far throughout our discussion we have taken one thing for granted—that operations are carried out in an orderly manner. Obviously, electrical pulses must not race all around the computer writing into, and reading from, any address that happens to be available while the printer is printing everything it can and the central processing unit adding everything all together. Order must be imposed on the entire system and this is done by *switching*. Series of pulses are switched to the appropriate addresses in the core store or on the magnetic tape, the reading- and writing-heads are switched on and off at the appropriate moments and so is the printer. In fact, every piece of on-line equipment and every component in such equipment must be carefully controlled by switching. Now to carry out any operation the switches must be turned on and off in a definite predetermined order. This predetermined order of switching is called *the program*. The program, therefore, specifies which switches are to be set at each and every stage of the operation.

2. Giving the program to the computer. Having prepared a program, the next thing is to give it to the computer. This is done in exactly the same way as ordinary data are given: the program is coded, the coded program punched into cards or paper tape and fed into the computer through the input reader. The computer will automatically store the program in part of the core store and, after the data which are to be processed have been fed in, will proceed step by step through the stored program.

3. Computer language. Computer *language* is really just another name for computer *code*. However, the whole field of computer languages is complicated by the fact that operating a computer requires so many detailed but repetitive switching instructions that a hierarchy of codes has had to be evolved to enable work to be handled effectively. Thus at the lowest level there must be a code (called *machine language*) that enables us to specify each individual switching instruction. Then groups of such instructions that always occur in a specific operation can themselves be coded. The process can be carried yet a stage further by coding groups of these latter operations so that in the end one symbol can instruct the computer to perform quite complex and relatively long series of operations. Codes at these higher levels of the hierarchy are, not surprisingly, referred to as *higher languages*.

4. Sub-routines. When processing commercial data we frequently find that a particular enterprise may wish to follow a particular procedure over and over again, *e.g.* compare stock balance in hand of each item with its re-order level. To avoid re-writing the program over and over again we can write it once, store it on magnetic tape, and then arrange for the computer to incorporate this special piece of program into the main program as and when we call for it. Such a special piece of program is called a *sub-routine* and sub-routines will obviously be prepared for any operation likely to repeat itself.

5. Software "equipment." Again we have been working throughout this chapter on an assumption—namely, that the computer can translate programs from one language to another and can also insert sub-routines into a main program as required. However, the computer is quite incapable of doing this on its own initiative; it must be specially programmed to manipulate these programs, *i.e.* we need programs to tell the computer how to handle programs. These "higher" programs are termed *software equipment* and form an important part in setting up a computer installation.

HOW TO USE A COMPUTER

Now we have seen in outline how a computer "works," we can consider how it can be used.

6. A super-clerk. Essentially a computer should be regarded as a completely moronic but highly accurate and very, very fast clerk. Indeed, so fast is our "clerk" that he can add thirty thousand ten-digit figures in less than one second. His accuracy is guaranteed, as all computers have special built-in checks to ensure both accurate computations and accurate recordings. The only place for error lies in the inadequacy of the instructions given by his human employer.

7. The "moronic" catch. Unfortunately there is just one catch—our "clerk" is moronic, so moronic in fact that he has to be told everything in the minutest detail. It is rather as if one had to instruct a human clerk to move his hand three inches forward, lower it two inches, close first finger and thumb on pen, raise hand three inches, move it four inches to inkwell—all this and we have not even got ink on the nib yet, let alone made an entry!

If such a clerk needs to be so completely instructed, the question arises as to whether he is worth employing. In the case of a computer he is, for once told how to carry out a simple repetitive task (*i.e.* given a sub-routine), he never forgets. Although it takes a long time detailing the instructions for this one task, if it is repeated over and over again then the time saved in the long run more than pays the cost of the initial instructions.

8. How to think about computer operations. If we are considering whether a computer can tackle a job or not, all we need to do is think in terms of instructing a clerk to add this, subtract that, and so on, while looking up figures and recording answers in various files. Addresses, in fact, should simply be regarded as file names or numbers, so in an "add" operation for example we would say: "Add the figure in file name X (1st address) to that filed under Y (2nd address) and record the answer in file Z (3rd address)." Remember *all* figures must be filed somewhere; the computer has no head in which it can keep numbers (though it is interesting to note that, just as we use a scrap of paper to jot down intermediate figures in a calculation, so computers have an address called *the accumulator* that serves just this function).

A computer, like a clerk, can make decisions. If you say to it: "See if the figure in file P is the same as (or more or less than) the figure in file Q; if it is, then follow this set of instructions, and if not, follow that set of instructions," the computer will subtract the first figure from the second and, according to whether the answer is zero or otherwise, select the appropriate set of instructions.

Basically, this is all the management accountant needs to consider. How to prepare the program that will instruct the computer to carry out these tasks is not his worry. That is the work of the programmer (*see* **13**).

9. Computer limits. There must, of course, be some limitations on the work you can give the computer. These, however, do not so much depend on the *type* of work as the *capacity* of the hardware. There are only so many core addresses and a very long program that requires more may not be possible to run. Individual addresses also have a capacity limit; each address can only record a limited number of magnetic spots. Any item of data requiring more spots than this creates "filing" difficulties.

A limit is also imposed on work by the fact that preparing programs is a long operation and, if such a program will only be used on rare occasions, then it may be uneconomical to prepare it at all. In other words, there is an economic limitation on the work that can be put on a computer.

10. The golden rule of operation. The golden rule in computer operation is to remember that you should not, as the proverb says, keep a dog and bark yourself. The computer can do a great deal and, to make the most effective use of it, you should let it. This requires considerable imagination in devising ways of getting the computer to do various jobs; humans should only do the work that you cannot possibly envisage putting on a computer economically. But remember, you must spend a long time envisaging.

MANAGEMENT AND THE COMPUTER

Having seen how to use a computer, we can now look at the most important thing of all—where it fits into the enterprise. It is, of course, employed to help management to manage, but this help can only be given if the computer and the personnel involved are properly "slotted" into the enterprise. In Fig. 28

the relationship between the manager, the computer and all the required personnel links is shown diagrammatically. This section discusses the elements shown in that Figure.

11. The manager. To manage an enterprise properly it is vital for managers to have *relevant information about events as quickly and as economically as possible.* Each manager must decide what he feels is relevant to enable him to do his job, be it weekly sales or output statistics, daily absenteeism or cost variances, for example. Whatever it is, he must clearly state his requirements.

12. The systems analyst. Knowing the manager's requirements, it is the task of the systems analyst to design a system that will give the manager what he wants.

(*a*) *Designing the system.* To do this the analyst will need to investigate the type of events to be reported and decide what, where and how the data describing them shall be recorded. This may mean arranging for a clerk to fill in a carefully-designed form from which punched cards or tape are later prepared, or it may mean arranging for a piece of equipment (*e.g.* a cash register) to punch a paper tape recording data at the moment the event occurs, so that the tape can be fed into the computer input-reader without need for further coding and punching. Often data recorded in one place or emerging after some computer processing operation can be further used in three or four other contexts and the systems analyst must bear such possible uses in mind so as to minimise work and time and, therefore, costs.

(*b*) *Recording the system design.* When the systems analyst has designed his system, he must then advise the next person in the chain, the programmer, of the steps to be taken in handling the data. This is often best done in the form of a *flow chart*, which is simply a list of steps laid out diagrammatically so that it is clear what happens at each stage and which step follows which (*see* Appendix II). The analyst then designs all the necessary forms, stipulates other recording methods and concludes by publishing a clear and detailed manual of instructions for all the people involved in the system.

13. The programmer. The task of the programmer is to turn the analyst's data-handling steps into a set of instructions for the computer. The actual working of the system does not concern him at all, he concentrates only on instructing the

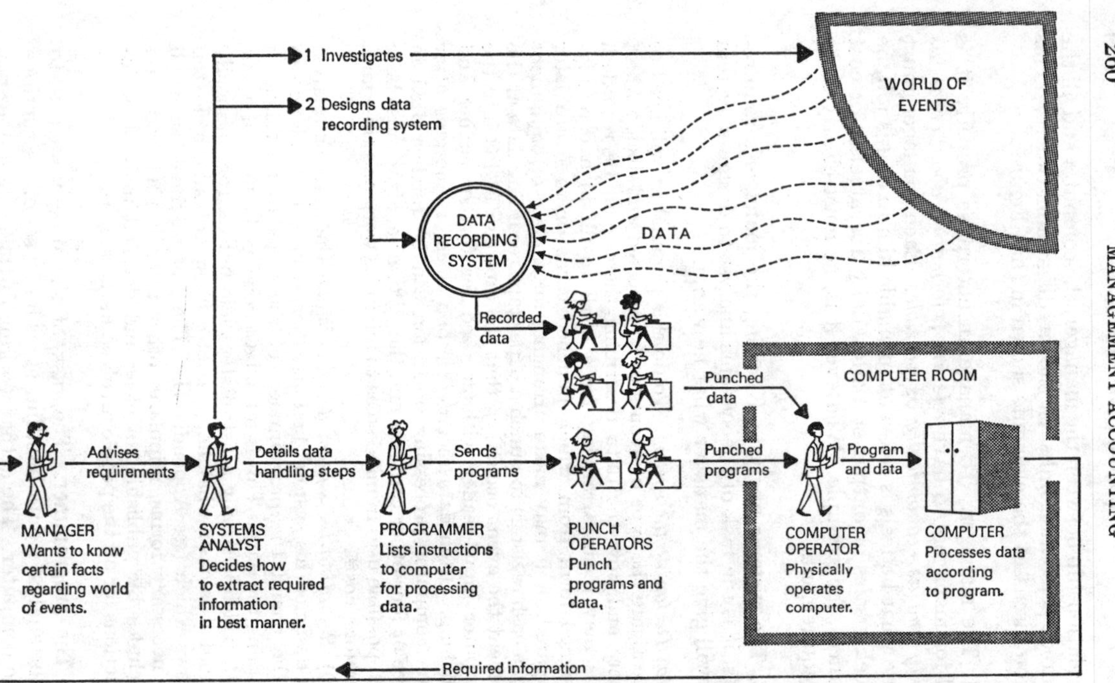

FIG. 28.—*The relationship between the manager, the computer personnel and the computer*

This diagram outlines the whole sequence of the relationships involved in using a computer to provide management with information.

computer to do what the analyst wants it to do. The programmer knows his computer well and knows just what software is available to help him. He can, therefore, decide how best to program the computer for maximum effectiveness. He accepts its moronic character and patiently lists all the instructions needed, using, of course, an appropriate computer language and marking which sub-routines must be inserted in the main program, and where.

14. The computer. Once the program is written and punched, the computer takes over. First the program is converted into machine language either on punched cards, punched paper tape or magnetic tape. Then, when the input data (*i.e.* data relating to events) have been collected and punched, both the program and data are fed into the central processing unit. In due course (sometimes only a fraction of a second later) the printer prints out the information the manager wants in the form in which he wants it.

15. The computer operator. Although a computer can carry out many complex technical functions, it is quite immobile. Somebody, therefore, must be made available to load and unload tapes and cards and generally act as arms and legs to the computer. Such a person is called a *computer operator*. Essentially his work will entail loading and unloading tapes on to the tape-deck; loading and unloading cards or paper tape on the input reader; removing and dispatching all print-out material; carrying out all instructions given to him by the computer via the console typewriter; taking the initiative if the computer runs into any sort of trouble; and generally over-seeing the operation of all pieces of equipment so that should any break down or begin to malfunction, the computer engineer can be quickly called.

16. Feasibility studies. Computers often fascinate managers. However, before management buy a computer, they should remember that the hardware *and its installation* involve complex physical factors; that system analysing involves much brainpower; and that programming requires much time. All this means high costs and that it is essential that any proposal to buy or use a computer should be preceded by a very detailed study. Even if a computer is already owned, any proposal to put a particular operation on to it should still be preceded by such a study.

Such studies are termed *feasibility studies* and involve:

(*a*) Analysing the existing system and provisionally designing one that could be used in conjunction with the computer.

(*b*) Assessing the programming requirements. If a computer is not already owned, this will be some guide as to the type and size of computer required. If a computer is owned, this will indicate if it is capable of handling the work, and for how many hours it will be engaged on the work.

(*c*) Estimating the costs and determining the benefits. This will indicate whether the proposition is an economic one or not, though of course, it is difficult to put values on some kinds of benefits, such as speed or reliability.

PROGRESS TEST 24

Principles

1. What is a program? (1)
2. What are:

   (*a*) computer languages? (3)
   (*b*) sub-routines? (4)

3. Within the data-processing context, distinguish between:

   (*a*) a manager; (11)
   (*b*) a systems analyst; (12)
   (*c*) a programmer; (13)
   (*d*) a computer operator. (15)

4. What are feasibility studies and what do they involve? (16)

APPENDIX I

PRESENT VALUE TABLES

PRESENT VALUE OF THE FUTURE £ IN n YEARS TIME AT 2%—24%.

n	2%	4%	6%	8%	10%	12%	14%	16%	18%	20%	22%	24%
1	0·9804	0·9615	0·9434	0·9259	0·9091	0·8929	0·8772	0·8621	0·8475	0·8333	0·8197	0·8065
2	0·9612	0·9246	0·8900	0·8573	0·8264	0·7972	0·7695	0·7432	0·7182	0·6944	0·6719	0·6504
3	0·9423	0·8890	0·8396	0·7938	0·7513	0·7118	0·6750	0·6407	0·6086	0·5787	0·5507	0·5245
4	0·9238	0·8548	0·7921	0·7350	0·6830	0·6355	0·5921	0·5523	0·5158	0·4823	0·4514	0·4230
5	0·9057	0·8219	0·7473	0·6806	0·6209	0·5674	0·5194	0·4761	0·4371	0·4019	0·3700	0·3411
6	0·8880	0·7903	0·7050	0·6302	0·5645	0·5066	0·4556	0·4104	0·3704	0·3349	0·3033	0·2751
7	0·8706	0·7599	0·6651	0·5835	0·5132	0·4523	0·3996	0·3538	0·3139	0·2791	0·2486	0·2218
8	0·8535	0·7307	0·6274	0·5403	0·4665	0·4039	0·3506	0·3050	0·2660	0·2326	0·2038	0·1789
9	0·8368	0·7026	0·5919	0·5002	0·4241	0·3606	0·3075	0·2630	0·2255	0·1938	0·1670	0·1443
10	0·8203	0·6756	0·5584	0·4632	0·3855	0·3220	0·2697	0·2267	0·1911	0·1615	0·1369	0·1164
11	0·8043	0·6496	0·5268	0·4289	0·3505	0·2875	0·2366	0·1954	0·1619	0·1346	0·1122	0·0938
12	0·7885	0·6246	0·4970	0·3971	0·3186	0·2567	0·2076	0·1685	0·1372	0·1122	0·0920	0·0757
13	0·7730	0·6006	0·4688	0·3677	0·2897	0·2292	0·1821	0·1452	0·1163	0·0935	0·0754	0·0610
14	0·7579	0·5775	0·4423	0·3405	0·2633	0·2046	0·1597	0·1252	0·0985	0·0779	0·0618	0·0492
15	0·7430	0·5553	0·4173	0·3152	0·2394	0·1827	0·1401	0·1079	0·0835	0·0649	0·0507	0·0397
16	0·7284	0·5339	0·3936	0·2919	0·2176	0·1631	0·1229	0·0930	0·0708	0·0541	0·0415	0·0320
17	0·7142	0·5134	0·3714	0·2703	0·1978	0·1456	0·1078	0·0802	0·0600	0·0451	0·0340	0·0258
18	0·7002	0·4936	0·3503	0·2502	0·1799	0·1300	0·0946	0·0691	0·0508	0·0376	0·0279	0·0208
19	0·6864	0·4746	0·3305	0·2317	0·1635	0·1161	0·0829	0·0596	0·0431	0·0313	0·0229	0·0168
20	0·6730	0·4564	0·3118	0·2145	0·1486	0·1037	0·0728	0·0514	0·0365	0·0261	0·0187	0·0135
21	0·6598	0·4388	0·2942	0·1987	0·1351	0·0926	0·0638	0·0443	0·0309	0·0217	0·0154	0·0109
22	0·6468	0·4220	0·2775	0·1839	0·1228	0·0826	0·0560	0·0382	0·0262	0·0181	0·0126	0·0088
23	0·6342	0·4057	0·2618	0·1703	0·1117	0·0738	0·0491	0·0329	0·0222	0·0151	0·0103	0·0071
24	0·6217	0·3901	0·2470	0·1577	0·1015	0·0659	0·0431	0·0284	0·0188	0·0126	0·0085	0·0057
25	0·6095	0·3751	0·2330	0·1460	0·0923	0·0588	0·0378	0·0245	0·0160	0·0105	0·0069	0·0046
26	0·5976	0·3607	0·2198	0·1352	0·0839	0·0525	0·0331	0·0211	0·0135	0·0087	0·0057	0·0037
27	0·5859	0·3468	0·2074	0·1252	0·0763	0·0469	0·0291	0·0182	0·0115	0·0073	0·0047	0·0030
28	0·5744	0·3335	0·1956	0·1159	0·0693	0·0419	0·0255	0·0157	0·0097	0·0061	0·0038	0·0024
29	0·5631	0·3207	0·1846	0·1073	0·0630	0·0374	0·0224	0·0135	0·0082	0·0051	0·0031	0·0020
30	0·5521	0·3083	0·1741	0·0994	0·0573	0·0334	0·0196	0·0116	0·0070	0·0042	0·0026	0·0016
35	0·5000	0·2534	0·1301	0·0676	0·0356	0·0189	0·0102	0·0055	0·0030	0·0017	0·0009	0·0005
40	0·4529	0·2083	0·0972	0·0460	0·0221	0·0107	0·0053	0·0026	0·0013	0·0007	0·0004	0·0002
45	0·4102	0·1712	0·0727	0·0313	0·0137	0·0061	0·0027	0·0013	0·0006	0·0003	0·0001	0·0001
50	0·3715	0·1407	0·0543	0·0213	0·0085	0·0035	0·0014	0·0006	0·0003	0·0001	0·0000	0·0000

APPENDIX II

EXAMINATION TECHNIQUE

To pass any examination you must:

1. Have the knowledge.
2. Convince the examiner you have the knowledge.
3. Convince him within the time allowed.

In the book so far we have considered the first of these only. Success in the other two respects will be much more assured if you apply the examination hints given below.

1. Answer the question. Apart from ignorance, *failure to answer the question is undoubtedly the greatest bar to success.* No matter how often students are told, they always seem to be guilty of this fault. If you are asked for a control report, *don't* give a product cost statement; if asked to give the advantages of standard costs, *don't* detail the steps for computing them. You can write a hundred pages of brilliant exposition, but if it's not in answer to the set question you will be given no more marks than if it had been a paragraph of utter drivel. To ensure you answer the question:

(a) *Read the question carefully.*
(b) *Decide what the examiner wants.*
(c) *Underline the nub of the question.*
(d) *Do just what the examiner asks.*
(e) *Keep referring to the question in your mind as you write.*

2. Put your ideas in logical order. It's quicker, more accurate and gives a greater impression of competence if you follow a predetermined logical path instead of jumping about from place to place as ideas come to you.

3. Maximise the points you make. Examiners are more impressed by a solid mass of points than an unending development of one solitary idea—no matter how sophisticated and exhaustive. Don't allow yourself to become bogged down with your favourite hobby-horse.

4. Allocate your time. Question marks often bear a close relationship to the time needed for an appropriate answer. Consequently the time spent on a question should be in proportion to the marks. Divide the total exam marks into the total exam time (less planning time) to obtain a "minutes per mark" figure, and allow that many minutes per mark of each individual question.

5. Attempt all questions asked for. Always remember that the first 50% of the marks for any question is the easier to earn. Unless you are working in complete ignorance, you will always earn more marks per minute while answering a new question than while continuing to answer one that is more than half done. So you can earn many more marks by half-completing two answers than by completing either one individually.

6. Don't show your ignorance. Concentrate on displaying your knowledge—not your ignorance. There is almost always one question you need to attempt and are not happy about. In answer to such a question put down all you *do* know—and then devote the unused time to improving some other answer. Certainly you won't get full marks by doing this, but nor will you if you fill your page with nonsense. By spending the saved time on another answer you will at least be gaining the odd mark or so.

7. If time runs out. What should you do if you find time is running out? The following are the recommended tactics:

(*a*) If it is a numerical answer, don't bother to work out the figures. Show the examiner by means of your layout that you know what steps need to be taken and which pieces of data are applicable. He is very much more concerned with this than with your ability to calculate.
(*b*) If it is an essay answer, put down your answer in the form of notes. It is surprising what a large percentage of the question marks can be obtained by a dozen terse, relevant notes.
(*c*) Make sure that every question and question part has some answer—no matter how short—that summarises the key elements.
(*d*) Don't worry. Shortage of time is more often a sign of knowing too much than too little.

8. Avoid panic, but welcome "nerves." "Nerves" are a great aid in examinations. Being nervous enables one to work at a much more concentrated pitch for a longer time without fatigue. Panic, on the other hand, destroys one's judgment. To avoid panic:

(*a*) Know your subject (this is your best "panic-killer").
(*b*) Give yourself a generous time allowance to read the paper. Quick starters are usually poor performers.
(*c*) Take two or three deep breaths.
(*d*) Concentrate simply on maximising your marks. Leave considerations of passing or failing until after.
(*e*) Answer the easiest questions first—it helps to build confidence.
(*f*) Don't let first impressions of the paper upset you. Given a few minutes, it is amazing what one's subconscious will throw up. This, too, is a good reason for answering the easiest question first; it gives your subconscious more time to "crack" the difficult ones.

REPORT-WRITING IN EXAMINATIONS

9. Purpose of report-writing: in practice. In practice reports are written so that the person reported to receives in a permanent form information which has been selected and presented *with a specific objective in mind.*

Good report-writing involves *clear, logical and attractive presentation of information that is pertinent to the basic objective.* Usually action is taken on the basis of a report, and in order that appropriate action is taken the report must embody these qualities. The extent to which a report aids the achievement of the objective that initially gave rise to its commission is the ultimate measure of the quality of a report.

10. Purpose of report-writing: in examinations. Examiners ask for reports in examinations to see if:

(*a*) Candidates appreciate the qualities needed to write a good report and can embody these qualities in their own writing. In other words, it is a test of lucid, logical and attractive presentation and the ability to select the relevant from the irrelevant.

(*b*) Candidates know their subject. Clearly knowledge (or the converse) of subject matter shows itself in the candidate's report.

(*c*) Candidates know how to lay out a report properly.

11. Report layout. A report should be laid out in the following order:

(*a*) *Heading.* A simple heading for an examination report is as follows:

TO: .....(Person's title).. REPORT REFERENCE:.....

FROM:....(Persons's title).. DATE: ....

COPIES TO: ..(Persons' titles) ....

TITLE

The "Copies to" space enables candidates to indicate that they appreciate which people in the organisation are likely to be affected by the contents of the report.

Titles are sometimes difficult to compose on the spur of the moment, but the attempt shows the examiner that the candidate is aware of the need of a title for a report.

(*b*) *Reason for report.* If possible the first paragraph should outline the reason for the report. The time available for the question will indicate whether this outline should be given or whether a higher priority should be put on getting down to the subject matter.

(*c*) *Main body.* This will usually be the major part of the examination report and will state the findings and arguments in a lucid and logical manner.

(*d*) *Conclusions and/or recommendations.* Candidates should *never* forget this part of the report. It is absolutely essential that some conclusions and/or recommendations are given. This will indicate the extent to which the candidate is able to appreciate the significance of the information he has reported. Often candidates leave the examiners to dig out the conclusions. To be blunt, they won't—they prefer to regard the omission as indicating the candidate's lack of ability to do this himself.

(*e*) *Signature.* A report must be signed. In addition it is usual to add the title of the person signing (*e.g.* Management Accountant). Beware of using "Yours faithfully" (or "Dear Sir", at the beginning). This only applies to reports to *clients*, and even then can be omitted if it is assumed that a covering letter (not given in the answer, of course) is sent with the report.

(*f*) *Appendixes.* These give all the details upon which the main body of the report was built (in practice they often form the bulk of the report). Time in the examination does not usually allow appendixes to be given, though use of an appendix to give specimen figures or suggested form design should be borne in mind.

Finally, note that a good report layout requires *all paragraphs to be numbered.*

12. Report-writing technique.

(*a*) *Length.* The shorter a report, the better—provided all relevant information is given. Brevity not only saves time, it also improves clarity. If an idea can be given in a sentence it is better understood than if two pages are used to express it. This may be paradoxical but it's a psychological fact. Length only keeps a person thinking about it *longer* (which has been the sole function of the last three sentences).

(*b*) *Paragraphs.* Decide before you start writing what each paragraph will contain. This will aid logical writing.

(*c*) *Style.* Keep sentences short. Good reports state facts and opinions tersely.

(*d*) *Technical jargon.* The reader of the report must always be borne in mind and jargon that would not be clearly understood by him should not be used. Candidates should check the question carefully to see what level of sophistication the reader may be assumed to have—some examiners make this a major factor in their questions.

(*e*) *Assumptions.* Some reports require assumptions to be made. Other reports do not, as there is enough "meat" in the question without conjuring up more (though whether the candidate will appreciate this is another matter). As a general rule do *not* make assumptions in your answer unless it is absolutely necessary.

(*f*) *Specimen figures.* If the subject matter allows it, try and give specimen figures. A few simple but well-chosen figures will often make a point much more effectively than a paragraph of writing.

(*g*) *Presentation of data.* When presenting data consider the possible use of tables and graphs. Figures should be presented wherever possible in a comparative form (*i.e.* in adjacent columns, headed, for example "This year/Last year"; "Current/Proposed").

13. Reporting is a form of communication. A report is not an end-product, it is a device for communicating information to somebody who wants to *use* such information. If this person cannot understand it, or is misled by it, or is repelled by its appearance so that he cannot get to grips with it, then no matter how accurate and painstaking the collection and analysis of detail, no matter how comprehensive the arguments, no matter how brilliant the conclusions and recommendations, the writer has failed and *all* his work (not just the writing of the report) is to no avail. After all, the writer alone has the choice of matter to be included, its order, and the words used to express it—the onus is on him for the comprehension of the report. Always remember that:

If the reader hasn't understood, the writer hasn't reported.

14. Practise. Students should now look at other people's reports (*e.g.* model answers) and criticise them. Make a start by criticising this part of the appendix as a *report*. Criticising others will teach the student to look at his own reports with a critical eye.

FLOW-CHARTING

Occasionally the examiner will ask the student to present his answer in the form of a flow-chart, and occasionally the alert student will see for himself that a particular question will be more effectively answered in the form of a flow-chart than by a narrative statement. In either situation it is necessary for the student to know something of flow-charting.

15. Definition. Essentially *flow-charting* is just listing a series of required operations and connecting these listed operations appropriately by arrows. The simplest kind of flow-chart, then, is one prepared in a similar way to that below, which depicts the operations needed to stamp an employee's insurance card:

→ Take employee's card and open it

↓

Ascertain from the bottom right-hand side the class of contribution applicable

↓

Obtain appropriate stamp from the Stamp Book

↓

Stick stamp on the card in the space marked with the relevant week

↓

Cancel stamp with date stamp

↓

Discard card

↓

Look for next employee's card

↓

NOTE: A continuously repetitive cycle can be indicated by an arrow that starts at a later operation and leads back to an earlier operation that starts the cycle. This form of representation is called a *loop*.

16. Parallel procedures. Flow charting is more often and more effectively used where there are parallel procedures. In these cases individual operations are usually recorded in small, rectangular boxes that are connected by the appropriate arrows. As clarity is very much improved if the arrows do not cross each other it does mean that frequently some thought has to be given in advance to the layout of the chart. This form of chart is illustrated in Fig. 29, where a hypothetical material re-ordering procedure is charted.

17. Use with computers. Flow-charts, of course, are very much used in computer work, where it is vital that every step is clearly and logically depicted. In this field there is a whole list of symbols having different meanings which enable quite complex procedures to be charted clearly. Of these symbols the most common after the rectangular box (which is the symbol for a "processing

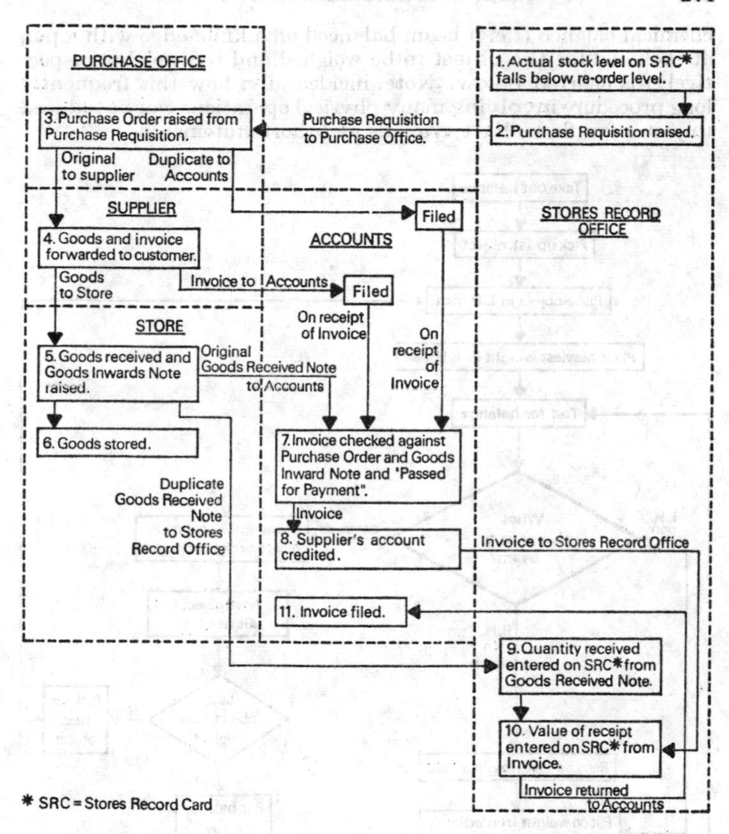

FIG. 29.—*Flow-chart of a material re-ordering procedure*

function") is a *diamond* which is used to depict the need for making a decision. Inside the diamond the question that is at the root of the decision is stated and lines emerging from the points of the diamond are labelled with the various possible answers—the subsequent processes being shown at the end of the appropriate line.

18. Illustration. To illustrate simply this more difficult form of charting, the procedure for weighing a set of objects using a chemical balance (*i.e.* a beam balanced on a knife-edge with a pan at each end for the object to be weighed and the weights respectively) is charted below. Note, incidentally, how this frequently long procedure involving many physical operations can be reduced to just a few flow-chart symbols and short statements.

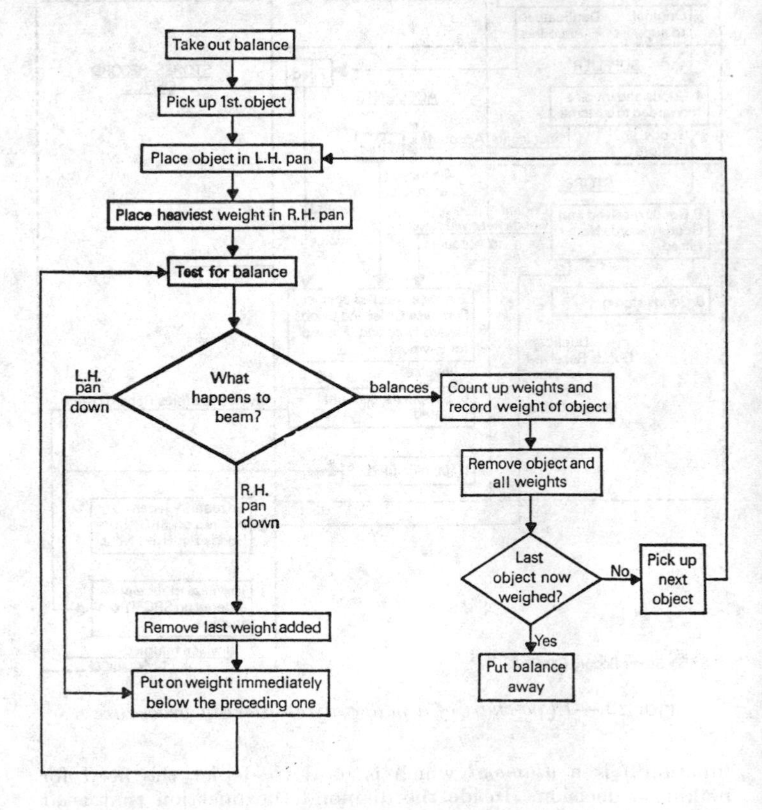

APPENDIX III

SUGGESTED ANSWERS

Progress Test 4

11. The most straightforward method of solving this problem is by use of the projected balance sheet technique. An important point to remember in this question is that fixed assets will need to be replaced regularly—£50,000 worth at the end of the 4th, 12th, 20th year, etc. (since the balance sheet given in the question shows a depreciation provision equal to one-half the fixed assets, these assets must be just halfway through their life) and £70,000 worth at the end of the 8th, 16th year, and so on. The analysis, then, would be as follows (all figures in thousands of pounds):

YEAR:	1st	2nd	3rd	4th	5th	6th	7th	8th	9th	10th	11th
Operating Data:											
Sales	200	220	240	260	280	300	320	340	360	380	*400*
Profit 20%	40	44	48	52	56	60	64	68	72	76	*80*
Tax 50%	20	22	24	26	28	30	32	34	36	38	*40*
Dividend 20%	10	10	10	10	10	10	10	10	10	10	*10*
To Reserves (*a*)	10	12	14	16	18	20	22	24	26	28	*30*
Assets:											
Fixed	120	120	120	120	120	120	120	120	120	120	*120*
Stocks	80	88	96	104	112	120	128	136	144	152	*160*
Debtors	40	44	48	52	56	60	64	68	72	76	*80*
Cash (balancing fig.)	—	9	30	53	28	55	84	115	78	113	*80*
	240	261	294	329	316	355	396	439	414	461	*440*
Capital & Liabilities:											
Capital	50	50	50	50	50	50	50	50	50	50	*50*
Reserves	30	42	56	72	90	110	132	156	182	210	*240*
Debentures	70	70	70	70	70	70	70	70	70	70	—
Tax	20	22	24	26	28	30	32	34	36	38	*40*
Creditors	20	22	24	26	28	30	32	34	36	38	*40*
Depreciation provision	40 (b)	55	70	85(c)	50(d)	65	80	95(c)	40(d)	55	*70*
Overdraft	10	—	—	—	—	—	—	—	—	—	—
	240	261	294	329	316	355	396	439	414	461	*440*
One-half current liabilities	20	22	24	26	28	30	32	34	36	38	*40*

↑ (5th year) *Replace* Fixed Assets £50,000

↑ (9th year) *Replace* Fixed Assets £70,000

(*a*) The net figure after deducting tax and dividend from the profit.
(*b*) Previous provision of £25,000 + one year's new annual depreciation of £15,000.
(*c*) Provision immediately prior to retirement of worn-out assets.
(*d*) Balance of provision after removal of provision for retired assets plus one year's depreciation (£15,000).

As we prepare our analysis we find that any repayment of debentures before the end of the 9th year will result in only £8000 cah remaining at the end of that year, well below half the current liabilities. However, repayment at the end of the 10th year will leave a cash balance of £43,000, *i.e.* in excess of half current liabilities. There is, of course, just the possibility that in replacing the £50,000 worth of plant at the end of the 12th year cash will be reduced below the policy limit, but projecting into the 11th year we find the cash balance is only £10,000 below the combined total of the £50,000 and half current liabilities. Clearly with cash building up at over £30,000 per annum there is no danger and therefore Mr Bencher's debentures should be dated to run for ten years.

NOTES: It will be seen that preparing a set of projected balance sheets is not as big a task as may first appear. Some figures don't change at all and most others follow a pattern (*e.g.* stocks increase by £8000 p.a.) so it is only a moment's work completing a line of the analysis.

(There is, incidentally, a much shorter solution to this problem based on computing a formula for the yearly net cash flow and then applying a short cash flow analysis. The student may like to see if he can find this solution on his own.)

12. As this problem deals with a situation where stability does not establish itself until quite late on, a cash flow approach is considered the best here. The analysis, then, will proceed as shown opposite (all figures in thousands of pounds).

Looking at the analysis we see that a deficit of £186,000 exists at the end of April and this is the worst figure visible. Clearly, then, the worst moment is around the end of April. However, it must be remembered that the creditors for Popular tents must be paid at the end of the first quarter of May. We must, therefore, next estimate the cash deficit that will exist immediately after this payment:

May:	Opening cash deficit	£186,000
	Popular creditors	81,000
	Overheads payable by end of 1st quarter	500
		£267,500
	Deduct receipts from debtors ($\frac{1}{4}$ × £150,000)	37,500
	Deficit end of 1st quarter May	£230,000

Since the bank will provide an overdraft of £50,000 the amount needed to finance the working capital will be £230,000 − £50,000 = £180,000.

	Jan.	Feb.	March	April	May	June
Operating Data:						
Sales—Popular	30	60	90	120	90	90
De-luxe	10	20	30	40	30	30
Purchases (*a*)—Popular	81 (*b*)	81 (*c*)	108	81	81	$67\frac{1}{2}$(*d*)
De-luxe	24 (*b*)	24 (*c*)	32	24	24	20(*d*)
Cash in:						
Debtors—Popular	—	30	60	90	120	90
De-luxe	—	—	10	20	30	40
Total	—	30	70	110	150	130
Cash out:						
Creditors—Popular (*e*)	—	81	81	108	81	81
De-luxe	24	24	32	24	24	20
Salaries	4	4	4	4	4	4
Overheads	—	2	2	2	2	2
Profit	—	—	—	—	—	23 (*f*)
Total	28	111	119	138	111	130
Negative net cash flow to date:						
Opening cash deficit	0	28	109	158	186	147
plus cash out	28	111	119	138	111	130
	28	139	228	296	297	277
less cash in	—	30	70	110	150	130
Closing cash deficit	28	109	158	186	147	147

(*a*) Purchases are at cost price, of course.
(*b*) Cost of sales for January + stock build-up equal in quantity to February sales (i.e. cost of sales January + cost of sales February).
(*c*) Purchases for stock equal in quantity to next month's sales.
(*d*) July sales are Popular £75,000 and De-luxe £25,000. Purchases in June, then, are equal to cost of sales for these sales. (Actually these figures come too late to be relevant.)
(*e*) Paid at end of 1st quarter of the month.
(*f*) Profit for the six months (£000s):

Sales (for which payment has been received):	Popular		£390
	De-luxe		100
			490
Cost of Sales:	Popular	£351	
	De-luxe	80	
		431	
Salaries		24	
Overheads		12	467
	Profit:		£23

Progress Test 5

9.

		Cost
Debt:	£500 at 10%	£50
Equity:	£300 at 20%	£60
	£800	£110

Therefore enterprise cost of capital $= \frac{110}{800} \times 100 = 13{\cdot}75\%$

Progress Test 7

8. (*a*) (*i*) The total costs for the two periods can be plotted at 10,000 and 12,000 units respectively. By joining these points and extending the line to the *y* axis, the fixed cost is found to be £28,000. Alternatively, the fixed cost can be found as follows:

	Period 1	*Period* 2	*Difference*
Total material, labour and overheads	£93,000	£106,000	£13,000
Production (units)	10,000	12,000	2,000

∴ 2,000 extra units incurred additional (*i.e.* variable) cost of £13,000

∴ 10,000 units have a variable cost of $\frac{13,000}{2,000} \times 10,000 = £65,000$

But the *total* cost of 10,000 units = £93,000 (*see* above)

∴ The fixed cost must be 93,000 − 65,000 = £28,000

(*ii*) See chart below when break-even = 8000 units

(*b*) See chart below where (*i*) break-even = 8800 units.

(*ii*) The plan will obviously not be worth operating as long as the new total cost exceeds the old. This situation holds until a production level of 11,600 units is achieved (*i.e.* on the graph the new total cost line lies above the old until they meet at this point). Therefore, unless a minimum sales of 11,600 units can be achieved the new plan should not be put into operation.

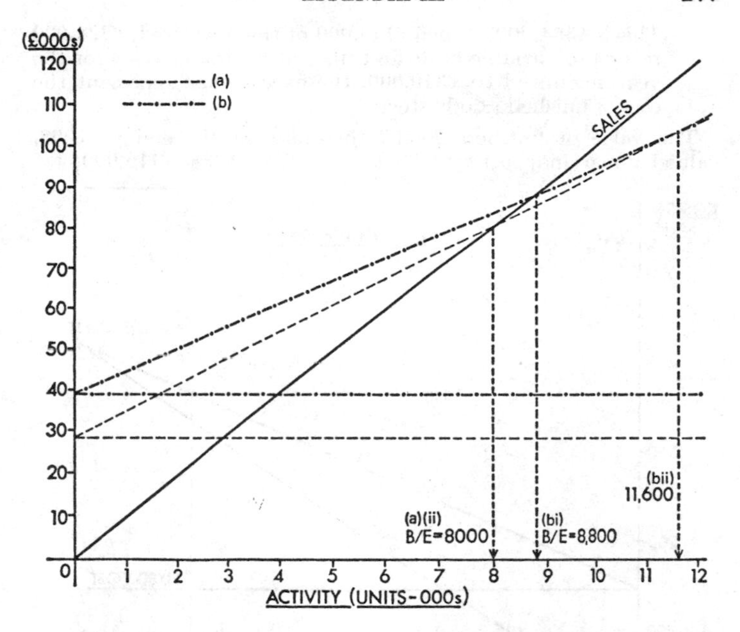

NOTE: In examinations the examiners almost invariably want mathematical-type questions answered on a basis of pure break-even theory.

9. This problem is solved taking the following steps:

(*a*) Prepare the break-even chart with appropriate axes (*see* Chart below).

(*i*) Insert the fixed cost line at £140,000.

(*ii*) Find the break-even point. This is simply £336,000 + 25% = £420,000. Plot this point on the graph. (At the break-even point sales and total costs are the same, of course.)

(*iii*) Join the break-even point to the origin. This gives the "sales" curve.

(*iv*) Join the break-even point to vertical axis at the point where the fixed cost line cuts the axis. This gives the "total cost" curve.

(*b*) As we now have a complete break-even chart it only remains to read off the total cost of sales at the £336,000 sales level.

This is £364,000. Since £140,000 of this was fixed, £224,000 related to variable costs and since also variable costs for the year amounted to £340,000, the excess must represent the cost of finished goods stock.

The value of finished goods, therefore, at the end of 1968, valued at marginal cost was £340,000 − £224,000 = £116,000

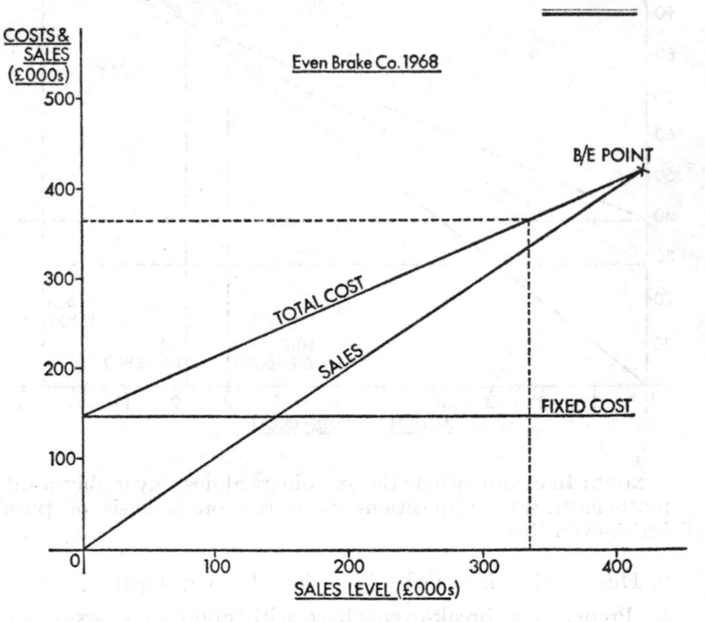

Progress Test 8

7. (*a*) Since Profit = Contribution − Fixed costs, then Contribution = Profit + Fixed costs, *i.e.* in this case £60,000 brings in a contribution of £5000 + £15,000 = £20,000. At the break-even point contribution from sales equals fixed costs. As £20,000 contribution came from £60,000 sales, then £15,000 contribution will come from $\frac{£15,000}{£20,000} \times £60,000 = £45,000$

Therefore, break-even point = £45,000

(*b*) At break-even point the contribution equals the fixed costs. Therefore £80,000 sales brought in a contribution of £20,000 and so the P/V ratio is 25%. With a P/V ratio of 25%, sales of

£100,000 will bring in a total of £25,000 contribution; and after deducting fixed costs of £20,000 the profit remaining is £5000.

(*c*) Again sales of £20,000 brings a contribution equal to the fixed costs, *i.e.* £10,000. Therefore the P/V ratio is 50%. Since profit is all the contribution earned above the break-even point, the £5000 profit equals the contribution from sales above break-even. With a P/V ratio of 50%, a contribution of £5000 is earned from £10,000 sales. Therefore total sales are £10,000 + sales at break-even = £10,000 + £20,000 = £30,000

8. (*a*) Current contribution = Profit + Fixed overheads
= £30,000 + £130,000 = £160,000

(*b*) Contribution from home sales (50% capacity)

$$= \frac{50^*}{80} \times 160{,}000 = £100{,}000$$

Contribution from overseas sales

= Contribution from home sales − 10% discount on sales

$$= 100{,}000 - \frac{1}{10}\left(\frac{50}{80} \times 320{,}000\right)$$

$$= 100{,}000 - 20{,}000 = £80{,}000$$

∴ Total contribution from home and overseas sales = £180,000

	% *Capacity*	
(*c*) Contribution from home sales (as in (*a*))	80	£160,000
Contribution from overseas sales (as in (b))	50	80,000
	130	£240,000

Penalties:

Extra fixed costs to gain extra 10% capacity	£20,000	
Overtime premium to meet remaining 20% capacity requirement $\frac{1}{2}\left(\frac{20}{80} \times 40{,}000\right)$	£5,000	25,000
Net Gain		£215,000

Clearly (*c*) is the most profitable alternative as it gives the enterprise the maximum contribution.

* Note again that both marginal costs and contribution are always in direct proportion to sales. If sales then drop from 80% capacity to 50%, contribution will fall to $\frac{50}{80}$ths of what it was before.

9. (*a*) In view of the scarcity of labour, labour hours are obviously a key factor. Since any new work undertaken by the company will entail diverting labour from the standard product (for which there is a heavy demand) the first thing that must be done is find the contribution per hour sacrificed by such a diversion:

Standard product:

Selling price of product			£10
Marginal cost:	Materials	£4	
	Labour: 2 hr at £0·50	1	5
	Contribution		5
	Contribution per labour hour		£2·50

(*b*) The next step is to determine whether to make or buy the special component in the event of accepting the contract:

Make cost for component:

Materials	£20
Labour: 12 hr at £0·50	6
Opportunity cost: 12 hrs at £2·50	30
Total	£56

Since this component can be purchased for only £50, the company should buy it rather than make it.

(*c*) Knowing the component will cost £50, the cost of the contract can now be computed:

Contract cost:

Materials	£190
Special component	50
Labour: 200 hr at £0·50	100
Opportunity cost: 200 hr at £2·50	500
Total	£840

Since the total cost, including lost contribution from the 100 standard units to be displaced, is less than the contract price of £900, the contract should be accepted.

(*d*) *Conclusion:* Management, therefore, will be advised to accept the contract and buy the component from an outside supplier. Company profit as a result will be £900 − £840 = £60 higher.

NOTE: The fixed costs given in the question are, in fact, irrelevant to the solution.

Progress Test 9

4.

Alternative: Volume of production and sales p.a. (units)	*Old Product* 5,000		*New Product* 20,000*	
Income per year		£50,000		£80,000
Direct material cost per year	£5,000		£30,000	
Additional fixed cost per year	—	5,000	3,000	33,000
Net differential income†		£45,000		£47,000

Since new product shows highest net differential income it should be manufactured in lieu of the old product.

* Since the labour time per unit of the new product is only a quarter that of the old, four times as many units can be made in a year.

† No other figures are needed to determine the net differential income as all other amounts (labour and normal fixed costs) remain unchanged. The unrecovered tooling cost is quite irrelevant (though if the tools had any scrap value this would have been a credit to the *new* product).

5. Limit of own production—200 tons material = 100 halves.

Alternative: Sales	*Both halves made* 100 units		*R.h. halves bought* 200 *units*	
Sales at £200 per unit		£20,000		£40,000
Assembly costs at £20 per unit	£2,000		£4,000	
Transport costs	—	2,000	400	4,400
Net differential income* (excluding cost of bought halves)		£18,000		£35,600

Since the relative differential income when the halves are bought (excluding purchase price) is 35,600 − 18,000 = £17,600, then the foundry could afford to pay up to £17,600 for these halves.

∴ since 200 right-hand halves will be required, maximum price will be $\frac{17,600}{200}$ = £88 per R.h. half.

* Casting costs do not enter the analysis for whichever alternative is selected they will be the same, *i.e.* 200 halves will be cast in either event.

Progress Test 10

4.

Alternative	*Existing Machine**	*New Machine**
Cash In: †		
Receipts from production	£50,000	£60,000
Residual value	4,000	2,000
From sale of existing machine	—	10,000
	+£54,000	+£72,000
Cash Out:		
Cash running costs	45,000	30,000
Purchase of new machine	—	30,000
	−£45,000	−£60,000
Net cash flow	+£9,000	+£12,000

* Take one alternative at a time and consider what cash would actually flow in and out if that alternative were the one selected.
† Take all figures over the full life of the project, *i.e.* five years.

Since the net cash flow from the new machine is higher than that from the existing, the correct decision is *to replace the existing machine.*

Finally, note that the book value of £24,000 for the existing machine does not enter the computation anywhere. It is important to appreciate that book values relate to book-keeping only and *have no relevance whatsoever in decision-making.* Only actual current and future economic values should be used in this type of work.

Progress Test 11

7. (a)

	Machine *Units per annum*		*Present* 8,000		*A* 8,000		*B* 12,000	
Annual Net Cash Flow	Sales			48,000		£48,000		£72,000
	Costs: Materials		£8,000		£8,000		£12,000	
	Variable		12,000		6,000		15,000	
	Fixed*		4,000		7,000		11,000	
	Advertising		—		—		2,000	
	Total			24,000		21,000		40,000
	Annual NCF			+24,000		+ 27,000		+ 32,000
DCF Analysis	*Year*	*Discount Factor* (10%)	*NCF*	*PV*	*NCF*	*PV*	*NCF*	*PV*
	0.	1·000	−85,000†	−85,000	−100,000	−100,000	−110,000	−110,000
	1.	0·909	+24,000	+21,800	− 27,000	+ 24,500	+ 32,000	+ 29,050
	2.	0·826	+24,000	+19,800	+ 27,000	+ 22,300	+ 32,000	+ 26,400
	3.	0·751	+14,000‡	+10,500	+ 17,000‡	+ 12,750	+ 22,000‡	+ 16,550
	4.	0·683	+24,000	+16,400	+ 27,000	+ 18,400	+ 32,000	+ 21,850
	5.	0·621	+24,000	+14,900	+ 27,000	+ 16,750	+ 32,000	+ 19,850
	Net present value			£−1,600		£−5,300		£+3,700

* After deducting depreciation (since this is not a cash cost).

† The re-sale value, not the book value, must be used since keeping present machine in effect means sacrificing the cash that could be obtained from its sale.

‡ After deducting the £10,000 overhaul costs in year 3.

(*b*) If no overhaul in year 3 is required, then all three machines have constant annual net cash flows from year 1 onwards. Buying (or retaining) one of the machines, therefore, is equivalent to buying a five-year annuity of an amount equal to the annual net cash flow. The yield, then, is the percentage return that makes the present value of the annuity equal to the initial cost of the machine. Now the present value of £*a* annuity = £*a* × *PV* of £1 annuity. Since this must equal initial machine cost, we can write:

$$£a \times PV \text{ of } £1 \text{ annuity} = \text{Initial machine cost}$$
$$\therefore PV \text{ of } £1 \text{ annuity} = \text{Initial machine cost} \div £a.$$

We use this equation in respect of each of the machines:

Present machine:	*PV* of £1 annuity	= 85,000 ÷ 24,000	= £3·52
Machine A:	*PV* of £1 annuity	= 100,000 ÷ 27,000	= £3·71
Machine B:	*PV* of £1 annuity	= 110,000 ÷ 32,000	= £3·44

Since each "annuity" is to run for five years we merely examine the tables for *PV* of £1 annuities for five years and determine the yields. These, it can be seen, to the nearest per cent are as follows:

Present machine — 13%
Machine A — 11%
Machine B — 14%

Progress Test 12

The methods used in the first two answers given here were chosen to illustrate how decision-making problems can be solved by applying decision-making principles in a less conventional manner. The student should always endeavour to pinpoint the essence of a problem and solve it by logical analysis rather than by standardised procedure. Indeed, the ability to do this is probably the main distinction between the able management accountant and a person simply holding that title.

5. The solution to this question clearly involves maximising the contribution and since space is the key factor, this means maximising the contribution per counter. The procedure is, though, complicated by the sudden changes of product contribution in different circumstances. However, the following is a possible method of solution:

(*a*) First we find the standard product contribution:

Product	*Selling Price new pence*	*P/V Ratio*	*Turnover*	*Standard Counter Contribution (S.P. × P/V × turnover ÷ 100)*
A	200	25%	336	£168
B	40	25%	1,320	132
C	80	25%	1,020	204
D	12½	30%	320	120
E	20	25%	3,840	192
F	12½	20%	12,000	300
G	100	25%	576	144
H	400	50%	30	60
I	100	30%	600	180
J	50	30%	1,040	156

(*b*) To find the maximum counter contribution we must first look at the Front Counters, then the Main Store and finally the

AREA LOCATION	PRODUCT	COUNTER CONTRIBUTION (£)				
		1st counter	*2nd counter* (one-half 1st counter)	*3rd counter* (one-third 1st counter)	*4th counter* (one-quarter 1st counter)	*5th counter* (one-fifth 1st counter)
Front Counters	A	504				
	B	396				
(1st counter	C	612(*2*)	306			
contribution =	D	360				
3 × Standard)	E	576(*3*)	288			
	F	900(*1*)	450			
	G	432				
4 counters	H	180				
available	I	540(*4*)				
	J	468				
Main	A	336(*5*)	168			
Store	B	264(*9*)	132			
(1st counter	C	*	204(*11*)	136		
contribution =	D	240(*10*)	120			
2 × Standard)	E	*	192(*13*)	128		
	F	*	300(*7*)	200(*12*)	150	
10 counters	G	288(*8*)	144			
available	H	120				
	I	*	180(*14*)			
	J	312(*6*)	156			
Basement	A	*	84(*15*)	56		
(1st counter)	B	*	66			
contribution =	C	*	*	68(*19*)	51	
Standard)	D	*	60			
	E	*	*	64		
	F	*	*	*	75(*17*)	60
	G	*	72(*18*)	48		
counters	H	60				
available	I	*	*	60		
	J	*	78(*16*)	52		

* Allocated in different area.

Basement. In the lay-out above figures are only inserted as they become relevant to the analysis. Note that the italic numbers in brackets indicate the order in which products are allocated counters. Also note that once a counter has been filled all figures relating to that counter status (*i.e.* 1st, 2nd, 3rd, etc.) become inapplicable to the rest of the analysis.

Now after the 19th selection it is clear that every product has been included in the allocation except H. To comply with the company policy of carrying all products, the 20th product selected must therefore be H, and it is to be allocated a basement counter.

(*c*) Finally we simply write out the allocations, add the contributions and deduct the fixed costs:

Location	*Order of selection*	*Product*	*Contribution* (£)
Front Counters	1	F	900
	2	C	612
	3	E	576
Main Store	4	I	540
	5	A	336
	6	J	312
	7	F	300
	8	G	288
	9	B	264
	10	D	240
	11	C	204
	12	F	200
	13	E	192
	14	I	180
Basement	15	A	84
	16	J	78
	17	F	75
	18	G	72
	19	C	68
	20	H	60
	Total contribution		5581
	Less Fixed costs		4000
Maximum potential monthly profit			£1581

6. The existence of hours as a key factor in this question indicates that a solution could be approached by maximising the

contribution per hour. However, a quicker way is to apply a somewhat more sophisticated differential costing technique.

First note that it always pays the company to manufacture a component rather than sub-contract it and have idle time, since the marginal costs of all components are less than the sub-contract prices. Therefore whichever components are sub-contracted, profit is only maximised when the factory is working at its capacity of 50,000 hours. This in turn means that whatever sub-contracting is done, the combined labour and variable overheads will *always* be 50,000 × (60p + 40p) = £50,000. If this figure is added to the fixed cost of £60,000 we see that whatever alternative is selected we will always have constant costs of £110,000 in respect of labour and overheads, and therefore these factors can be ignored in our analysis.

All this means that we need only take into consideration material costs and sub-contract prices. Note next that if the company makes a component as against sub-contracting it, it saves the difference between the material cost and the sub-contract price. Such a saving, however, is only obtained at the expense of using valuable key factor hours. This shows that profit will be maximised *by maximising the savings per hour*. This approach will underlie our solution to this question.

(*a*) Note that currently the sub-contract price of a complete suite (1 × 50 + 2 × 20 + 4 × 15 = £150) exactly equals the selling price. If, then, we sub-contract all the components the sales income will exactly cover our sub-contract costs no matter how many suites are sold. Let us assume we adopt this approach and at the same time have the factory *working at capacity producing nothing*. Our factory costs will clearly be our constant cost of £110,000 (no material costs will be incurred in such a situation) and our loss, therefore, also £110,000.

Next let us compute the saving we can make by manufacturing components instead of sub-contracting them and find the saving per hour (remember material costs only are the additional factory costs incurred):

	COMPONENT		
	Settee	*Armchair*	*Armless chair*
Sub-contract price saved	£50	£20	£15
Direct material cost incurred	£20	£10	£11
Saving per component	£30	£10	£4
Hours required per component	10	5	1
Saving per hour	£3	£2	£4

Making armless chairs maximises our saving. However, only $8000 \times 4 = 32{,}000$ chairs are required to meet current sales. These chairs will use only 32,000 of our 50,000 hours and so 18,000 hours can be allocated to the next most profitable alternative, namely manufacturing settees. In 18,000 hours 1800 settees will be made, leaving 6200 to be sub-contracted.

The company therefore should manufacture 32,000 armless chairs and 1800 settees, and should sub-contract 6200 settees and 16,000 armchairs.

(*b*) (*i*) Profit = Saving from manufacture *less* constant costs. Now savings while manufacturing armless chairs and settees are at £4 and £30 per component respectively. Therefore profit at current level of sales:

$$(32{,}000 \times £4) + (1{,}800 \times £30) - £110{,}000 = \underline{\underline{£72{,}000}}$$

(*ii*) If sales are unlimited then profit is maximised by manufacturing armless chairs only. Since the saving per hour is £4, the 50,000 hours available will give a total saving of £200,000 which, after deduction of constant costs of £110,000 leaves a profit of $\underline{\underline{£90{,}000}}$

(*c*) If the selling price drops to £139 then it is no longer true that the selling price of a suite exactly equals its sub-contract cost, and indeed selling wholly sub-contracted suites gives a direct loss.

In this case, therefore, let us assume that the factory works to capacity making nothing, selling nothing and sub-contracting nothing. Now if we compute the various material and sub-contract costs of a suite using all the combinations of manufacturing and sub-contracting, deduct these costs from £139 to find the "gain" per suite from each combination, and divide this gain by the total manufacturing hours per suite for the combination, we will obtain a saving per hour figure, and maximising profit simply involves selecting the highest of these. The calculations are as follows:

Combination:	Settees	S	S	S	M	S	M	M	M
	Armchairs	S	S	M	S	M	S	M	M
	Armless chairs	S	M	S	S	M	M	S	M
(S = Sub-contract (M = Manufacture									
Hours:	1 settee	—	—	—	10	—	10	10	10
	2 armchairs	—	—	10	—	10	—	10	10
	4 armless chairs	—	4	—	—	4	4	—	4
Total		—	4	10	10	14	14	20	24
Costs (£)	1 settee	50	50	50	20	50	20	20	20
	2 armless	40	40	20	40	20	40	20	20
	4 armless chairs	60	44	60	60	44	44	60	44
Total		150	134	130	120	114	104	100	84
Gain (£): (£139 − total costs)		−11	5	9	19	25	35	39	55
Gain per hour (£):		Loss	1·25	0·90	1·90	1·80	2·50	1·95	2·30

Here we can see that the combination—manufacture settees and armless chairs and sub-contract armchairs—gives us a maximum gain of £2·50 per hour. Using all the 50,000 hours on this combination,* then, will give us a total gain of 50,000 × £2·50 = £125,000. Deducting the constant costs of £110,000 we are left with a profit of £15,000

* Since 50,000 hours is not divisible by 14 we cannot use all the hours in this way. In actual fact we could employ 49,994 hours on this combination, the remaining 6 hours being perhaps partially used to make 4 armless chairs for a final suite. Note, incidentally, 49,994 hours will enable only 3571 suites to be produced for sale. Thus profit is maximised *by cutting sales by over 50%*.

7. As no figures are given regarding costs and incomes (these being the same for both machines), then the problem is simply, do tax considerations warrant the purchase of a brand-new machine costing £5120 more than a second-hand machine? This really means that a relative cash flow approach is called for (X, **7**). To prepare the analysis, therefore, it is assumed that the second-hand machine is selected and the relative cash payments and receipts that would follow if the new machine was bought instead are detailed. After discounting at 20% the net present value of the relative cash flow is found.

To simplify the analysis lay-out the realisable value of the existing machine is left until after the analysis has been prepared.

Year	New Machine		2nd-hand Machine		Relative Allowance	Relative Tax Payment (b)	Discount Factor (20%)	Present Value
	Book Value (a)	Depreciation Allowance	Book Value (a)	Depreciation Allowance				
0.	£25,600	Grant only	£20,480	£0				£−5,120 (d)
1.	20,480 (e)	£5,120	20,480	{6,144 (c) {5,120	£−6,144	£+5,120 (f)	0·833	+4,265
2.	15,360	3,840	9,216	2,304	+1,536	−2,457·6	0·694	−1,706
3.	11,520	2,880	6,912	1,728	+1,152	+ 614·4	0·579	+ 356
4.	8,640	2,160	5,184	1,296	+ 864	+ 460·8	0·482	+ 222
5.	6,480	1,620	3,888	972	+ 648	+ 345·6	0·402	+ 139
6.	4,860	3,860 (g)	2,916	1,916 (g)	+1,944	+ 259·2	0·335	+ 87
7.						+ 777·6	0·279	+ 216
						Net Present	Value	£−1,541

(a) Book value at beginning of year (except year 0 where amounts are purchase prices).
(b) Tax in respect of allowance of previous year at 40% (except year 1, *see* (f)).
(c) 30% Initial depreciation allowance.
(d) Extra initial cash payment for purchase of new machine.
(e) After deduction of investment grant.
(f) Grant in full.
(g) Book value minus £1000 realised value.

Now this analysis shows that the purchase of a brand-new machine leads to a *NPV* of £−1541. However, £2000 extra would be received in this instance for the existing machine, but this figure would clearly affect the balancing allowance or charge—it can, in fact, be regarded as taxable income here. This £2000 can, then, have its own analysis as follows:

Cash receipt in year 0		*PV* = £+2000
Tax payable in year 1 on £2000 at 40% with 20% discount factor = 2000 × 0·4 × 0·833		*PV* = −666
	NPV	= £+1334

Therefore the overall *NPV* following the acquirement of a brand-new machine rather than a second-hand one is £−1541 + £1334 = £−207. This is still just negative, so on these figures it is better to buy the second-hand machine, though the margin here is very slight.

Progress Test 13

7. (*a*) Budget for month:

Rental	£1,000
Fuel costs—20,000 articles at £0·50 per article	10,000
	£11,000

(*b*) Allowances:

Fuel cost: 14,000 articles at £0·50 per article	£7,000

(*c*) Variances:

Fuel costs: Allowance		£7,000
Actual		7,400
	Variance	£400 (A)

Only the fuel costs are controllable by the foreman. The annual rental is a cost which he clearly will have no authority to alter in any way.

Progress Test 15

8. (*a*) *Profit variance.* First we will compute the profit variance by finding the difference between the budgeted and actual profits:

Budgeted profit			
Budgeted contribution, 500 × £20			£10,000
Less Budgeted fixed costs:	Test	£600	
	Administration	5,000	
	Stores	400	
	Selling	1,000	7,000
Budgeted profit			£3,000
Actual profit			
Sales of 450 Cyberloops			£21,810
Scrap sales, 50 spoiled units			125
			21,935
Costs: Materials—	Opening stock: 4000 × 60p	£2,400	
	Purchases	625	
		3,025	
	Closing stock: 1400 × 60p	840	
	Cost of materials consumed	2,185	
Wages		7,875	
Overheads:	Test	1,820	
	Administration	10,500	
	Stores	2,450	
	Selling	2,790	
		27,620	
Finished goods:	Opening stock: 200 × £26	5,200	
		32,820	
	Closing stock: 350 × £26	9,100	
Cost of sales			23,720
	Net loss		1,785

∴ *Profit variance* = 3000 − (−1785) = £4,785 (A)

(*b*) *Spoilage variance.* Next we will compute the spoilage variance. Since no spoilage was planned the whole loss is the variance.

Units spoiled 50		
Standard cost per unit £26		
Cost of spoilage: 50 × £26	=	£1,300
Less scrap sales: 50 × £2·50	=	125
∴ *Spoilage variance* =		£1,175 (A)

Now we have taken account of the whole of the loss from the 50 spoiled units, other variances must be based on the *actual production of* 650 *units*, *i.e.* from the point of view of such variances it is now irrelevant whether or not any of the 650 units actually manufactured were spoiled or not.

(*c*) *Material price variance*

Allowed cost of actual purchases = 1000 × 60p	= £600
Actual cost	= £625
∴ *Material price variance* =	£25 (A)

Note that 4% of £625 = £25. Therefore the whole of the variance is due to the expected loss of the quantity discount.

(*d*) *Material usage variance.* First let us analyse the movements of physical material:

	Feet
Opening stock	4,000
Purchases	1,000
	5,000
Scrapped	400
	4,600
Closing stock	1,400
Actual usage	3,200

Material usage variance:

Allowed usage = 650 × 5 =	3,250 ft
Actual usage	3,200 ft
Saving	50 ft

∴ *Material usage variance* = 50 × 60p = £30 (F)

(*e*) *Stores loss variance.*
Stores loss variance = 400 × 60p = £240 (A) (*i.e.* the whole of the loss since none was planned).

(*f*) *Labour efficiency variance*

Allowed hours for 650 units	= 650 × 20 =	13,000
Actual hours	=	13,500
Excess hours	=	500

∴ *Labour efficiency variance* = 500 × 50p = £250 (A)

(Note that the extra hours required through this inefficiency would have had to be worked as overtime hours.)

(*g*) *Wage rate variance*

Allowed wages	= 13,500 × 50p =	£6,750
Actual wages	=	£7,875
∴ *Wage rate variance*.......	=	£1,125 (A)

However, this is accounted for wholly by the overtime premium, *i.e.*:

Normal monthly hours	10,000
Absenteeism	1,000
Actual normal hours	9,000
Total hours	13,500
∴ Overtime hours =	4,500

4,500 overtime hours leads to an overtime premium of 4,500 × ½ × 50p = £1125, the whole of the rate variance.

The wage rate variance can be analysed according to the factors that gave rise to overtime, *i.e.*:

Cause of variance	*Hours*	*O/T Premium (at 25p per hr)*
Absenteeism	1,000	£250
Planned extra 100 Cyberloops	2,000	500
Replacement batch of 50 Cyberloops	1,000	250
Labour inefficiency (*see* (*f*) above)	500	125
∴ *Wage rate variance*		£1,125

(h) Overhead expenditure variances

Service	*Activity Unit*	*Actual Activity*	*Standard Activity Price*	*Allowed Variable Cost*	*Fixed Cost*	*Total Allowance*	*Actual Cost*	*Variance*
Test	Test hours	315	£4	£1,260	£600	£1,860	£1,820	£40 (F)
Administration	Dir. Lab. hr	13,500	40p	5,400	5,000	10,400	10,500	100 (A)
Stores	Points	1,015*	£2	2,030	400	2,430	2,450	20 (A)
Selling	Units sold	450	£4	1,800	1,000	2,800	2,790	10 (F)
							Total	£70 (A)

* Stores actual activity:	*Points*
Batches guillotined: 13 at 25 points a batch	325
Cybersheet issues: 3200 ft at 1 point per 5 ft	640
Spoiled Cyberloops: 50 units at 1 point per unit	50
Total	1,015

(i) Variable overhead efficiency variances

Service	*Activity Unit*	*Allowed Activity per Cyberloop*	*Allowed Activity for 650 Cyberloops*	*Actual Activity*	*Difference*	*Standard Price*	*Variance*
Test	Test hr	½	325	315	10 hr (F)	£4	£40 (F)
Administration	Dir. lab. hr	20	13,000	13,500	500 hr (A)	40p	200 (A)
Stores	Points	1½	975	1,015	40 points (A)*	£2	80 (A)
						Total	240 (A)

* Difference accounted for as follows:

50 spoiled units at 1 point each, unallowed for in standard	=	50 points
Less 50 ft Cybersheet at 1 point for 5 ft saved on issue	=	10 points
		40 points

NOTE: There can be no efficiency variance for selling as activity in that service is measured by cost units.

(*j*) *Contribution variances*

Allowed sales value = 450 × £50 = £22,500
Actual sales value = £21,810

∴ *Contribution price variance* = £690 (A)

Budgeted sales quantity = 500 units
Actual quantity sold = 450

Shortfall = 50

∴ *Contribution quantity variance* = 50 × £20 = £1,000 (A)

(*k*) *Cross-check*

Summary of variances:	*Adverse*	*Favourable*
Spoilage	£1,175	
Material price	25	
Material usage		£30
Stores loss	240	
Labour efficiency	250	
Wage rate	1,125	
Overhead expenditure	70	
Variable overhead efficiency	240	
Contribution price	690	
Contribution quantity	1,000	
	£4,815	£30

Adverse variances	£4,815
Favourable variance	30
Net variance	£4,785 (A)

Since the net variance equals the profit variance found earlier, the analysis is arithmetically proved.

Progress Test 16

10. (*a*)

Profit Statement for May

BUDGETED PROFIT				
Budgeted contribution, 500 Cyberloops at £20				£10,000
Less budgeted fixed costs for one month				7,000*
Unamended budgeted profit				3,000
Amendments accepted by Planning Committee at planning stage:				
Overtime premium on 100 extra units			−£500	
Quantity discount loss			−25	−525
Final budgeted profit				2,475
VARIANCES				
Sales:				
Contribution price		690 (A)		
Contribution quantity		1,000 (A)	1,690 (A)	
Production:				
Spoilage: 50 Cyberloops	1,300			
Less Scrap sales	125			
	1,175 (A)			
Overtime premium on replacements	250 (A)			
Additional store costs†	100 (A)	1,525 (A)		
Overtime premium:				
Absenteeism	250 (A)			
Labour efficiency	125 (A)	375 (A)		
Labour efficiency		250 (A)		
Variable overhead efficiency‡		140 (A)		
		2,290 (A)		
Material usage		30 (F)	2,260 (A)	
Stores:				
Deterioration, 400 ft Cybersheet		240 (A)		
Overhead expenditure		20 (A)	260 (A)	
Administration: Overhead expenditure			100 (A)	
Test: Overhead expenditure			40 (F)	
Selling: Overhead expenditure			10 (F)	
∴ *Profit variance*				4,260 (A)
Actual net loss				£1,785

* Fixed costs: Test £600 + Administration £5,000 + Stores £400 + Selling £1,000 = Total: £7,000

† 1 spoiled unit carries 1 stores point. Therefore 50 units carry 50 points at £2 a point = £100.

‡ £240 shown in suggested answer to Question 8 (*i*) Progress Test 15 (see p. 296) less £100 stores costs applicable to, and shown under, spoiled units (*see* † above).

NOTES: The finished goods stock is now 50 Cyberloops in excess of plan, due to actual sales being 50 units below budget. Had this sales failure been notified quickly enough to production, the final batch could have been cancelled with the result that an overtime premium of £250 would have been saved.

10(*b*)

DEPARTMENTAL OPERATING STATEMENT

Department..................Production.. Production: Actual 600 Cyberloops* ....

Manager.........................M. Underwood.................................. Budget 600 Cyberloops ....

Position......Production Centre Manager .... Working Hours......13,500 ....

Period.......................May, 1968... Budgeted Hours (for actual month) 12,000 ....

Control Ratios:

Activity..............100%.............. Efficiency..............96%.............. Capacity..............112%..............

* 600 good Cyberloops and 50 defective units produced.

All allowances based on a total production of 650 units.

(Note: Overspending +; Saving −; All costs and variances in £s.)

Direct Materials:

Material	Unit	Allowed Quantity	Actual Quantity	Difference	Standard Price	Usage Variance	Reason
Cybersheet	Ft	3250	3200	−50	60*p*	−30	Not known

Direct Labour—Efficiency:

Allowed Hours	Actual Hours	Difference	Standard Rate	Efficiency Variance	Reason
13,000	13,500	+500	50*p*	+250	Probably due to reduced efficiency as a result of heavy O/T

DEPARTMENTAL OPERATING STATEMENT—*continued*

Direct Labour—Overtime Premiums:

Cause of Overtime	O/T Hours	O/T Premium	Comments
Absenteeism	1000	+250	10% of normal time, investigation indicated
Replacement batch	1000	+250	Wholly due to spoiled units
Labour efficiency	500	+125	See "Labour Efficiency" detail above
Total	2500	+625	
(Planned extra production	2000	+500	authorised by Planning Committee.)

Variable Overhead Efficiency*

Service	Activity Unit	Allowed Activity	Actual Activity	Difference	Standard Price	Efficiency Variance	Reason
Test	Test hr	325	315	−10	£4	−40	Probably because the 50 units that failed test did not require full test time
Administration	Direct Labour hr	13,000	13,500	+500	40*p*	+200	See "Labour Efficiency" detail above.
Stores	Points	975	1015	+40	£2	+80	50 spoiled units = +50 50 ft issue saved = −10 Points +40
						+240	

NOTE: No overhead expenditure variances here as these are all controllable by other managers.

Spoilage:

Units spoiled as result of faulty production set-up:

Number of units	50		
Standard marginal cost £26 each			
Total cost of loss	50 × £26	=	£1300
Less scrap sales: 50 at £2.50 each		=	£125
∴ *Spoilage variance*		=	£1175(A)

Summary:

VARIANCE	£
Direct materials—usage	−30
Direct labour—efficiency	+250
Direct labour—overtime premiums	+625
Variable overhead efficiency	+240
Spoilage	+1175
Total	+2260

Comments:

A very bad month. The spoilage was a major disaster—the cost of £1175 certainly being a low valuation, for at least an additional £250 was spent on overtime premiums replacing the lost batch and 50 stores points incurred for £100 giving a total cost of at least £1525. More could probably be attributed to this loss in the shape of a share in the cause of the drop in labour efficiency, so the total cost could easily reach £1600.

The saving on material usage is a little worrying. Are we really cutting more efficiently or is the customer receiving "short measure"?

The absenteeism is very high. Quite apart from the inevitable cost of extra overtime could this be another reason for labour efficiency being below 100%?

For your general information:

Last month's budgeted profit:	£2475
Last month's actual profit: *Loss*	£1785
Profit variance	£4260 (A)

Date...........June, 19........

Copies to: Works Manager
Managing Director
Planning Committee Secretary

Signed...........A. Student...........
Management Accountant

Progress Test 20

11. *Dreamboats Ltd—Analysis of Balance Sheet**

(*a*) *Initial testing.*

Current ratio:
(6,000 + 4,000) to (10,000 + 25,000 + 10,000) = 1:4½

Liquid ratio: 4,000 to 45,000 = worse than 1:11
These ratios at once suggest overtrading.
(*b*) *Deeper probe.* Check ratios that test for overtrading.

Equity turnover: $\frac{60,000}{25,000}$ = 2·4 times per year.

Stock turnover: $\frac{60,000\dagger}{6,000}$ = 10 times per year.

Debtors turnover: $\frac{60,000}{4,000}$ = 15 times per year (*i.e.* less than 1 month's sales).

Current liabilities liquidation period: ‡ With profits of £10,000 p.a. net of tax it will take *3½ years* to pay off creditors and overdraft.
These figures show heavy overtrading. Dreamboats is very precariously placed financially and a disastrous slide into liquidation is liable to start at any time. (Indeed a suspicious analyst may well wonder if it has not already begun—hence the tragedy!)
(*c*) *Shares valuation.* (*i*) Earnings basis:

To assess the *true* return from this company it is first necessary to reconstruct the balance sheet so that the enterprise is in normal financial good health. (Note that a "normal" return of 20% implies a return from a financially sound business, not an expiring freak. Hence 100% return is *not* the appropriate figure to use for this company.)

Now if our balance sheet is to have £101,000 assets and £23,000 liabilities, then the equity will be £101,000 − £23,000 = £78,000. However, the existing equity is only £25,000.

* As only one balance sheet is given, priority should be given to analysing for financial health.
† Strictly speaking, this should be cost-of-sales figure.
‡ This measure was specially devised for this particular analysis. Students should always create measures that illustrate points they feel the analysis is revealing.

*Reconstructed Balance Sheet**

ASSETS	*Estimated appropriate value* (to nearest £000)
Fixed: Assume (*a*) fixed assets fairly valued in balance sheet; (*b*) Nelson was using an absolute minimum of fixed assets and additional equipment worth, say £10,000 is needed.	80,000
Stocks: Assume Nelson would have stocks at a minimum. Suggested appropriate stock levels: Showroom, say 10% turnover; Raw material and W.I.P., say 30% turnover.	16,000†
Debtors: Assume (*a*) £50,000 of annual sales on hire-purchase, *i.e.* only 1 week wait = £1000; (*b*) £10,000 of sales on credit, with 5 weeks' average credit = £1000.	2,000
Cash: Nominal cash float to meet fluctuations in cash flow, say 5% sales	3,000
Total Assets	£101,000
LIABILITIES	
Loan and Taxation: As previously.	20,000
Creditors: Say 1 month's cost of sales = 1/12 (60,000 − 20,000).	3,000
Overdraft: To be used only in emergencies.	Nil
Total Liabilities	23,000

* Students may legitimately differ regarding the assumptions made in this reconstruction. In this type of question examiners are only concerned with the quality of the analysis, not the student's intimate knowledge of the trade involved.

† Stocks are computed on cost-of-sales basis, *i.e.* since £60,000 sales gave £20,000 profit, then cost of sales was £40,000 = 2/3 sales. Since total stock figure is to be 40% of the turnover, then cost of these stocks = 2/3 × 40% of £60,000 = £16,000.

Therefore an additional £78,000 − £25,000 = £53,000 will need to be invested in the company.

Next, note that the value of a *financially sound* business returning £20,000 is worth $\frac{20,000 \times 100}{20}$ = £100,000 (*i.e.* 20% return on £100,000 = £20,000). We are, therefore, prepared to pay in total £100,000 to acquire this company in good financial health.

However, we will need to invest £53,000 immediately on acquiring Dreamboats, and consequently this will only leave £100,000 − £53,000 = £47,000 available for buying the whole of the existing equity (which is represented by 20,000 shares).

$$\therefore \textit{Share value} \text{ (earnings basis)} = \frac{£47,000}{20,000} = \underline{\underline{£2{\cdot}35}}$$

Shares valuation. (*ii*) Assets basis:

Estimated break-up value (*optimistic*)

ASSETS		
Fixed:	Assume (*a*) fairly valued at market value in balance sheet; (*b*) 10% realisation cost.	£63,000
Stocks:	Assume (*a*) all stock merchantable. (*b*) 10% realisation cost.	5,400
Debtors:	Since Nelson was so short of cash he was probably selling wholly on hire-purchase, *i.e.* £1000 debtors. The other £3000, then possibly represents old and difficult debts. Assume, therefore, £2000 of these bad debts. ∴ Good debts, 1000 + 1000	2,000
		70,400
LIABILITIES		
As per balance sheet:		55,000
	Net Assets Value	£15,400

$$\therefore \textit{Share value} \text{ (assets basis)} = \frac{£15,400}{20,000} = \underline{\underline{£0{\cdot}77 \text{ per share}}}$$

(*d*) *Conclusion*

As the valuation on an earnings basis is higher than that on even an optimistic assets basis, then the company will be bought to be run and the earnings basis valuation is the appropriate one to use, *i.e.* £2·35 per share.

However, it should be appreciated that Dreamboats is only a small business and Mr Nelson almost certainly dominated it. He knew boats well (tested new design himself) and had the energy of youth (only 30 at death) and if he founded the company (as seems likely since he and his wife were the only shareholders) he must have been enterprising (earning some £20,000 per annum at 25). He also had had the experience of running that particular business.

Taking all these factors into account it is unlikely that any purchaser could match his profit-making ability, at least, not for some time. Consequently £2·35 would be much too high a price for us to pay, particularly if we were complete outsiders to the trade. In practice, of course, the price will be fixed by negotiation, though a floor is set by the assets basis valuation.*

* It is interesting to note that even if the company was *given away* the recipient would need to earn at least £10,000 p.a. from it in order to give himself a 20% return on the £53,000 that must necessarily be injected to make it financially sound.

APPENDIX IV

EXAMINATION QUESTIONS

1. (*a*) What is the significance of cash budgeting for management purposes and why is the cash budget dependent on both the operating and the capital budgets?

(*b*) From the following information taken from the budget of the A.B. Co. Ltd prepare a statement showing the average amount of working capital required by the company.

(*i*) Annual sales are estimated at 100,000 units at £1 per unit.

(*ii*) Production quantities coincide with sales and will be carried on evenly throughout the year and production cost is:

Material	10*s*. per unit
Labour	4*s*. per unit
Expenses	3*s*. 6*d*. per unit

(*iii*) Customers are given 60 days credit, and 50 days credit is taken from suppliers.

(*iv*) Forty days supply of raw materials and 15 days supply of finished goods are kept.

(*v*) The production cycle is 20 days and all material is issued at the commencement of each production cycle.

(*vi*) A cash balance equivalent to one-third of the average other working capital requirements is kept for contingencies. (*A.C.C.A.*)

2. You are in consultation with the Directors of a company manufacturing fountain pens. They tell you:

1. The company's year-end is 31st December.
2. They are employing, in 1968, 50 salesmen at a total fixed cost of £2000 per annum each and expect that each salesman will achieve fountain pen sales equivalent to 2½ times his fixed cost.
3. They expect each salesman's costs will rise by £200 per annum each year and that his performance, in terms of sales of fountain pens, will remain at 2½ times. They plan to increase the number of salesmen by ten each year.

4. The direct manufacturing cost of pens represents one-third of sales value. Other fixed overheads, excluding salesmen, will amount to £55,000 in 1968 and are estimated to amount to £70,000 in 1969, £85,000 in 1970 and £100,000 in 1971.
5. The Sales Director has put forward the proposal that another manufacturer should be approached to produce a complementary propelling pencil for marketing with the pens. He has been quoted a buying price of 6*s*. each, which would be reduced to 5*s*. each should the orders fulfilled in a year exceed 500,000. He plans to sell them at an average price of 6*s*. 8*d*. each. He forecasts that each salesman will sell 2000 pencils in 1969, 5000 in 1970 and 7500 in 1971.
6. The Production Director is proposing alternatively that the company should manufacture a similar pencil together with the fountain pens but the Cost Accountant has advised that the company could only do so at a total cost, including a proportion of fixed overheads, of 6*s*. 6*d*. each. The Production Director is nevertheless arguing that no extra production facilities will be needed and that the average direct costs of material and labour will amount to only 4*s*. for each pencil. There would be no increase in overhead costs.
7. The Directors propose to compensate salesmen with commission of 1% on their total sales when they introduce pencil sales in 1969.

You are required to:

(*a*) prepare forecast statements of the company's operations for the four years 1968 to 1971 showing the profitability of fountain pens and the effect of adopting the proposals made by the Sales and Production Directors respectively, and
(*b*) advise the Directors which of the two proposals they should adopt, giving reasons for your choice based upon the company's cost structure and the performance of its salesmen.
(Prepare the forecasts and do all workings to the nearest £1000). (*C.A.*)

3. XYZ Engineering Ltd proposes to increase its output by re-organising the factory layout, installing some additional plant and increasing the labour force.

The plan is intended to be put into operation during the four months to 31st December 1966, and has the following financial implications:

1. The forecast balance sheet as on 31st August 1966 is as follows:

Issued Share Capital	£700,000	Plant and machinery	
Reserves	100,000	at cost	£600,000
		Less: Depreciation	264,000
			336,000
Profit and Loss		Raw material stocks	115,000
Account	140,000	Work-in-progress and	
		finished stocks	125,000
	940,000	Debtors	300,000
Trade creditors	85,000	Cash	163,000
Accrued charges:			
Rent £8,000			
Other 6,000			
	14,000		
	£1,039,000		£1,039,000

NOTE: Trade creditors represent the purchases of raw materials during August 1966. Debtors represent sales in July and August, 1966 at the rate of £150,000 per month.

2. The additional plant, costing £200,000, will be delivered and paid for in September.
3. Raw materials to be consumed per month:

September	October to December
£70,000	£100,000

4. Stocks of raw materials are to be increased to £130,000 at the end of September and maintained at that level.
5. Monthly figures of other costs of production:

	September	October to December per month
Direct wages	£16,000	£24,000
Indirect wages	5,000	7,000
Other factory expenses	3,000	5,000

One quarter of each of the above costs would be outstanding at the end of the respective month and would be paid in the following month.

Rent of the factory at £4000 per month is paid quarterly in arrears on 30th September and 31st December, etc.

Depreciation on plant and machinery is to be provided throughout at the rate of £7000 per month.

6. Administration and selling expenses monthly:

	September	October to December per month
Salaries	£20,000	£22,000
Other office expenses	2,000	3,000

Advertising and publicity will continue at £10,000 monthly, but will be increased to £30,000 in October and November.

Each of the above expenses is to be considered as paid in the month in which they arise.

7. Forecast sales are:

September and October	£150,000 per month
November	£160,000
December	£250,000

8. To meet the higher level of sales planned, work-in-progress and finished stocks are to be increased to £160,000 at the end of October and to £195,000 at the end of November.

A fall to £175,000 is expected at 31st December.

9. It is expected that existing credit terms will continue to be observed.

10. The parent company has agreed to advance on a loan account monthly such sums as may be necessary to limit to £100,000 the bank overdraft of XYZ Engineering Ltd. (Interest on overdraft and loan is to be ignored.)

As Chief Accountant you are required to prepare the following for discussion with your Managing Director:

(*a*) A forecast Trading and Profit and Loss Account for each of the four months September to December 1966, and a supporting forecast Balance Sheet as on 31st December 1966.

(*b*) A cash forecast, month by month, for the four months to 31st December 1966, showing when any advance on the Parent Company Loan Account will be required.

Ignore taxation and investment grants. (*C.A.*)

4. The following figures relate to a manufacturing company:

Annual sales		£700,000
Direct material	£100,000	
Direct wages	150,000	
Semi-variable overhead	120,000	
Fixed overhead	80,000	
Fixed administrative and selling cost	40,000	
Variable selling and distribution cost	100,000	

Apart from the cost described as fixed overhead there is included in the semi-variable overhead figure a fixed element amounting to £50,000.

On a single graph, display the cost-volume relationship for each category of cost, and also for the total costs.

Plot the sales line on the graph. What is the break-even point?

(*I.C.W.A., Advanced Cost & Management Accountancy,* June 1966)

5. Your company operates a factory which is working at full machine capacity producing the total requirements of three component parts, A, B and C, used in equal proportions in an assembly type product. Data concerning one unit of the product are as follows:

	Machine hours	COSTS		
		Variable	*Fixed*	*Total*
Component parts:				
A	5	£24	£8	£32
B	8	30	10	40
C	10	30	30	60
Assembly	—	50	20	70
Total	23	£134	£68	£202
Selling price				£250

In preparing a budget for the coming year an increase of sales and production is being considered. It is ascertained that the present machine capacity of the factory will be capable of producing the requirements of only two of the three component parts. No increase of machine capacity can be effected during the course of the next year although other facilities can be increased at very short notice.

In the circumstances it has been decided to consider purchasing supplies of one component part from outside suppliers and quotations have been received as follows:

Part	Each
A	£34
B	44
C	52

The Sales Manager feels that the minimum increase on existing sales and production that should be considered is 50% and that he could sell up to an increase of 80% provided the factory capacity is available.

You are required to prepare a report for management giving

your recommendations as to which component part should be ordered from outside suppliers for the coming year if production is increased by 50% and also if full factory capacity is utilised.

(*I.C.W.A.*, *A.C.&M.A.*, May 1968)

6. Your organisation has a plant at Barchester which owing to technological developments will shortly have to cease production of the existing products—as the demand for these is coming to an end. Hence your Board has to consider what to do with the Barchester factory. The buildings are comparatively new and good for another 50 years—although it would be wise to reckon on maintenance of the fabric of the premises at around £500 p.a. An offer has been received for a seven-year lease at £10,000 p.a.: alternatively, they would fetch £100,000 if sold. The existing equipment is obsolete and will fetch no more than the cost of dismantling and carting away.

At this time your company is considering launching on the U.K. market one or both of two new products, Ace and Trumps, for which an excellent demand is expected until superseded by further technical advances expected seven to eight years hence. The factory at Barchester, suitably re-equipped would allow for the production of either one of these products at a normal budgeted production of 100,000 units p.a. The new plant required (estimated life seven years) would cost £40,000 for the manufacture of Ace and £50,000 for Trumps. In addition, £10,000 manufacturing working capital would then be required for each product.

The normal production capacity could be extended to 150,000 units p.a. by overtime working. The additional costs for stepping up production (by overtime working or extra shifts), etc., and conversely the under recovery of overheads and other losses due to under production are estimated as:

Ace 2*s*. per unit
Trumps 6*s*. per unit

The products are perishable and cannot be stored for longer than to allow for the carrying of the usual small buffer stocks.

Other forecasted figures are:

(*on normal production basis*)	*Ace*	*Trumps*
Production costs p.a.	£52,000	£47,000
Distribution costs p.a.	19,200	18,300
Selling costs p.a.	5,000	4,000
Administration costs p.a.	10,000	10,000

The products could be bought in completed from Germany which with selling, distribution and administrative costs would amount to a price per unit of: **20*s*.** **17*s*. 6*d*.**

Both products are expected to sell at 22*s*. per unit delivered to wholesalers and bulk buyers.

A market research survey has been conducted and from this the following annual demand pattern has been forecast for the seven years' period:

Year	*Ace* Units	*Trumps* Units
1.	50,000	20,000
2.	90,000	80,000
3.	120,000	120,000
4.	120,000	150,000
5.	110,000	120,000
6.	100,000	100,000
7.	50,000	70,000

You will appreciate from the foregoing that your Board is faced with a policy decision as to whether to sell or let out the Barchester premises or to continue manufacture there with a new product—and there may be other factors which should be taken into account. You are fully to appraise the position and write a report, including therein any statements you consider relevant, to assist the board to make a decision.

The Board considers 7% per annum as a reasonable return for capital tied up. The annuity which may be obtained for a current outlay of £1 (that is, to return capital and provide an interest rate of 7% on the remaining balance) is, for a seven-year period, £0·185553.

To provide for return of capital only and taking into account 7% compound interest on the annual amounts set aside requires an annuity of £0·00246 for a 50-year period. (*A.C.C.A.*)

7. The annual flexible budget of a company is as follows:

Production capacity	40%	60%	80%	100%
Costs:				
Direct labour	£16,000	£24,000	£32,000	£40,000
Direct material	12,000	18,000	24,000	30,000
Production overhead	11,400	12,600	13,800	15,000
Administration overhead	5,800	6,200	6,600	7,000
Selling and distribution overhead	6,200	6,800	7,400	8,000
	£51,400	£67,600	£83,800	£100,000

Owing to trading difficulties the company is operating at 50% capacity. Selling prices have had to be lowered to what the directors maintain is an uneconomic level and they are considering whether or not their single factory should be closed down until the trade recession has passed.

A market research consultant has advised that in about twelve months' time there is every indication that sales will increase to about 75% of normal capacity and that the revenue to be produced in the second year will amount to £90,000. The present revenue from sales at 50% capacity would amount to only £49,500 for a complete year.

If the Directors decide to close down the factory for a year it is estimated that:

(*a*) the present fixed costs would be reduced to £11,000 per annum;
(*b*) closing down costs (redundancy payments, etc.) would amount to £7500;
(*c*) necessary maintenance of plant would cost £1000 per annum;
(*d*) on re-opening the factory, the cost of overhauling plant, training and engagement of new personnel would amount to £4000.

Prepare a statement for the Directors, presenting the information in such a way as to indicate whether or not it is desirable to close the factory. (*I.C.W.A., A.C.&M.A.*, June 1967)

8. On a farm of 200 acres, the farmer plans to sow 100 acres of barley, 20 acres of kale, and to use 80 acres on which to graze milk cattle.

For the barley, seed will cost £2 10*s.* 0*d.* per acre, and fertilisers £3 10*s.* 0*d.* per acre. It is expected that the yield will be 30 cwt per acre, which will be sold at £25 per ton.

The kale will cost £2 per acre for seed and £5 per acre for fertilisers. The kale produced will be fed to the cattle.

On the 80 acres, 40 milking cows will be kept, and in addition to the kale, other feeding stuffs will cost £1000 in all for the year. Each cow should produce one calf which will be sold at £10 each, together with an annual milk yield sold at £120. Cows will "depreciate" at the rate of £10 per annum.

Other farm costs (which are unlikely to change, however the farm is worked) are, per annum:

Farmworkers' wages	£1,800
Rent, rates, etc.	1,200
General charges	3,000

A suggestion is made that kale should be purchased instead of grown: if this is done it is estimated that kale will cost £12 10*s.* 0*d.* per cow, per annum.

Prepare figures to indicate to the farmer whether the kale should be purchased or grown. If the kale is purchased, show how the 20 acres could be used to best advantage.

(*I.C.W.A.*, *A.C.&M.A.*, Dec. 1964)

9. The MN Company Ltd has decided to increase its productive capacity to meet an anticipated increase in demand for its products. The extent of this increase in capacity has still to be determined and a management meeting has been called to decide which of the following two mutually exclusive proposals—I and II—should be undertaken. On the basis of the information given below you are required to:

1. evaluate the profitability (ignoring taxation and investment grants) of each of the proposals; and
2. on the assumption of a cost of capital of 8% advise management of the matters to be taken into consideration when deciding between Proposal I and Proposal II.

Capital expenditure	*I*	*II*
Buildings	£50,000	£100,000
Plant	200,000	300,000
Installation	10,000	15,000
Working capital	50,000	65,000
Net Income		
Annual pre-depreciation profits (Note (i))	70,000	95,000
Other relevant income/expenditure		
Sales promotion (Note (ii))	—	15,000
Plant scrap value	10,000	15,000
Buildings disposable value (Note (iii))	30,000	60,000

NOTES: (*i*) The investment life is ten years.

(*ii*) An exceptional amount of expenditure on sales promotion of £15,000 will require to be spent in year 2 on Proposal II. This has not been taken into account in calculating pre-depreciation profits.

(*iii*) It is not the intention to dispose of the buildings in ten years time; however, it is company policy to take a notional figure into account for project evaluation purposes. (*A.C.C.A.*)

Present value tables are given in Appendix I.

10. The AB Company Limited uses the payoff criterion for selecting investments in that a project which does not recoup all the capital outlays within four years is automatically rejected. The cash budget for the ensuing year indicates that there will be £100,000 available for investment. Three projects have been submitted to the directors, all of which pay back within four years and all of which, over this period, show an identical suplus cash inflow.

Prepare a report advising the directors as to which should be accepted, commenting on the present method for selecting investments and any other matters you think relevant.

Project A—Lend the £100,000 to a subsidiary company at 8% for four years interest to be withdrawn each year.

Project B—A property developer with whom the AB Company is associated wishes the company to construct a supermarket, which will cost in total £100,000. It is anticipated that the net cash inflow for the first two years will be £3000 and £5000 respectively, all of which will go to the company and at the end of the second year the property developer will purchase a half share in the supermarket for £52,500. During the next two years the net cash inflow will be £12,000 and £16,000 respectively, to be shared equally between the company and the developer, and at the end of the period the property developer will purchase the remaining share in the supermarket for £57,500.

Project C—Invest the £100,000 in new machinery which will provide net cash inflows for four years of £30,000, £35,000, £35,000 and £32,000 respectively.

NOTE:

1. Taxation and investment grants can be ignored.
2. The AB Company's capital structure is as follows:

8% debentures	£600,000
5% redeemable preference shares	200,000
Ordinary £1 shares	200,000
	£1,000,000

3. Ordinary dividends of the AB Company have been

1963— 9%
1964— 9%
1965— 9½%
1966—10%
1967—10%

(*A.C.C.A.*)

Present value tables are given in Appendix I.

11. The standard costs of the three products manufactured by your company are as follows:

PER UNIT

	Product 1		Product 2		Product 3	
	Quantity units	*Cost shillings*	*Quantity units*	*Cost shillings*	*Quantity units*	*Cost shillings*
Materials: A	15	30	—	—	22	44
B	50	25	64	32	12	6
C	20	15	24	18	—	—
	hours		hours		hours	
Direct labour	2½	25	2	20	3	30
Factory overhead:						
variable		10		8		12
fixed		5		4		6
Standard cost		110		82		98

Transactions for the past month were:

		Quantity units	*Cost*
Materials purchased:	A	100,000	£10,719
	B	300,000	7,971
	C	100,000	3,560
Materials issued:	A	75,000	
	B	267,560	
	C	98,960	

Direct labour costs amounted to £7345 and the wages analysis for the month provided the following information:

Product	*Direct labour hours*	*Number of products manufactured*
1	6200	2500
2	3900	2000
3	4550	1500

Actual overhead:	fixed	£1550
	variable	2925

Normal manufacturing capacity for the month is fixed at:

Product	*Units*
1	2600
2	2050
3	1800

There was no work-in-progress at the beginning or end of the month. Materials were held in stock at standard prices.

You are required from the information given above to prepare a report on variances. In this report variances should be analysed not only into elements of cost and causes but also, where applicable, into types of product.

(*I.C.W.A.*, *A.C.&M.A.*, Dec. 1967)

12. The following is a summary of the accounts of a company over a period of 23 years:

Balance sheets at year end

	1944	1951	1958	1966	1967
	£'000	£'000	£'000	£'000	£'000
Fixed assets at cost	200	200	317	504	519
less depreciation	25	132	148	235	243
	175	68	169	269	276
Trading assets, net	200	300	460	560	580
Quick resources	35	66	(−5)	3	1
Equity capital and retained profits	410	434	624	832	857

Profit and Loss Accounts for the year

	1944	1951	1958	1966	1967
Trading profit	80	120	184	224	232
Depreciation	25	10	24	39	40
Profit before taxation	55	110	160	185	192
Taxation	15	56	80	95	97
Dividend, gross	24	30	50	70	70
Retained	16	24	30	20	25
	55	110	160	185	192

Index numbers

	1944	1951	1958	1966	1967
Wholesale prices	100	150	230	280	290

A financial commentator suggests that, because of the changing value of money, the company has in effect been paying dividends out of capital.

You are asked to comment on this statement, saying whether:

(*a*) you agree with the commentator's calculations and with his interpretation of the facts; and

(*b*) in your view the company has fulfilled its obligations to its shareholders. (*I.C.W.A., Advanced Accountancy & Financial Management*, May 1968)

13. A holding company has decided to apply return on capital employed in assessing the performance of its Subsidiary Companies. However, to obtain realistic figures, certain adjustments, based on price level indices to book values, will have to be made.

From information relating to the subsidiary companies, A and B, you are required first to calculate:

(*i*) the current replacement cost of the asset involved;

(*ii*) the accumulated depreciation to date, assuming the asset is to be reported at current value;

(*iii*) the depreciation figure for the present year based on current values.

Secondly, using the calculated figures, you are required to state, with reasons, why you do/do not feel that in assessing capital employed, assets should be valued at current rather than historic cost.

	Subsidiary Company A Asset	*Subsidiary Company B Asset*
Year of purchase	1940	1950
Purchase price	£200,000	£550,000
Life	40 years	40 years
Disposable value	Nil	Nil
Price level index at date of acquisition	40	100
Price level index now	150	150
Depreciation method	Straight line	Straight line

(*A.C.C.A.*)

14. The summarised balance sheets of companies X and Y as at 31st August 1964 are as follows:

	X	Y
Share capital, £1 ordinary shares fully paid	£62,500	£10,000
Revenue reserves:		
General	7,500	6,250
Profit and loss account	6,000	5,650
Reserve for future taxation	5,000	2,315
	£81,000	£24,215

Current assets:		
4½% stock at cost	—	3,150
Stocks, debtors and cash	37,500	15,650
	37,500	18,800
Current liabilities	10,250	3,935
	27,250	14,865
Fixed assets:		
Land and buildings at cost	25,000	—
Plant, etc., at cost less depreciation	19,375	9,350
Goodwill	9,375	—
	£81,000	£24,215

An independent valuation of the tangible fixed assets gives the following values:

Land and buildings	(X)	£32,000
Plant, etc.	(X)	21,000
	(Y)	10,750

The profits for the past three years, after eliminating exceptional items, have been:

		X	Y
		£	£
Year ended 31st August:	1962	8,925	3,250
	1963	9,720	3,497
	1964	10,545	4,210

The boards of the two companies have been considering the possibility of an amalgamation as from 1st September 1964. You are asked to value the two undertakings on such bases as you consider appropriate, and to suggest a fair exchange ratio of the shares in the two companies.

(*I.C.W.A., A.A.&F.M.*, Dec. 1965)

15. It is recommended that profits should be sufficient to finance the replacement of assets as this becomes necessary, to make a contribution towards growth, to provide adequate dividends on share capital and to cover taxation on these items so far as they are not allowable for tax purposes.

You are given the following information relating to the present position of the company:

Fixed assets at cost (replacement value £17,500)	£10,000
Current assets (net)	10,000
Total capital employed	£20,000
Represented by:	
Ordinary share capital	8,000
Retained earnings	12,000
	£20,000

Capital allowances for the year on existing fixed assets: £1000 at 40% = £400.
Average overall life of fixed assets: 25 years.
Target dividend on ordinary share capital: 15% (gross).
Target growth rate per annum in new capital investment in fixed assets (at replacement values): 3%.
Proportion of new capital investment to be financed out of retained earnings from current year's profits: 70%.
Rate of taxation: 40%.
Capital grants (not taxable) on capital cost of new assets: 20%.
Annual allowances for tax purposes on capital cost of new assets after deducting investment grant: 20%.

On the basis recommended in the first sentence of this question state:

(*a*) the target profit you would aim for in the year ahead;
(*b*) the rate of return it would represent on the total capital employed at the commencement of the year.

(*I.C.W.A., A.A.&F.M.*, June 1967)

16. Your company proposes to acquire, as at 31st December 1963, the whole of the issued ordinary shares of the XYZ Engineering Company Ltd., which are currently quoted at par.

(*a*) From a study of the following information, available to you at the above date, do you consider that from the point of view of your company a price of 23*s*. 6*d*. per share would be a satisfactory basis of valuation for the purpose of the acquisition? Explain your reasoning and set out in your answer any calculations involved in arriving at your opinion on this matter.

The XYZ Engineering Company Ltd

	1958	1959	1960	1961	1962	1963 (probably)
1. Profit and loss account—year to 31st December.	£'000	£'000	£'000	£'000	£'000	£'000
Sales		141	213	177	187	266
Materials		70	106	108	96	138
Direct labour		12	18	18	18	23
General overhead		28	32	32	33	45
Depreciation		3	3	3	3	4
Selling and publicity		7	11	12	26	15
Loan stock interest		—	—	—	1	4
Profit before tax		21	43	4	10	37
		141	213	177	187	266
2. Balance sheet—at 31st December.						
Land and buildings	14	14	14	14	14	20
Other fixed assets (both at cost less depreciation)	30	27	24	27	35	55
Stock and work-in-progress	25	30	43	42	35	75
Debtors	27	35	54	44	36	51
Cash	18	20	22	9	86	46
	114	126	157	136	206	247
Creditors	9	12	18	22	22	39
Future taxation	4	10	21	2	5	18
6% convertible loan stock, 1965	—	—	—	—	70	70
Profit and loss account	1	4	18	12	9	20
Ordinary shares of £1 each, fully paid	100	100	100	100	100	100
	114	126	157	136	206	247
3. Orders on hand—at 31st December	70	107	108	90	120	150

No budget has been prepared for the year 1964.

The rate of earnings on total capital employed which could be expected from a company of this nature is 12½% after taxation, 60% of the earnings being retained in the business. The XYZ Engineering Company Ltd has in fact paid dividends of 8% free of tax each year.

The rate of company taxation may be taken as 10*s*. in the £.

(*b*) Assuming that the proposed acquisition is effected by the issue on a one-for-one basis of £1 ordinary shares in your company, having a market value of 23*s*. 6*d*. per share, what entries would you make in the books of your company to reflect the investment? Would any alternative method of presentation be legally permissible?

(*I.C.W.A., A.A.&F.M.*, June, 1964)

17. Towards the end of 1964 the directors of Wholesale Merchants Ltd decided to expand their business. The annual accounts of the company for 1964 and 1965 may be summarised as follows:

	Year 1964		*Year* 1965	
Sales				
Cash	£30,000		£32,000	
Credit	270,000		342,000	
		£300,000		£374,000
Cost of sales		£236,000		£298,000
Gross margin		64,000		76,000
Expenses				
Warehousing		13,000		14,000
Transport		6,000		10,000
Administration		19,000		19,000
Selling		11,000		14,000
Debenture interest		—		2,000
		49,000		59,000
Net profit		£15,000		£17,000

	On 31st December 1964		*On 31st December* 1965	
Fixed assets (less depreciation)		£30,000		£40,000
Current assets				
Stock	£60,000		£94,000	
Debtors	50,000		82,000	
Cash	10,000		7,000	
		120,000		183,000
Less Current liabilities				
Trade creditors		50,000		76,000
Net current assets		70,000		107,000
		£100,000		£147,000
Share capital		75,000		75,000
Reserves and undistributed profit		25,000		42,000
Debenture loan		—		30,000
		£100,000		£147,000

You are informed that:

1. All sales were from stocks in the company's warehouse.
2. The range of merchandise was not changed and buying prices remained steady throughout the two years.
3. Budgeted total sales for 1966 were £390,000.
4. The debenture loan was received on 1st January 1965 and additional fixed assets were purchased on that date.

You are required to state the internal accounting ratios that you would use in this type of business to assist the management of the Company in measuring the efficiency of its operation, including its use of capital.

Your answer should name the ratios and give the figures (calculated to one decimal place) for 1964 and 1965, together with possible reasons for changes in the ratios for the two years. Ratios relating to capital employed should be based on the capital at the year end. Ignore taxation. (*C.A.*)

18.

	Profit/ Net Assets	*Profit/ Sales*	*Sales/ Net Assets*	*Fixed Assets/ Total Assets*	*Sales/ Net Worth*
	%	%	*Times*	%	*Times*
COMPANY A	13·3	8·3	1·6	52·0	2·1
Average of other companies in same industry	17·4	11·6	1·5	60·0	2·1

The above information which has been prepared from the published accounts of companies has led your managing director to conclude that other companies are obviously much more efficient than Company A. Comment on the figures disclosed above giving a brief description of the significance of each figure in the table and discuss the dangers which might exist in basing an opinion on figures which have been arrived at from the published accounts of companies. (*A.C.C.A.*)

19. The punched card equipment in the data processing department of your company consists of two tabulators with one summary punch and one reproducer, one sorter, one interpreter, and punches and verifiers.

Your company sells 100 products, but orders must be for standard quantities and there are only 278 different "standard packs" (possible combinations of product and quantity). The country is divided into nine sales areas. Discounts are not given. Goods ordered are never out of stock, and goods are never returned from customers. The data processing department is given a daily list of finished goods received into stock.

You are required to describe (in narrative or flow-chart form) a procedure for producing, from edited customers' orders and the goods received lists, with the punched card equipment available in the data processing department, the following:

(*a*) Combined despatch note/invoice sets.
(*b*) A weekly finished stock ledger showing, for each of the 278 different standard packs, quantity brought forward, a list of stock movements, and quantity carried forward.
(*c*) A weekly sales analysis showing, for each of the nine sales areas, total sales for the week of each standard pack. (*C.A.*)

20. A company is divided into a number of profit centres (or "divisions") each of which is expected to show a profit return before tax of 10% on the book value of its capital employed.

One such division, engaged in custom-built heavy engineering and employing a capital of £6 million, is anticipating a profit break-even in 1966/67, forecast as follows:

Product	*Quantity*	*Sales value*		*Variable costs*		*Marginal*
		per unit	*Total*	*per unit*	*Total*	*contribution*
		£'000	£'000	£'000	£'000	£'000
A	50	40	2,000	24	1,200	800
B	40	7·5	300	5	200	100
C	200	5	1,000	3	600	400
D	50	4	200	2	100	100
			£3,500		£2,100	£1,400
Less divisional fixed costs, including depreciation						£1,400
Divisional profit						Nil

Early in 1966 the Sales Director had forecast the market potential as follows:

Quantities of product	1966/67	1967/68	1968/69	1969/70	1970/71
A	50	50	50	60	50
B	50	20			
B.2		20	40	40	40
C	210	210	220	230	240
D	60	40	30	10	
E			20	40	60

B.2 and E are new products; the former selling at £8000 and the latter at £30,000 per unit on average, subject to customer modifications. The marginal contribution in each case may be taken as 40% of sales value.

The production director states that to produce these quantities, capital expenditure on plant and equipment totalling £1,000,000 would be needed; the timing of cash outlay being £600,000 in 1967/68; and £200,000 in each of the years 1968/69 and 1969/70.

The increase in stocks and other working capital would be £500,000 spread evenly over the years 1967/68–1970/71.

It is expected that apart from an increased depreciation charge (at say 10% per annum on cost), any increases in cost would be offset by increases in selling prices.

As financial director you are asked for a preliminary opinion:

(*a*) whether the project would make the division adequately profitable;
(*b*) whether the project itself is financially sound;
(*c*) what would be the maximum requirement of finance for the project.

In answering these questions, you should indicate what further information you might require.

The cost of capital to the company is 8% per annum gross.

For this preliminary appraisal, taxation may be ignored.

(*I.C.W.A.*, *A.A.&F.M.*, Dec. 1967)

Present value tables are given in Appendix I.

INDEX